# Dialogue of Comfort
# Against Tribulation

**St. Thomas More**

**Dialogue of Comfort Against Tribulation**

Copyright © 2014 by Bibliotech Press
All rights reserved.

Contact:
BibliotechPress@gmail.com

The present edition is a reproduction of 1951 publication of this work. Minor typographical errors may have been corrected without note, however, for an authentic reading experience the spelling, punctuation, and capitalization have been retained from the original text.

ISBN: 978-1-61895-189-2

# **NOTE**

This edition of the Dialogue of Comfort has been transcribed from the 1557 version as it appears in Everyman's Library. The Everyman edition is heartily recommended to readers who would like to taste the dialogue in its original form.

The first plan was to change only the spelling. It soon became evident that the punctuation would have to be changed to follow present usage. The longest sentences were then broken up into two or three, and certain others were rearranged into a word order more like that of today. Nothing was omitted, however, and nothing was added except relative pronouns, parts of "to be," and other such neutral connectives. Finally, obsolete words were changed to more familiar equivalents except when they were entirely clear and too good to lose. Thus "wot" became "know" but "gigglot" and "galp up the ghost" were retained. Words that have come to have a quite different meaning for us, such as "fond" and "lust" were replaced by less ambiguous ones—wherever possible, by ones that More himself used elsewhere.

The text has not been cut or expanded, re-interpreted or edited. Any transcription seems to involve some interpretation, conscious or otherwise, but an effort has been made to keep it to a minimum. Passages that seemed to make no sense have therefore been left unaltered. If other readers find solutions for them their suggestions will be welcomed.

This is not in any sense a scholarly piece of work. That would require a very different method, as well as a far more thorough knowledge of sixteenth-century English. It would be a most commendable undertaking, but it might result in an edition for the learned. This one is for everyone who has the two essentials, faith and intelligence, presupposed by Anthony in Chapter II.

MONICA STEVENS
Middlebury, Vermont.
Feast of St. Benedict, 1950

# BOOK ONE

VINCENT: Who would have thought, O my good uncle, a few years past, that those in this country who would visit their friends lying in disease and sickness would come, as I do now, to seek and fetch comfort of them? Or who would have thought that in giving comfort to them they would use the way that I may well use to you? For albeit that the priests and friars be wont to call upon sick men to remember death, yet we worldly friends, for fear of discomforting them, have ever had a way here in Hungary of lifting up their hearts and putting them in good hope of life.

But now, my good uncle, the world is here waxed such, and so great perils appear here to fall at hand, that methinketh the greatest comfort a man can have is when he can see that he shall soon be gone. And we who are likely long to live here in wretchedness have need of some comforting counsel against tribulation to be given us by such as you, good uncle. For you have so long lived virtuously, and are so learned in the law of God that very few are better in this country. And you have had yourself good experience and assay of such things as we do now fear, as one who hath been taken prisoner in Turkey two times in your days, and is now likely to depart hence ere long.

But that may be your great comfort, good uncle, since you depart to God. But us of your kindred shall you leave here, a company of sorry comfortless orphans. For to all of us your good help, comfort, and counsel hath long been a great stay—not as an uncle to some, and to others as one further of kin, but as though to us all you had been a natural father.

ANTHONY: Mine own good cousin, I cannot much deny but what there is indeed, not only here in Hungary but also in almost all places in Christendom, such a customary manner of unchristian comforting. And in any sick man it doth more harm than good, by drawing him in time of sickness, with looking and longing for life, from the meditation of death, judgment, heaven, and hell, with which he should beset much of his time—even all his whole life in his best health. Yet is that manner of comfort to my mind more than mad when it is used to a man of mine age. For as we well know that a young man may die soon, so are we very sure that an old man cannot live long. And yet there is (as Tully saith) no man so old but that, for all that, he hopeth yet that he may live one year more, and of a frail folly delighteth to think thereon and comfort himself therewith. So other men's words of such comfort, adding more sticks to that fire, shall (in a manner) quite burn up the pleasant moisture that should most refresh him—the wholesome dew, I mean, of God's grace, by which he should wish with God's will to be hence, and long to be with him in Heaven.

Now, as for your taking my departing from you so heavily (as that of one from whom you recognize, of your goodness, to have had here before help and comfort), would God I had done to you and to others half so much as I myself reckon it would have been my duty to do! But whensoever God may take me hence, to reckon yourselves then comfortless, as though your chief comfort stood in me—therein would you make, methinketh, a reckoning very much as though you would cast away a strong staff and lean upon a rotten reed. For God is, and must be, your comfort, and not I. And he is a sure comforter, who (as he said unto his disciples) never leaveth his servants comfortless orphans, not even when he departed from his disciples by death. But he both sent them a comforter, as he had promised, the Holy Spirit of his Father and himself, and he also made them sure that to the world's end he would ever dwell with them himself. And therefore, if you be part of his flock and believe his promise, how can you be comfortless in any tribulation, when Christ and his Holy Spirit, and with them their inseparable Father, if you put full trust and confidence in them, are never either one finger-breadth of space nor one minute of time from you?

VINCENT: O, my good uncle, even these selfsame words, with which you prove that because of God's own gracious presence we cannot be left comfortless, make me now feel and perceive how much comfort we shall miss when you are gone. For albeit, good uncle, that while you tell me this I cannot but grant it for true, yet if I had not now heard it from you, I would not have remembered it, nor would it have fallen to my mind. And moreover, as our tribulations shall increase in weight and number, so shall we need not only one such good word or twain, but a great heap of them, to stable and strengthen the walls of our hearts against the great surges of this tempestuous sea.

ANTHONY: Good cousin, trust well in God and he shall provide you outward teachers suitable for every time, or else shall himself sufficiently teach you inwardly.

VINCENT: Very well, good uncle, but yet if we would leave the seeking of outward learning, when we can have it, and look to be inwardly taught by God alone, then should be thereby tempt God and displease him. And since I now see the likelihood that when you are gone we shall be sore destitute of any other like you, therefore methinketh that God bindeth me of duty to pray you now, good uncle, in this short time that we have you, that I may learn of you such plenty of good counsel and comfort, against these great storms of tribulation with which both I and all mine are sore beaten already, and now upon the coming of this cruel Turk fear to fall in far more, that I may, with the same laid up in remembrance, govern and stay the ship of our kindred and keep it afloat from peril of spiritual drowning.
You are not ignorant, good uncle, what heaps of heaviness have of late fallen among us already, with which some of our poor family are fallen into such dumps that scantly can any such comfort as my poor wit can give

them at all assuage their sorrow. And now, since these tidings have come hither, so hot with the great Turk's enterprise into these parts here, we can scantly talk nor think of anything else than his might and our danger. There falleth so continually before the eyes of our heart a fearful imagination of this terrible thing: his mighty strength and power, his high malice and hatred, and his incomparable cruelty, with robbing, spoiling, burning, and laying waste all the way that his army cometh; then, killing or carrying away the people thence, far from home, and there severing the couples and the kindred asunder, every one far from the other, some kept in thraldom and some kept in prison and some for a triumph tormented and killed in his presence; then, sending his people hither and his false faith too, so that such as are here and still remain shall either both lose all and be lost too, or be forced to forsake the faith of our Saviour Christ and fall to the false sect of Mahomet. And yet—that which we fear more than all the rest—no small part of our own folk who dwell even here about us are, we fear, falling to him or already confederated with him. If this be so, it may haply keep this quarter from the Turk's invasion. But then shall they that turn to his law leave all their neighbours nothing, but shall have our goods given them and our bodies too, unless we turn as they do and forsake our Saviour too. And then—for there is no born Turk so cruel to Christian folk as is the false Christian that falleth from the faith—we shall stand in peril, if we persevere in the truth, to be more hardly handled and die a more cruel death by our own countrymen at home than if we were taken hence and carried into Turkey. These fearful heaps of peril lie so heavy at our hearts, since we know not into which we shall fortune to fall and therefore fear all the worst, that (as our Saviour prophesied of the people of Jerusalem) many among us wish already, before the peril come, that the mountains would overwhelm them or the valleys open and swallow them up and cover them.

Therefore, good uncle, against these horrible fears of these terrible tribulations—some of which, as you know, our house hath already, and the rest of which we stand in dread of—give us, while God lendeth you to us, such plenty of your comforting counsel as I may write and keep with us, to stay us when God shall call you hence.

ANTHONY: Ah, my good cousin, this is a heavy hearing. And just as we who dwell here in this part now sorely fear that thing which a few years ago we feared not at all, so I suspect that ere long they shall fear it as much who now think themselves very sure because they dwell further off.

Greece feared not the Turk when I was born, and within a while afterward that whole empire was his. The great Sultan of Syria thought himself more than his match, and long since you were born hath he that empire too. Then hath he taken Belgrade, the fortress of this realm. And since that hath he destroyed our noble young goodly king, and now two of them strive for us—our Lord send the grace that the third dog carry not away the bone from them both! What of the noble strong city of Rhodes, the winning of which he counted as a victory against the whole body of

Christendom, since all Christendom was not able to defend that strong town against him? Howbeit, if the princes of Christendom everywhere would, where there was need, have set to their hands in time, the Turk would never have taken any one of all those places. But partly because of dissensions fallen among ourselves, and partly because no man careth what harm other folk feel, but each part suffereth the other to shift for itself, the Turk has in a few years wonderfully increased and Christendom on the other hand very sorely decayed. And all this is worked by our wickedness, with which God is not content.

But now, whereas you desire of me some plenty of comforting things, which you may put in remembrance, to comfort your company with—verily, in the rehearsing and heaping of your manifold fears, I myself began to feel that there would be much need, against so many troubles, of many comforting counsels. For surely, a little before you came, as I devised with myself upon the Turk's coming, it happened that my mind fell suddenly from that to devising upon my own departing. Now, albeit that I fully put my trust in God and hope to be a saved soul by his mercy, yet no man is here so sure that without revelation he may stand clean out of dread. So I bethought me also upon the pain of hell, and afterward, then, I bethought me upon the Turk again. And at first methought his terror nothing, when I compared with it the joyful hope of heaven. Then I compared it on the other hand with the fearful dread of hell, casting therein in my mind those terrible fiendish tormentors, with the deep consideration of that furious endless fire. And methought that if the Turk with his whole host, and all his trumpets and timbrels too, were to come to my chamber door and kill me in my bed, in respect of the other reckoning I would regard him not a rush. And yet, when I now heard your lamentable words, laying forth as though it were present before my face that heap of heavy sorrowful tribulations that (besides those that are already befallen) are in short space likely to follow, I waxed myself suddenly somewhat dismayed. And therefore I well approve your request in this behalf, since you wish to have a store of comfort beforehand, ready by you to resort to, and to lay up in your heart as a remedy against the poison of all desperate dread that might arise from occasion of sore tribulation. And I shall be glad, as my poor wit shall serve me, to call to mind with you such things as I before have read, heard, or thought upon, that may conveniently serve us to this purpose.

# I

First shall you, good cousin, understand this: The natural wise men of this world, the old moral philosophers, laboured much in this matter. And many natural reasons have they written by which they might encourage men to set little by such goods—or such hurts, either—the going and coming of which are the matter and cause of tribulation. Such are the goods of fortune, riches, favour, friends, fame, worldly honour, and such other things: or of the body, as beauty, strength, agility, liveliness, and health. These things, as you know, coming to us, are matter of worldly wealth. And, taken from us by fortune or by force or the fear of losing them, they are matter of adversity and tribulation. For tribulation seemeth generally to signify nothing else but some kind of grief, either pain of the body or heaviness of the mind. Now that the body should not feel what it feeleth, all the wit in the world cannot bring that about. But that the mind should not be grieved either with the pain that the body feeleth or with occasions of heaviness offered and given unto the soul itself, this thing the philosophers laboured very much about. And many goodly sayings have they toward strength and comfort against tribulation, exciting men to the full contempt of all worldly loss and the despising of sickness and all bodily grief, painful death and all.

Howbeit, indeed, for anything that ever I read in them, I never could yet find that those natural reasons were ever able to give sufficient comfort of themselves. For they never stretch so far but that they leave untouched, for lack of necessary knowledge, that special point which not only is the chief comfort of all but without which also all other comforts are nothing. And that point is to refer the final end of their comfort unto God, and to repute and take for the special cause of comfort that by the patient sufferance of their tribulation they shall attain his favour and for their pain receive reward at his hand in heaven. And for lack of knowledge of this end, they did, as they needs must, leave untouched also the very special means without which we can never attain to this comfort, which is the gracious aid and help of God to move, stir, and guide us forward in the referring of all our ghostly comfort—yea, and our worldly comfort too—all unto that heavenly end. And therefore, as I say, for the lack of these things, all their comforting counsels are very far insufficient.

Howbeit, though they be far unable to cure our disease of themselves and therefore are not sufficient to be taken for our physicians, some good drugs have they yet in their shops. They may therefore be suffered to dwell among our apothecaries, if their medicines be made not of their own brains but after the bills made by the great physician God, prescribing the medicines himself and correcting the faults of their erroneous recipes. For unless we take this way with them, they shall not fail to do as many bold blind apothecaries do who, either for lucre or out of a foolish pride, give sick folk medicines of their own devising. For therewith do they kill up in corners many such simple folk as they find so foolish as to put their lives in the hands of such ignorant and unlearned Blind Bayards.

We shall therefore neither fully receive these philosophers' reasons in this matter, nor yet utterly refuse them. But, using them in such order as may beseem them, we shall fetch the principal and effectual medicines against these diseases of tribulation from that high, great, and excellent physician without whom we could never be healed of our very deadly disease of damnation. For our necessity in that regard, the Spirit of God spiritually speaketh of himself to us, and biddeth us give him the honour of all our health. And therein he thus saith unto us: "Honour thou the physician, for him hath the high God ordained for thy necessity." Therefore let us pray that high physician, our blessed Saviour Christ, whose holy manhood God ordained for our necessity, to cure our deadly wounds with the medicine made of the most wholesome blood of his own blessed body. And let us pray that, as he cured our mortal malady by this incomparable medicine, it may please him to send us and put in our minds at this time such medicines as may so comfort and strengthen us in his grace against the sickness and sorrows of tribulation, that our deadly enemy the devil may never have the power, by his poisoned dart of murmur, grudge, and impatience, to turn our short sickness of worldly tribulation into the endless everlasting death of infernal damnation.

## II

Since all our principal comfort must come from God, we must first presuppose, in him to whom we shall give any effectual comfort with any ghostly counsel, one ground to begin with, on which all that we shall build may be supported and stand; that is, the ground and foundation of faith. Without this, had ready before, all the spiritual comfort that anyone may speak of can never avail a fly.

For just as it would be utterly vain to lay natural reasons of comfort to him who hath no wit, so would it undoubtedly be frustrate to lay spiritual causes of comfort to him who hath no faith. For unless a man first believe that holy scripture is the word of God, and that the word of God is true, how can he take any comfort in that which the scripture telleth him? A man must needs take little fruit of scripture, if he either believe not that it be the word of God, or else think that, though it were, it might yet for all that be untrue! As this faith is more strong or more faint, so shall the comforting words of holy scripture stand the man in more stead or less.

This virtue of faith can no man give himself, nor yet any man to another. But though men may with preaching be ministers unto God therein; and though a man can, with his own free will, obeying freely the inward inspiration of God, be a weak worker with almighty God therein; yet is the faith indeed the gracious gift of God himself. For, as St. James saith, "Every good gift and every perfect gift is given from above, descending from the Father of lights." Therefore, feeling our faith by many tokens very faint, let us pray to him who giveth it to us, that it may please him to help and increase it. And let us first say with him in the gospel, "I believe, good Lord, but help thou the lack of my belief." And afterwards, let us pray with the apostles, "Lord, increase our faith." And finally, let us consider, by Christ's saying unto them, that, if we would not suffer the strength and fervour of our faith to wax lukewarm—or rather key-cold—and lose its vigour by scattering our minds abroad about so many trifling things that we very seldom think of the matters of our faith, we should withdraw our thought from the respect and regard of all worldly fantasies, and so gather our faith together into a little narrow room. And like the little grain of mustard seed, which is by nature hot, we should set it in the garden of our soul, all weeds being pulled out for the better feeding of our faith. Then shall it grow, and so spread up in height that the birds—that is, the holy angels of heaven—shall breed in our soul, and bring forth virtues in the branches of our faith. And then, with the faithful trust that through the true belief of God's word we shall put in his promise, we shall be well able to command a great mountain of tribulation to void from the place where it stood in our heart, whereas with a very feeble faith and faint, we shall be scantly able to remove a little hillock.

And therefore, as for the first conclusion, since we must of necessity before any spiritual comfort presuppose the foundation of faith, and since no man can give us faith but only God, let us never cease to call upon God for it.

VINCENT: Forsooth, good uncle, methinks that this foundation of faith which, as you say, must be laid first, is so necessarily requisite, that without it all spiritual comfort would be given utterly in vain. And therefore now shall we pray God for a full and fast faith. And I pray you, good uncle, proceed you farther in the process of your matter of spiritual comfort against tribulation.

ANTHONY: That shall I, cousin, with good will.

## III

I will in my poor mind assign, for the first comfort, the desire and longing to be comforted by God. And not without some reason call I this the first cause of comfort. For, as the cure of that person is in a manner desperate, who hath no will to be cured, so is the comfort of that person desperate, who desireth not his own comfort.

And here shall I note you two kinds of folk who are in tribulation and heaviness: one sort that will not seek for comfort, and another sort that will.

And again, of those that will not, there are also two sorts. For the first there are the sort who are so drowned in sorrow that they fall into a careless deadly dullness, regarding nothing, thinking almost of nothing, no more than if they lay in a lethargy. With them it may so befall that wit and remembrance will wear away and fall even fair from them. And this comfortless kind of heaviness in tribulation is the highest kind of the deadly sin of sloth.

Another sort there are, who will seek for no comfort, nor yet receive none, but in their tribulation (be it loss or sickness) are so testy, so fuming, and so far out of all patience that it profiteth no man to speak to them. And these are as furious with impatience as though they were in half a frenzy. And, from a custom of such behaviour, they may fall into one full and whole. And this kind of heaviness in tribulation is even a dangerous high branch of the mortal sin of ire.

Then is there, as I told you, another kind of folk, who fain would be comforted. And yet are they of two sorts too. One sort are those who in their sorrow seek for worldly comfort. And of them shall we now speak the less, for the divers occasions that we shall afterwards have to touch upon them in more places than one. But here will I say this, which I learned of St. Bernard: He who in tribulation turneth himself unto worldly vanities, to get help and comfort from them, fareth like a man who in peril of drowning catcheth whatsoever cometh next to hand, and that holdeth he fast, be it never so simple a stick. But then that helpeth him not, for he draweth that stick down under the water with him, and there they lie both drowned together. So surely, if we accustom ourselves to put our trust of comfort in the delight of these childish worldly things, God shall for that foul fault suffer our tribulation to grow so great that all the pleasures of this world shall never bear us up, but all our childish pleasure shall drown with us in the depth of tribulation.

The other sort is, I say, of those who long and desire to be comforted by God. And as I told you before, they undoubtedly have a great cause of comfort even in that point alone, that they consider themselves to desire and long to be comforted by almighty God. This mind of theirs may well be cause of great comfort to them, for two great considerations.

One is that they see themselves seek for their comfort where they cannot fail to find it. For God both can give them comfort, and will. He can, for he is all-mighty; he will, for he is all-good, and hath himself promised, "Ask and you shall have." He who hath faith—as he must needs have who shall take comfort—cannot doubt but what God will surely keep his promise. And therefore hath he a great cause to be of good comfort, as I say, in that he considereth that he longeth to be comforted by him who, his faith maketh him sure, will not fail to comfort him.

But here consider this: I speak here of him who in tribulation longeth to be comforted by God, and who referreth the manner of his comforting to God. Such a man holdeth himself content, whether God comfort him by taking away or diminishing the tribulation itself, or by giving him patience and spiritual consolation therein. For if he long only to have God take his trouble from him, we cannot so well warrant that mind for a cause of so great comfort. For a man may desire that who never mindeth to be the better, and also may he miss the effect of his desire, because his request is haply not good for him. And of this kind of longing and requiring, we shall have occasion hereafter to speak further. But he who, referring the manner of his comforting to God, desireth of God to be comforted, asketh a thing so lawful and so pleasing to God that he cannot fail to fare well. And therefore hath he, as I say, great cause to take comfort in the very desire itself.

Another cause hath he to take of that desire a very great occasion of comfort. For since his desire is good, and declareth to him that he hath a good faith in God, it is a good token unto him that he is not an abject, cast out of God's gracious favour, since he perceiveth that God hath put such a virtuous, well-ordered appetite in his mind. For as every evil mind cometh of the world and ourselves and the devil, so is every such good mind inspired into man's heart, either immediately or by the mean of our good angel or other gracious occasion, by the goodness of God himself. And what a comfort then may this be to us, when we by that desire perceive a sure undoubted token that towards our final salvation our Saviour is himself so graciously busy about us!

## IV

VINCENT: Forsooth, good uncle, this good mind of longing for God's comfort is a good cause of great comfort indeed—our Lord in tribulation send it to us! But by this I see well, that woe may they be who in tribulation lack that mind and who desire not to be comforted by God, but either are of sloth or impatience discomfortless, or else of folly seek for their chief ease and comfort anywhere else.

ANTHONY: That is, good cousin, very true, as long as they stand in that state. But then you must consider that tribulation is a means to drive them from that state, and that is one of the causes for which God sendeth it unto man. For albeit that pain was ordained by God for the punishment of sins (so that they who never do now but sin cannot but be ever punished in hell) yet in this world, in which his high mercy giveth men space to be better, the punishment that he sendeth by tribulation serveth ordinarily for a means of amendment.

St. Paul himself was sorely against Christ, till Christ gave him a great fall and threw him to the ground, and struck him stark blind. And with that tribulation he turned to him at the first word, and God was his physician and healed him soon after both in body and in soul by his minister Ananias and made him his blessed apostle. Some are in the beginning of tribulation very stubborn and stiff against God, and yet at length tribulation bringeth them home. The proud king Pharaoh did abide and endure two or three of the first plagues, and would not once stoop at them. But then God laid on a sorer lash that made him cry to him for help. And then sent he for Moses and Aaron and confessed himself for a sinner and God for good and righteous. And he prayed them to pray for him and to withdraw that plague, and he would let them go. But when his tribulation was withdrawn, then was he wicked again. So was his tribulation occasion of his profit, and his help in turn was cause of his harm. For his tribulation made him call to God, and his help made hard his heart again. Many a man who in an easy tribulation falleth to seek his ease in the pastime of worldly fantasies, in a greater pain findeth all those comforts so feeble that he is fain to fall to the seeking of God's help.

And therefore is, I say, the very tribulation itself many times a means to bring the man to the taking of the aforementioned comfort therein—that is, to the desire of comfort given by God. For this desire of God's comfort is, as I have proved you, great cause of comfort itself.

## V

Howbeit, though the tribulation itself be a means oftentimes to get a man this first comfort in it, yet sometimes itself alone bringeth not a man to it. And therefore, since unless this comfort be had first, there can in tribulation no other good comfort come forth, we must consider the means by which this first comfort may come.

Meseemeth that if the man of sloth or impatience or hope of worldly comfort have no mind to desire and seek for comfort of God, those who are his friends, who come to visit and comfort him, must before everything put that point in his mind, and not spend the time (as they commonly do) in trifling and in turning him to the fantasies of the world. They must also move him to pray God to put this desire in his mind. For when he once getteth it, he then hath the first comfort—and, without doubt, if it be well considered, a comfort marvellously great. His friends who thus counsel him must also, to the attaining thereof, help to pray for him themselves, and cause him to desire good folk to help him to pray for it. And then, if these ways be taken to get it, I doubt not but the goodness of God shall give it.

## VI

VINCENT: Verily methinketh, good uncle, that this counsel is very good. For unless a person have first a desire to be comforted by God, I cannot see what it can avail to give him any further counsel of any spiritual comfort.

Howbeit, what if the man have this desire of God's comfort: that is, that it may please God to comfort him in his tribulation by taking that tribulation from him—is not this a good desire of God's comfort, and a desire sufficient for him who is in tribulation?

ANTHONY: No, cousin, that it is not. I touched before upon this point and passed it over, because I thought it would fall in our way again, and so know I well that it will, oftener than once. And now am I glad that you yourself move it to me here.

A man may many times, well and without sin, desire of God that the tribulation be taken from him. But neither may we desire that in every case, nor yet very well in any case (except very few) save under a certain condition, either expressed or implied. For tribulations are, as you know well, of many sundry kinds. Some are by loss of goods or possessions, some by the sickness of ourselves, and some by the loss of friends or by some other pain put unto our bodies. Some are by the dread of losing these things that we fain would save, under which fear fall all the same things that we have spoken of before. For we may fear loss of goods or possessions, or the loss of our friends, or their grief and trouble or our own by sickness, imprisonment, or other bodily pain. We may be troubled most of all with the fear of that thing which he feareth least of all who hath most need to do so—that is, the fear of losing through deadly sin the life of his blessed soul. And this last kind of tribulation, as the sorest tribulation of all, though we may touch some pieces of it here and there before, yet the chief part and the principal pain will I reserve to treat apart effectually at the end.

But now, as I said, since the kinds of tribulation are so diverse, a man may pray God to take some of these tribulations from him, and may take some comfort in the trust that God will do so. And therefore against hunger, sickness, and bodily hurt, and against the loss of either body or soul, men may lawfully many times pray to the goodness of God, either for themselves or for their friends. And toward this purpose are expressly prayed many devout orisons in the common services of our mother Holy Church. And toward our help in some of these things serve some of the petitions in the Pater Noster, in which we pray daily for our daily food, and to be preserved from the fall into temptation, and to be delivered from evil.

But yet may we not always pray for the taking away from us of every kind of temptation. For if a man should in every sickness pray for his health again, when should he show himself content to die and to depart unto God? And that mind must a man have, you know, or else it will not be well with him. It is a tribulation to good men to feel in themselves the conflict of the flesh against the soul and the rebellion of sensuality against the rule and governance of reason—the relics that remain in mankind of old original sin, of which St. Paul so sore complaineth in his epistle to the Romans. And yet may we not pray, while we stand in this life, to have this kind of tribulation utterly taken from us. For it is left us by God's ordinance to strive against it and fight with it, and by reason and grace to master it and use it for the matter of our merit.

For the salvation of our soul may we boldly pray. For grace may we boldly pray, for faith, for hope, and for charity, and for every such virtue as shall serve us toward heaven. But as for all the other things before mentioned (in which is contained the matter of every kind of tribulation), we may never well make prayers so precisely but that we must express or imply a condition therein—that is, that if God see the contrary better for us, we refer it wholly to his will. And if that be so, we pray that God, instead of taking away our grief, may send us of his goodness either spiritual comfort to take it gladly or at least strength to bear it patiently.

For if we determine with ourselves that we will take no comfort in anything but the taking of our tribulation from us, then either we prescribe to God that he shall do us no better turn, even though he would, than we will ourselves appoint him; or else we declare that we ourselves can tell better than he what is better for us. And therefore, I say, let us in tribulation desire his help and comfort, and let us remit the manner of that comfort unto his own high pleasure. When we do this, let us nothing doubt but that, as his high wisdom better seeth what is best for us than we can see it ourselves, so shall his sovereign high goodness give us that thing that shall indeed be best.

For otherwise, if we presume to stand to our own choice—unless God offer us the choice himself, as he did to David in the choice of his own punishment, after his high pride conceived in the numbering of the people—we may foolishly choose the worst. And by prescribing unto God ourselves so precisely what we will that he shall do for us, unless of his gracious favour he reject our folly, he shall for indignation grant us our own request, and afterward shall we well find that it shall turn us to harm.

How many men attain health of body for whom it would be better, for their soul's health, that their bodies were sick still? How many get out of prison who happen outside on such harm as the prison would have kept them from? How many who have been loth to lose their worldly goods have, in keeping of their goods, soon afterward lost their life? So blind is our mortality and so unaware what will befall—so unsure also what manner of mind we ourselves will have tomorrow—that God could not lightly do a man more vengeance than to grant him in this world his own foolish wishes.

What wit have we poor fools to know what will serve us? For the blessed apostle himself in his sore tribulation, praying thrice unto God to take it away from him, was answered again by God (in a manner) that he was but a fool in asking that request, but that the help of God's grace in that tribulation to strengthen him was far better for him than to take that tribulation from him. And therefore, perceiving well by experience the truth of the lesson, he giveth us good warning not to be too bold of our minds, when we require aught of God, at his own pleasure. For his own Holy Spirit so sore desireth our welfare that, as men say, he groaneth for us, in such wise as no tongue can tell. "What we may pray for, that would be behovable for us, we cannot ourselves tell," saith St. Paul, "but the Spirit himself desireth for us with unspeakable groanings."

And therefore I say, for conclusion of this point, let us never ask of God precisely our own ease by delivery from our tribulation, but pray for his aid and comfort by such ways as he himself shall best like, and then may we take comfort even of our such request. For we may be sure that this mind cometh of God. And also we may be very sure that as he beginneth to work with us, so—unless we ourselves fly from him—he will not fail to tarry with us. And then, if he dwell with us, what trouble can do us harm? "If God be with us," saith St. Paul, "who can stand against us?"

## VII

VINCENT: You have, good uncle, well opened and declared the question that I demanded you—that is, what manner of comfort a man might pray for in tribulation. And now proceed forth, good uncle, and show us yet farther some other spiritual comfort in tribulation.

ANTHONY: This may be, methinketh, good cousin, great comfort in tribulation: that every tribulation which any time falleth unto us is either sent to be medicinable, if men will so take it; or may become medicinable, if men will so make it; or is better than medicinable, unless we will forsake it.

VINCENT: Surely this is very comforting—if we can well perceive it!

ANTHONY: There three things that I tell you, we shall consider thus: Every tribulation that we fall in, either cometh by our own known deserving deed bringing us to it, as the sickness that followeth our intemperate surfeit or the imprisonment or other punishment put upon a man for his heinous crime; or else it is sent us by God without any certain deserving cause open and known to ourselves, either for punishment of some sins past (we know not certainly which) or for preserving us from sin in which we would otherwise be like to fall; or finally it is not due to the man's sin at all but is for the proof of his patience and increase of his merit. In all the former cases tribulation is, if we will, medicinable. In this last case of all, it is better than medicinable.

## VIII

VINCENT: This seemeth to me very good, good uncle, save that it seemeth somewhat brief and short, and thereby methinketh somewhat obscure and dark.

ANTHONY: We shall therefore, to give it light withal, touch upon every member of it somewhat more at large.
One member is, as you know, of them that fall in tribulation through their own certain well-deserving deed, open and known to themselves, as when we fall in a sickness following upon our own gluttonous feasting, or when a man is punished for his own open fault. These tribulations, and others like them, may seem not to be comfortable, in that a man may be sorry to think himself the cause of his own harm. Yet hath he good cause of comfort in them, if he consider that he may make them medicinable for himself if he will. For whereas there was due to that sin, unless it were purged here, a far greater punishment after this world in another place, this worldly tribulation of pain and punishment, by God's good provision for him put upon him here in this world before, shall by the mean of Christ's passion, if the man will in true faith and good hope by meek and patience sufferance of his tribulation so make it, serve him for a sure medicine to cure him. And it shall clearly discharge him of all the sickness and disease of those pains that he should otherwise suffer afterward. For

such is the great goodness of almighty God that he punisheth not the same thing twice.

And albeit that this punishment is put unto the man, not of his own election and free choice but by force, so that he would fain avoid it and falleth in it against his will, and therefore it seemeth worthy of no thanks; yet the great goodness of almighty God so far surpasseth the poor imperfect goodness of man, that though men make their reckoning here one with another such, God yet of his high bounty in man's account alloweth it toward him far otherwise. For though a man fall in his pain by his own fault, and also at first against his will, yet as soon as he confesseth his fault and applieth his will to be content to suffer that pain and punishment for the same, and waxeth sorry not only that he shall sustain such punishment but also that he hath offended God and thereby deserved much more, our Lord from that time counteth it not for pain taken against his will. But it shall be a marvellous good medicine, and work as a willingly taken pain the purgation and cleansing of his soul with gracious remission of his sin, and of the far greater pain that otherwise would have been prepared for it, peradventure forever in hell. For many there are undoubtedly who would otherwise drive forth and die in their deadly sin, who yet in such tribulation, feeling their own frailty so effectually and the false flattering world failing them, turn full goodly to God and call for mercy. And so by grace they make virtue of necessity, and make a medicine of their malady, taking their trouble meekly, and make a right godly end.

Consider well the story of Acham, who committed sacrilege at the great city of Jericho. Thereupon God took a great vengeance upon the children of Israel, and afterward told them the cause and bade them go seek the fault and try it out by lots. When the lot fell upon the very man who did it—being tried by the lot falling first upon his tribe and then upon his family and then upon his house and finally upon his person—he could well see that he was deprehended and taken against his will. But yet at the good exhortation of Josue saying unto him, "Mine own son, give glory to the God of Israel, and confess and show me what thou hast done, and hide it not," he confessed humbly the theft and meekly took his death for it. And he had, I doubt not, both strength and comfort in his pain, and died a very good man. Yet, if he had never come in tribulation, he would have been in peril never haply to have had just remorse in all his whole life, but might have died wretchedly and gone to the devil eternally. And thus made this thief a good medicine of his well-deserved pain and tribulation.

Consider well the converted thief who hung on Christ's right hand. Did not he, by his meek sufferance and humble knowledge of his fault, asking forgiveness of God and yet content to suffer for his sin, make of his just punishment and well-deserved tribulation a very good special medicine to cure him of all pain in the other world, and win him eternal salvation?

And thus I say that this kind of tribulation, though it seem the most base and the least comfortable, is yet, if the man will so make it, a very marvellous wholesome medicine. And it may therefore be, to the man who will so consider it, a great cause of comfort and spiritual consolation.

## IX

VINCENT: Verily, mine uncle, this first kind of tribulation have you to my mind opened sufficiently. And therefore, I pray you, resort now to the second.

ANTHONY: The second kind, you know, was of such tribulation as is so sent us by God that we know no certain cause deserving that present trouble, as we certainly know that upon such-and-such a surfeit we fell in such-and-such a sickness, or as the thief knoweth that for a certain theft he is fallen into a certain punishment. But yet, since we seldom lack faults against God worthy and well-deserving of great punishment, indeed we may well think—and wisdom it is to do so—that with sin we have deserved it and that God for some sin sendeth it, though we know not certainly for which. And therefore thus far is this kind of tribulation somewhat in effect to be taken alike unto the other. For you see, if we thus will take it, reckoning it to be sent for sin and suffering it meekly therefor, it is medicinable against the pain of the other world to come for our past sins in this world, And this is, as I have showed you, a cause of right great comfort.

But yet may then this kind of tribulation be, to some men of more sober living and thereby of more clear conscience, somewhat a little more comfortable. They may none otherwise reckon themselves than sinners, for, as St. Paul saith, "My conscience grudgeth me not of anything, but yet am I not thereby justified," and, as St. John saith, "If we say that we have no sin in us, we beguile ourselves and truth is there not in us." Yet, forasmuch as the cause is to them not so certain as it is to the others afore-mentioned in the first kind, and forasmuch as it is also certain that God sometimes sendeth tribulation to keep and preserve a man from such sin as he would otherwise fall in (and sometimes also for exercise of their patience and increase of merit), great cause of increase in comfort have those folk of the clearer conscience in the fervour of their tribulation. For they may take the comfort of a double medicine, and also of that thing that is of the kind that we shall finally speak of, that I call "better than medicinable."

But as I have before spoken of this kind of tribulation—how it is medicinable in that it cureth the sin past and purchaseth remission of the pain due for it—so let us somewhat consider how this tribulation sent us by God is medicinable in that it preserveth us from the sins into which we would otherwise be like to fall. If that thing be a good medicine that restoreth us our health when we lose it, as good a medicine must this one be that preserveth our health while we have it, and suffereth us not to fall into that painful sickness that must afterward drive us to a painful remedy!

Now God seeth sometimes that worldly wealth is coming so fast upon someone (who nevertheless is good) that, foreseeing how much weight of worldly wealth the man may bear and how much will overcharge him and enhance his heart up so high that grace should fall from him, God of his goodness, I say, doth anticipate his fall, and sendeth him tribulation betimes while he is yet good. And this he doth to make him know his maker and, by less liking the false flattering world, to set a cross upon the ship of his heart and bear a low sail thereon, so that the boisterous blast of pride blow him not under the water.

Some lovely young lady, lo, who is yet good enough—God seeth a storm come toward her that would, if her health and fat feeding should last a little longer, strike her into some lecherous love and, instead of her old-acquainted knight, lay her abed with a new-acquainted knave. But God, loving her more tenderly than to suffer her to fall into such shameful beastly sin, sendeth her in season a goodly fair fervent fever, that maketh her bones to rattle and wasteth away her wanton flesh. And it beautifieth her fair skin with the colour of a kite's claw, and maketh her look so lovely that her love would have little pleasure to look upon her. And it maketh her also so lusty that if her lover lay in her lap she should so sore long to throw up unto him the very bottom of her stomach that she should not be able to restrain it from him, but suddenly lay it all in his neck!

Did not, as I before told you, the blessed apostle himself confess that the high revelations that God had given him might have enhanced him into so high a pride that he might have caught a foul fall, had not the provident goodness of God provided for his remedy? And what was his remedy but a painful tribulation, so sore that he was fain thrice to call to God to take the tribulation from him. And yet would not God grant his request, but let him lie therein till he himself, who saw more in St. Paul than St. Paul saw in himself, knew well the time was come in which he might well without his harm take it from him.

And thus you see, good cousin, that tribulation is double medicine—both a cure of the sin past, and a preservative from the sin that is to come. And therefore in this kind of tribulation is there good occasion for a double comfort; but that is, I say, diversely to sundry diverse folk, as their own conscience is cumbered with sin or clear. Howbeit, I will advise no man to be so bold as to think that his tribulation is sent him to keep him from the pride of his holiness! Let men leave that kind of comfort hardly to St. Paul, till their living be like his. But of the rest men may well take great comfort and good besides.

## X

VINCENT: The third kind of tribulation, uncle, remaineth now—that is, that which is sent a man by God, and not for his sin either committed or which otherwise would come, and therefore is not medicinable, but is sent for exercise of our patience and increase of our merit, and therefore better than medicinable. Though it be, as you say (and as indeed it is) better for the man than any of the other two kinds in another world, where the reward shall be received, yet I cannot see by what reason a man can in this world, where the tribulation is suffered, take any more comfort in it than in any of the other twain that are sent him for his sin. For he cannot here know whether it be sent him for sin before committed, or for sin that otherwise should befall, or for increase of merit and reward after to come. For every man hath cause enough to fear and think that his sin already past hath deserved it, and that it is not without peril for a man to think otherwise.

ANTHONY: This that you say, cousin, hath place of truth in far the most part of men. And therefore must they not envy nor disdain, since they may take in their tribulation sufficient consolation for their part, that some other who is more worthy may take yet a great deal more. For, as I told you, cousin, though the best must confess himself a sinner, yet there are many men—though to the multitude, few—who for the kind of their living and the clearness of their conscience may well and without sin have a good hope that God sendeth them some great grief for the exercise of their patience and for increase of their merit. This appeareth not only by St. Paul, in the place before remembered, but also by the holy man Job, who in sundry places of his disputations with his burdensome comforters forbore not to say that the clearness of his own conscience declared and showed to himself that he deserved not that sore tribulation that he then had. Howbeit, as I told you before, I will not advise every man at adventure to be bold upon this manner of comfort. But yet know I some men such that I would dare, for their more ease and comfort in their great and grievous pains, to put them in right good hope that God sendeth it unto them not so much for their punishment as for exercise of their patience.

And some tribulations are there, also, that grow upon such causes that in those cases I would never forbear but always would, without any doubt, give that counsel and comfort to any man.

VINCENT: What causes, good uncle, are those?

ANTHONY: Marry, cousin, wheresoever a man falleth in tribulation for the maintenance of justice or for the defence of God's cause. For if I should happen to find a man who had long lived a very virtuous life, and had at last happened to fall into the Turks' hands; and if he there did abide by the truth of his faith and, with the suffering of all kinds of torments taken upon his body, still did teach and testify the truth; and if I should in his passion give him spiritual comfort—might I be bold to tell him no further but that he should take patience in his pain, and that God sendeth it to him for his sin, and that he is well worthy to have it, though it were yet much more? He might then well answer me, and other such comforters, as Job answered his: "Burdensome and heavy comforters be you." Nay, I would not fail to bid him boldly, while I should see him in his passion, to cast sin and hell and purgatory and all upon the devil's pate, and doubt not but—as, if he gave over his hold, all his merit would be lost and he would be turned to misery—so if he stand and persevere still in the confession of his faith, all his whole pain shall turn all into glory.

Yea, more shall I yet say than this. If there were a Christian man who had among those infidels committed a very deadly crime, such as would be worthy of death, not only by their laws but by Christ's too (as manslaughter, or adultery, or other such thing); and if when he were taken he were offered pardon of his life upon condition that he should forsake the faith of Christ; and if this man would now rather suffer death than so do—should I comfort him in his pain only as I would a malefactor? Nay, this man, though he would have died for his sin, dieth now for Christ's sake, since he might live still if he would forsake him. The bare patient taking of his death would have served for the satisfaction of his sin—through the merit of Christ's passion, I mean, without help of which no pain of our own could be satisfactory. But now shall Christ, for his forsaking of his own life in the honour of his faith, forgive the pain of all his sins, of his mere liberality, and accept all the pain of his death for merit of reward in heaven, and shall assign no part of it to the payment of his debt in purgatory, but shall take it all as an offering and requite it all with glory. And this man among Christian men, although he had been before a devil, nothing would I doubt afterward to take him for a martyr.

VINCENT: Verily, good uncle, methinketh this is said marvellous well. And it specially delighteth and comforteth me to hear it, because of our principal fear that I first spoke of, the Turk's cruel incursion into this country of ours.

ANTHONY: Cousin, as for the matter of that fear, I purpose to touch it last of all. Nor meant I here to speak of it, had it not been that the vehemency of your objection brought it in my way. But otherwise I would rather have put instead some example of those who suffer tribulation for maintenance of right and justice, and choose rather to take harm than to do wrong in any manner of matter. For surely if a man may—as indeed he may—have great comfort in the clearness of his conscience, who hath a false crime put upon him and by false witness proved upon him, and who is falsely punished and put to worldly shame and pain for it; a hundred times more comfort may he have in his heart who, where white is called black and right is called wrong, abideth by the truth and is persecuted for justice.

VINCENT: Then if a man sue me wrongfully for my own land, in which I myself have good right, it is a comfort yet to defend it well, since God shall give me thanks for it?

ANTHONY: Nay nay, cousin, nay, there walk you somewhat wide. For there you defend your own right for your temporal avail. But St. Paul counseleth, "Defend not yourselves, my more dear friends," and our Saviour counseleth, "If a man will strive with thee at the law and take away thy coat, leave him thy gown too." The defence therefore of our own right asketh no reward. Say you speed well, if you get leave; look hardly for no thanks!

But on the other hand, if you do as St. Paul biddeth, "Seek not for your own profit but for other folk's" and defend therefore of pity a poor widow or a poor fatherless child, and rather suffer sorrow by some strong extortioner than suffer them to take wrong; or if you be a judge and have such zeal to justice that you will abide tribulation by the malice of some mighty man rather than judge wrong for his favour—such tribulations, lo, are those that are better than only medicinable. And every man upon whom they fall may be bold so to reckon them, and in his deep trouble may well say to himself the words that Christ hath taught him for his comfort, "Blessed be the merciful men, for they shall have mercy given them. Blessed be they that suffer persecution for justice, for theirs is the kingdom of heaven."

Here is a high comfort, lo, for those that are in this case. And their own conscience can show it to them, and can fill their hearts so full with spiritual joy that the pleasure may far surmount the heaviness and grief of all their temporal trouble. But God's nearer cause of faith against the Turks hath yet a far surpassing comfort that by many degrees far excelleth this. And that, as I have said, I purpose to treat last. And for this time this sufficeth concerning the special comfort that men may take in this third kind of tribulation.

## XI

VINCENT: Of truth, good uncle, albeit that every one of these kinds of tribulations have cause of comfort in them, as you have well declared, if men will so consider them, yet hath this third kind above all a special prerogative therein.

ANTHONY: That is undoubtedly true. But yet even the most base kind of them all, good cousin, hath more causes of comfort than I have spoken of yet.

For I have, you know, in that kind that is sent us for our sin, spoken of no other comfort yet but twain: one that it refraineth us from sin that otherwise we would fall in; and one that it serveth us, through the merit of Christ's passion, as a means by which God keepeth us from hell and serveth for the satisfaction of such pain as we should otherwise endure in purgatory. Howbeit, there is therein another great cause of joy besides this. For surely those pains here sent us for our sin, in whatsoever wise they happen to us (be our sin never so sore nor never so open and evident unto ourselves and all the world too), yet if we pray for grace to take them meekly and patiently; and if, confessing to God that it is far too little for our fault, we beseech him nevertheless, since we shall come hence so void of all good works for which we should have any reward in heaven, to be not only so merciful to us as to take our present tribulation in relief of our pains in purgatory, but also so gracious unto us as to take our patience therein for a matter of merit and reward in heaven; I verily trust—and nothing doubt it—that God shall of his high bounty grant us our boon.

For as in hell pain serveth only for punishment without any manner of purging, because all possibility of purging is past; and as in purgatory punishment serveth only for purging, because the place of deserving is past; so while we are yet in this world in which is our place and our time of merit and well-deserving, the tribulation that is sent us for our sin here shall, if we faithfully so desire, beside the cleansing and purging of our pain, serve us also for increase of reward. And so shall, I suppose and trust in God's goodness, all such penance and good works as a man willingly performeth, enjoined by his ghostly father in confession, or which he willingly further doth of his own devotion beside. For though man's penance, with all the good works that he can do, be not able to satisfy of themselves for the least sin that we do, yet the liberal goodness of God, through the merit of Christ's bitter passion—without which all our works could never satisfy so much as a spoonful to a great vesselful in comparison with the merit and satisfaction that Christ has merited and satisfied for us himself—this liberal goodness of God, I say, shall yet at our faithful instance and request cause our penance and tribulation patiently taken in this world to serve us in the other world both for release and reward, tempered after such rate as his high goodness and wisdom shall see best for us, whereof our blind mortality cannot here imagine nor devise the stint.

And thus hath yet even the first and most base kind of tribulation, though not fully so great as the second and very far less than the third, far greater cause of comfort yet than I spoke of before.

## XII

VINCENT: Verily, good uncle, this pleaseth me very well. But yet are there, you know, some of these things now brought in question. For as for any pain due for our sin, to be diminished in purgatory by the patient sufferance of tribulation here, there are, you know, many who utterly deny that, and affirm for a sure truth that there is no purgatory at all. And then, if they say true, is the cause of the comfort gone, if the comfort that we should take be but in vain and needless.

They say, you know, also that men merit nothing at all, but God giveth all for faith alone, and that it would be sin and sacrilege to look for reward in heaven either for our patience and glad suffering for God's sake, or for any other good deed. And then is there gone, if this be thus, the other cause of our further comfort too.

ANTHONY: Cousin, if some things were as they be not, then should some things be as they shall not! I cannot indeed deny that some men have of late brought up some such opinions, and many more than these besides, and have spread them abroad. And it is a right heavy thing to see such variousness in our belief rise and grow among ourselves, to the great encouragement of the common enemies of us all, whereby they have our faith in derision and catch hope to overwhelm us all. Yet do three things not a little comfort my mind. The first is that, in some communications had of late together, there hath appeared good likelihood of some good agreement to grow together in one accord of our faith. The second is that in the meanwhile, till this may come to pass, contentions, disputations, and uncharitable behaviour are prohibited and forbidden in effect upon all parties—all such parties, I mean, as fell before to fight for it. The third is that in Germany, for all their diverse opinions, yet as they agree together in profession of Christ's name, so agree they now together in preparation of a common power, in defence of Christendom against our common enemy the Turk. And I trust in God that this shall not only help us here to strengthen us in this war, but also that, as God hath caused them to agree together in the defence of his name, so shall he graciously bring them to agree together in the truth of his faith. Therefore will I let God work, and leave off contention. And I shall now say nothing but that with which they who are themselves of the contrary mind shall in reason have no cause to be discontented.

First, as for purgatory: Though they think there be none, yet since they deny not that all the corps of Christendom for so many hundred years have believed the contrary, and among them all the old interpreters of scripture from the apostles' days down to our time, many of whom they deny not for holy saints, these men must, of their courtesy, hold my poor fear excused, that I dare not now believe them against all those. And I beseech our Lord heartily for them, that when they depart out of this wretched world, they find no purgatory at all—provided God keep them from hell!

As for the merit of man in his good works, neither are those who deny it fully agreed among themselves, nor is there any man almost of them all that, since they began to write, hath not somewhat changed and varied from himself. And far the more part are thus far agreed with us: Like as we grant them that no good work is worth aught toward heaven without faith; and that no good work of man is rewardable in heaven of its own nature, but through the mere goodness of God, who is pleased to put so high a price upon so poor a thing; and that this price God setteth through Christ's passion, and also because they are his own works with us (for no man worketh good works toward God unless God work with him); and as we grant them also that no man may be proud of his works for his own imperfect working, because in all that he may do he can do God no good, but is an unprofitable servant, and doth but his bare duty—as we, I say, grant them these things, so this one thing or twain do they grant us in turn: That men are bound to work good works if they have time and power, and that whosoever worketh in true faith most, shall be most rewarded. But then they add to this that all his reward shall be given him for his faith alone and nothing for his works at all, because his faith is the thing, they say, that forceth him to work well. I will not strive with them for this matter now. But yet I trust to the great goodness of God, that if the question hang on that narrow point, since Christ saith in the scripture in so many places that men shall in heaven be rewarded for their works, he shall never suffer our souls—who are but mean-witted men and can understand his words only as he himself hath set them and as old holy saints have construed them before and as all Christian people this thousand year have believed—to be damned for lack of perceiving such a sharp subtle thing. Especially since some men who have right good wits, and are beside that right well learned, too, can in no wise perceive for what cause or why these folk who take away the reward from good works and give that reward all whole to faith alone, give the reward to faith rather than to charity. For this grant they themselves, that faith serveth of nothing unless she be accompanied by her sister charity. And then saith the scripture, too, "Of these three virtues, faith, hope, and charity, of all these three, the greatest is charity." And therefore it seemeth as worthy to have the thanks as faith. Howbeit, as I said, I will not strive for it, nor indeed as our matter standeth I shall not greatly need to do so. For if they say that he who suffereth tribulation and martyrdom for the faith shall have high reward, not for his work but for his well-working faith, yet since they grant that have it he shall, the cause of high comfort in the third kind of tribulation standeth. And that is, you know, the effect of all my purpose.

VINCENT: Verily, good uncle, this is truly driven and tried unto the uttermost, it seemeth to me. And therefore I pray you proceed at your leisure.

## XIII

ANTHONY: Cousin, it would be a long work to peruse every comfort that a man may well take in tribulation. For as many comforts, you know, may a man take thereof, as there be good commodities therein. And of those there are surely so many that it would be very long to rehearse and treat of them. But meseemeth we cannot lightly better perceive what profit and commodity, and thereby what comfort, they may take of it who have it, than if we well consider what harm the lack of it is, and thereby what discomfort the lack should be to them that never have it.

So is it now that all holy men agree, and all the scripture is full, and our own experience proveth before our eyes, that we are not come into this wretched world to dwell here. We have not, as St. Paul saith, our dwelling-city here, but we are seeking for the city that is to come. And St. Paul telleth us that we do seek for it, because he would put us in mind that we should seek for it, as good folk who fain would come thither. For surely whosoever setteth so little by it that he careth not to seek for it, it will I fear be long ere he come to it, and marvellous great grace if ever he come thither. "Run," saith St. Paul, "so that you may get it." If it must then be gotten with running, when shall he come at it who lifteth not one step toward it?

Now, because this world is, as I tell you, not our eternal dwelling, but our little-while wandering, God would that we should use it as folk who were weary of it. And he would that we should in this vale of labour, toil, tears, and misery not look for rest and ease, game, pleasure, wealth, and felicity. For those who do so fare like a foolish fellow who, going towards his own house where he should be wealthy, would for a tapster's pleasure become a hostler by the way, and die in a stable, and never come home.

And would God that those that drown themselves in the desire of this world's wretched wealth, were not yet more fools than he! But alas, their folly as far surpasseth the foolishness of that silly fellow as there is difference between the height of heaven and the very depth of hell. For our Saviour saith, "Woe may you be that laugh now, for you shall wail and weep." And "There is a time of weeping," saith the scripture, "and there is a time of laughing." But, as you see, he setteth the weeping time before, for that is the time of this wretched world, and the laughing time shall come after in heaven. There is also a time of sowing and a time of reaping, too. Now must we in this world sow, that we may in the other world reap. And in this short sowing time of this weeping world, must we water our seed with the showers of our tears. And then shall we have in heaven a merry laughing harvest forever. "They went forth and sowed their seeds weeping," saith the prophet. But what, saith he, shall follow thereof? "They shall come again more than laughing, with great joy and exultation, with their handfuls of corn in their hands." Lo, they that in their going home towards heaven sow their seeds with weeping, shall at the day of judgment come to their bodies again with everlasting plentiful laughing. And to prove that this life is no laughing time, but rather the time of weeping, we find that our Saviour himself wept twice or thrice, but never find we that he laughed so much as once. I will not swear that he never did, but at least he left us no example of it. But on the other hand, he left us example of weeping.

Of weeping have we matter enough, both for our own sins and for other folk's, too. For surely so should we do—bewail their wretched sins, and not be glad to detract them nor envy them either. Alas, poor souls, what cause is there to envy them who are ever wealthy in this world, and ever out of tribulation? Of them Job saith, "They lead all their days in wealth, and in a moment of an hour descend into their graves and are painfully buried in hell." St. Paul saith unto the Hebrews that those whom God loveth he chastiseth, "And he scourgeth every son of his that he receiveth." St. Paul saith also, "By many tribulations must we go into the kingdom of God." And no marvel, for our Saviour Christ said of himself unto his two disciples that were going into the village of Emaus, "Know you not that Christ must suffer and so go into his kingdom?" And would we who are servants look for more privilege in our master's house than our master himself? Would we get into his kingdom with ease, when he himself got not into his own but by pain? His kingdom hath he ordained for his disciples, and he saith unto us all, "If any man will be my disciple, let him learn of me to do as I have done, take his cross of tribulation upon his back and follow me." He saith not here, lo, "Let him laugh and make merry." Now if heaven serve but for Christ's disciples, and if they be those who take their cross of tribulation, when shall these folk come there who never have tribulation? And if it be true, as St. Paul saith, that God chastiseth all them that he loveth and scourgeth every child whom he receiveth, and that to heaven shall not come but such as he loveth and receiveth, when shall they come thither whom he never chastiseth, nor never doth vouchsafe to defile his hands upon them or give them so much as one lash? And if we cannot (as St. Paul saith we cannot) come to heaven but by many tribulations, how shall they come thither who never have none at all? Thus see we well, by the very scripture itself, how true the words are of old holy saints, who with one voice (in a manner) say all one thing—that is, that we shall not have continual wealth both in this world and in the other too. And therefore those who in this world without any tribulation enjoy their long continual course of never-interrupted prosperity have a great cause of fear and discomfort lest they be far fallen out of God's favour, and stand deep in his indignation and displeasure. For he never sendeth them tribulation, which he is ever wont to send them whom he loveth. But they that are in tribulation, I say, have on the other hand a great cause to take in their grief great inward comfort and spiritual consolation.

## XIV

VINCENT: Verily, good uncle, this seemeth so indeed. Howbeit, yet methinketh that you say very sore in some things concerning such persons as are in continual prosperity. And they are, you know, not a few; and they are also those who have the rule and authority of this world in their hand. And I know well that when they talk with such great learned men as can, I suppose, tell the truth; and when they ask them whether, while they make merry here in earth all their lives, they may not yet for all that have heaven afterwards too; they do tell them "Yes, yes," well enough. For I have heard them tell them so myself.

ANTHONY: I suppose, good cousin, that no very wise man, and especially none that is also very good, will tell any man fully of that fashion. But surely such as so say to them, I fear me that they flatter them thus either for lucre or for fear.
Some of them think, peradventure, thus: "This man maketh much of me now, and giveth me money also to fast and watch and pray for him. But so, I fear me, would he do no more, if I should go tell him now that all that I do for him will not serve him unless he go fast and watch and pray for

himself too. And if I should add thereto and say further that I trust my diligent intercession for him may be the means that God should the sooner give him grace to amend, and fast and watch and pray and take affliction in his own body, for the bettering of his sinful soul, he would be wonderous wroth with that. For he would be loth to have any such grace at all as should make him go leave off any of his mirth, and so sit and mourn for his sin." Such mind as this, lo, have some of those who are not unlearned, and have worldly wit at will, who tell great men such tales as perilously beguile them. For the flatterer who so telleth them would, if he told a true tale, jeopard to lose his lucre.

Some are there also who tell them such tales for consideration of another fear. For seeing the man so sore set on his pleasure that they despair of any amendment of his, whatsoever they should say to him; and then seeing also that the man doth no great harm, but of a courteous nature doth some good men some good; they pray God themselves to send him grace. And so they let him lie lame still in his fleshly lusts, at the pool that the gospel speaketh of, beside the temple, in which they washed the sheep for the sacrifice, and they tarry to see the water stirred. And when his good angel, coming from God, shall once begin to stir the water of his heart, and move him to the lowly meekness of a simple sheep, then if he call them to him they will tell him another tale, and help to bear him and plunge him into the pool of penance over the hard ears! But in the meanwhile, for fear lest if he would wax never the better he would wax much the worse; and from gentle, smooth, sweet, and courteous, might wax angry, rough, froward, and sour, and thereupon be troublous and tedious to the world to make fair weather with; they give him fair words for the while and put him in good comfort, and let him for the rest take his own chance.

And so deal they with him as the mother doth sometimes with her child, when the little boy will not rise in time for her, but will lie slug-abed, and when he is up weepeth because he has lain so long, fearing to be beaten at school for his late coming thither. She telleth him then that it is but early days, and he shall come in time enough, and she biddeth him, "Go, good son. I warrant thee, I have sent to thy master myself. Take thy bread and butter with thee—thou shalt not be beaten at all!" And thus, if she can but send him merry forth at the door, so that he weep not in her sight at home, she careth not much if he be taken tardy and beaten when he cometh to school.

Surely thus, I fear me, fare many friars and state's chaplains too, in giving comfort to great men when they are both loth to displease them. I cannot commend their doing thus, but surely I fear me thus they do.

## XV

VINCENT: But, good uncle, though some do thus, this answereth not the full matter. For we see that the whole church in the common service uses divers collects in which all men pray, specially for the princes and prelates, and generally every man for others and for himself too, that God would vouchsafe to send them all perpetual health and prosperity. And I can see no good man praying God to send another sorrow, nor are there such prayers put in the priests' breviaries, as far as I can hear. And yet if it were as you say, good uncle, that perpetual prosperity were so perilous to the soul, and tribulation also so fruitful, then meseemeth every man would be bound of charity not only to pray God send his neighbour sorrow, but also to help thereto himself. And when folk were sick, they would be bound not to pray God send them health, but when they came to comfort them, they should say, "I am glad, good friend, that you are so sick—I pray God keep you long therein!" And neither should any man give any medicine to another nor take any medicine himself neither. For by the diminishing of the tribulation he taketh away part of the profit from his soul, which can with no bodily profit be sufficiently recompensed.

And also this you know well, good uncle, that we read in holy scripture of men that were wealthy and rich and yet were good withal. Solomon was, you know, the richest and most wealthy king that any man could in his time tell of, and yet was he well beloved with God. Job also was no beggar, perdy, nor no wretch otherwise. Nor did he lose his riches and his wealth because God would not that his friend should have wealth, but rather for the show of his patience, to the increase of his merit and the confusion of the devil. And, for proof that prosperity may stand with God's favour, "God restored Job double of all" that ever he lost, and gave him afterward long life to take his pleasure long. Abraham was also, you know, a man of great substance, and so continued all his life in honour and wealth. Yea, and when he died, too, he went unto such wealth that when Lazarus died in tribulation and poverty, the best place that he came to was that rich man's bosom!

Finally, good uncle, this we find before our eyes, and every day we prove it by plain experience that many a man is right wealthy and yet therewith right good, and many a miserable wretch is as evil as he is wretched. And therefore it seemeth hard, good uncle, that between prosperity and tribulation the matter should go thus, that tribulation should be given always by God to those that he loveth, for a sign of salvation, and prosperity sent for displeasure, as a token of eternal damnation.

## XVI

ANTHONY: I said not, cousin, that for an undoubted rule, worldly prosperity were always displeasing to God or tribulation evermore wholesome to every man—or else I meant not to say it. For well I know that our Lord giveth in this world unto either sort of folk either sort of fortune. "He maketh his sun to shine both upon the good and the bad, and his rain to fall both on the just and on the unjust." And on the other hand, "he scourgeth every son that he receiveth," yet he beateth not only good folk that he loveth, but "there are many scourges for sinners" also. He giveth evil folk good fortune in this world to call them by kindness—and, if they thereby come not, the more is their unkindness. And yet where wealth will not bring them, he giveth them sometimes sorrow. And some who in prosperity cannot creep forward to God, in tribulation they run toward him apace. "Their infirmities were multiplied," saith the prophet, "and after that they made haste." To some that are good men, God sendeth wealth here also; and they give him great thanks for his gift, and he rewardeth them for the thanks too. To some good folk he sendeth sorrow, and they thank him for that too. If God should give the goods of this world only to evil folk, then would men think that God were not the Lord thereof. If God would give the goods only to good men, then would folk take occasion to serve him but for them. Some will in wealth fall into folly: "When man was in honour, his understanding failed him; then was he compared with beasts and made like unto them." Some men with tribulation will fall into sin, and therefore saith the prophet, "God will not leave the rod of the wicked men upon the lot of righteous men, lest the righteous peradventure extend and stretch out their hands to iniquity." So I deny not that either state, wealth or tribulation, may be matter of virtue and matter of vice also.

But this is the point, lo, that standeth here in question between you and me: not whether every prosperity be a perilous token, but whether continual wealth in this world without any tribulation be a fearful sign of God's indignation. And therefore this mark that we must shoot at, set up well in our sight, we shall now aim for the shot and consider how near toward, or how far off, your arrows are from the mark.

VINCENT: Some of my bolts, uncle, will I now take up myself, and readily put them under my belt again! For some of them, I see well, are not worth the aiming. And no great marvel that I shoot wide, while I somewhat mistake the mark.

ANTHONY: Those that make toward the mark and light far too short, when they are shot, shall I take up for you.
To prove that perpetual wealth should be no evil token, you say first that for princes and prelates, and every man for others, we pray all for perpetual prosperity, and that in the common prayers of the church, too.
Then say you secondly, that if prosperity were so perilous and tribulation so profitable, every man ought to pray God to send others sorrow.
Thirdly, you furnish your objections with examples of Solomon, Job, and Abraham.
And fourthly, in the end of all, you prove by experience of our own time daily before our face, that some wealthy folk are good and some needy ones very wicked. That last bolt, since I say the same myself, I think you will be content to take up, it lieth so far wide.

VINCENT: That will I, with a good will, uncle.

ANTHONY: Well, do so, then, cousin, and we shall aim for the rest.
First must you, cousin, be sure that you look well to the mark, and that you cannot do so unless you know what tribulation is. For since that is one of the things that we principally speak of, unless you consider well what it is, you may miss the mark again.

I suppose now that you will agree that tribulation is every such thing as troubleth and grieveth a man either in body or mind, and is as it were the prick of a thorn, a bramble, or a briar thrust into his flesh or into his mind. And surely, cousin, the prick that very sore pricketh the mind surpasseth in pain the grief that paineth the body, almost as far as doth a thorn sticking in the heart surpass and exceed in pain the thorn that is thrust in the heel.

Now cousin, if tribulation be this that I call it, then shall you soon consider this: There are more kinds of tribulation peradventure than you thought on before. And thereupon it followeth also, since every kind of tribulation is an interruption of wealth, that prosperity (which is but another name for wealth) may be discontinued by more ways than you would before have thought. Then say I thus unto you, cousin: Since tribulation is not only such pangs as pain the body, but every trouble also that grieveth the mind, many good men have many tribulations that every man marketh not, and consequently their wealth is interrupted when other men are not aware. For think you, cousin, that the temptations of the devil, the world, and the flesh, soliciting the mind of a good man unto sin, are not a great inward trouble and grief to his heart? To such wretches as care not for their conscience, but like unreasonable beasts follow their foul affections, many of these temptations are no trouble at all, but matter of their bodily pleasure. But unto him, cousin, that standeth in dread of God, the tribulation of temptation is so painful that, to be rid of it or to be sure of the victory, he would gladly give more than half his substance, be it never so great. Now if he who careth not for God think that this trouble is but a trifle, and that with such tribulation prosperity is not interrupted, let him cast in his mind if he himself come upon a fervent longing for something which he cannot get (as a good man will not), as perchance his pleasure of some certain good woman who will not be caught. And then let him tell me whether the ruffle of his desire shall not so torment his mind that all the pleasures that he can take beside shall, for lack of that one, not please him a pin! And I dare be bold to warrant him that the pain in resisting, and the great fear of falling, that many a good man hath in his temptation, is an anguish and a grief every deal as great as this.

Now I say further, cousin, that if this be true, as indeed it is, that such trouble is tribulation, and thereby consequently an interruption of prosperous wealth, no man meaneth precisely to pray for another to keep him in continual prosperity without any manner of discontinuance or change in this world. For that prayer, without other condition added or implied, would be inordinate and very childish. For it would be to pray either that they should never have temptation, or else that if they had they might follow and fulfil their affection. Who would dare, good cousin, for shame or for sin, for himself or any other man, to make this kind of prayer?

Besides this, cousin, the church, you know, well adviseth every man to fast, to watch, and to pray, both for taming of his fleshly lusts and also to mourn and lament his sin before committed and to bewail his offence done against God, as they did at the city of Nineve, and as the prophet David did for his sin put affliction to his flesh. And when a man so doth, cousin, is this no tribulation to him because he doth it himself? For I know you would agree that it would be, if another man did it against his will. Then is tribulation, you know, tribulation still, though it be taken well in worth. Yea, and though it be taken with very right good will, yet is pain, you know, pain, and therefore so is it, though a man do it himself. Then, since the church adviseth every man to take tribulation for his sin, whatsoever words you find in any prayer, they never mean, do you be fast and sure, to pray God to keep every good man (nor every bad man neither) from every kind of tribulation.

Now he who is not in a certain kind of tribulation, as peradventure in sickness or in loss of goods, is not yet out of tribulation. For he may have his ease of body or mind disquieted (and thereby his wealth interrupted) with another kind of tribulation, as is either temptation to a good man, or voluntary affliction, either of body by penance or of mind by contrition and heaviness for his sin and offence against God. And thus I say that for precise perpetual wealth and prosperity in this world—that is to say, for the perpetual lack of all trouble and tribulation—no wise man prayeth either for himself or for any man else. And thus I answer your first objection.

Now before I meddle with your second, your third will I join to this. For upon this answer will the solution of your examples fittingly depend.

As for Solomon, he was, as you say, all his days a marvellous wealthy king, and much was he beloved with God, I know, in the beginning of his reign. But that the favour of God continued with him, as his prosperity did, that cannot I tell, and therefore will I not warrant it. But surely we see that his continual wealth made him fall into wanton folly, first in multiplying wives to a horrible number, contrary to the commandment of God, given in the law of Moses, and secondly in taking to wife among others some who were infidels, contrary to another commandment of God's written law. Also we see that finally, by means of his infidel wife, he fell into maintenance of idolatry himself. And of this we find no amendment or repentance, as we find of his father. And therefore, though he were buried where his father was, yet whether he went to the rest that his father did, through some secret sorrow for his sin at last—that is to say, by some kind of tribulation—I cannot tell, and am content therefore to trust well and pray God that he did so. But surely we are not so sure, and therefore the example of Solomon can very little serve you. For you might as well lay it for a proof that God favoureth idolatry as that he favoureth prosperity; for Solomon was, you know, in both.

As for Job, since our question hangeth upon prosperity that is perpetual, the wealth of Job, which was interrupted with so great adversity, can, as you yourself see, serve you for no example. And that God gave him here in this world all things double that he lost, little toucheth my matter, which denieth not prosperity to be God's gift, and given to some good men, too; namely, to such as have tribulation too.

But in Abraham, cousin, I suppose is all your chief hold, because you not only show riches and prosperity perpetual in him through the course of all his whole life in this world, but after his death also. Lazarus, that poor man, who lived in tribulation and died for pure hunger and thirst, had after his death his place of comfort and rest in Abraham's—that wealthy man's—bosom. But here must you consider that Abraham had not such continual prosperity but what it was discontinued with divers tribulations.

Was it nothing to him, think you, to leave his own country, and at God's sending to go into a strange land, which God promised him and his seed forever, but in all his life he gave him never a foot? Was it no trouble, that his cousin Loth and himself were fain to part company, because their servants could not agree together? Though he recovered Loth again from the three kings, was his capture no trouble to him, think you, in the meanwhile? Was the destruction of the five cities no heaviness to his heart? Any man would think so, who readeth in the story what labour he made to save them. His heart was, I daresay, in no little sorrow, when he was fain to let Abimelech the king have his wife. Though God provided to keep her undefiled and turned all to wealth, yet it was no little woe to him in the meantime. What continual grief was it to his heart, many a long day, that he had no child begotten of his own body? He that doubteth thereof shall find in Genesis Abraham's own moan made to God. No man doubteth but Ismael was great comfort unto him at his birth; and was it no grief, then, when he must cast out the mother and the child both? As for Isaac, who was the child of the promise, although God kept his life, that was unlooked for. Yet while the loving father bound him and went about to behead him and offer him up in sacrifice, who but himself can conceive what heaviness his heart had then? I should suppose (since you speak of Lazarus) that Lazarus' own death panged him not so sore. Then, as Lazarus' pain was patiently borne, so was Abraham's taken not only patiently but—which is a thing much more meritorious—of obedience willingly. And therefore, even if Abraham had not far excelled Lazarus in merit of reward (as he did indeed) for many other things besides, and especially for that he was a special patriarch of the faith, yet would he have far surpassed him even by the merit of that tribulation well taken here for God's sake too. And so serveth for your purpose no man less than Abraham!

But now, good cousin, let us look a little longer here upon the rich Abraham and Lazarus the poor. And as we shall see Lazarus set in wealth somewhat under the rich Abraham, so shall we see another rich man lie full low beneath Lazarus, crying and calling out of his fiery couch that Lazarus might, with a drop of water falling from his finger's end, a little cool and refresh the tip of his burning tongue. Consider well now what Abraham answered to the rich wretch: "Son, remember that thou hast in thy life received wealth, and Lazarus likewise pain, but now receiveth he comfort, and thou sorrow, pain, and torment." Christ described his wealth and his prosperity: gay and soft apparel with royal delicate fare, continually day by day. "He did fare royally every day," saith our Saviour; his wealth was continual, lo, no time of tribulation between. And Abraham telleth him the same tale, that he had taken his wealth in this world, and Lazarus likewise his pain, and that they had now changed each to the clean contrary—poor Lazarus from tribulation into wealth, and the rich man from his continual prosperity into perpetual pain. Here was laid expressly to Lazarus no very great virtue by name, nor to this rich glutton no great heinous crime but the taking of his continual ease and pleasure, without any tribulation or grief, of which grew sloth and negligence to think upon the poor man's pain. For that ever he himself saw Lazarus and knew that he died for hunger at his door, that laid neither Christ nor Abraham to his charge. And therefore, cousin, this story of which, by occasion of Abraham and Lazarus, you put me in remembrance, well declareth what peril there is in continual worldly wealth; and contrariwise what comfort cometh of tribulation. And thus, as your other examples of Solomon and Job nothing for the matter further you, so your example of rich Abraham and poor Lazarus hath not a little hindered you.

## XVII

VINCENT: Surely, uncle, you have shaken my examples sorely, and have in your aiming of your shot removed me these arrows, methinketh, further off from the mark than methought they stuck when I shot them! And I shall therefore now be content to take them up again.

But meseemeth surely that my second shot may stand. For of truth, if every kind of tribulation be so profitable that it be good to have it, as you say it is, then I cannot see why any man should either wish, or pray, or do any manner of thing to have any kind of tribulation withdrawn either from himself or from any friend of his.

ANTHONY: I think indeed tribulation so good and profitable that I might doubt, as you do, why a man might labour and pray to be delivered of it, were it not that God, who teacheth us the one, teacheth us also the other. For as he biddeth us take our pain patiently, and exhort our neighbours to do also the same, so biddeth he us also not forbear to do our best to remove the pain from us both. And then, since it is God who teacheth both, I shall not need to break my brain in devising wherefore he would bid us to do both, the one seeming opposed to the other.

If he send the scourge of scarcity and great famine, he will that we shall bear it patiently; but yet will he that we shall eat our meat when we can get it. If he send us the plague of pestilence, he will that we shall patiently take it; but yet will he that we let blood, and lay plasters to draw it and ripen it, and lance it, and get it away. Both these points teacheth God in scripture, in more than many places. Fasting is better than eating, and hath more thanks of God, and yet will God that we shall eat. Praying is better than drinking, and much more pleasing to God, and yet will God that we shall drink. Keeping vigil is much more acceptable to God than sleeping, and yet will God that we shall sleep. God hath given us our bodies here to keep, and will that we maintain them to do him service with, till he send for us hence.

Now we cannot tell surely how much tribulation may mar the body or peradventure hurt the soul also. Therefore the apostle, after he had commanded the Corinthians to deliver to the devil the abominable fornicator who forbore not the bed of his own father's wife, yet after he had been a while accursed and punished for his sin, the apostle commanded them charitably to receive him again and give him consolation, "that the greatness of his sorrow should not swallow him up." And therefore, when God sendeth the tempest, he will that the shipmen shall get them to their tackling and do the best they can for themselves, that the sea eat them not up. For help ourselves as well as we can, he can make his plague as sore and as long-lasting as he himself please.

And as he will that we do for ourselves, so will he that we do for our neigbour too. And he will that we shall in this world have pity on each other and not be sine affectione, for which the apostle rebuketh them that lack their tender affection here. So of charity we should be sorry too for the pain of those upon whom, for necessary cause, we ourselves be driven to put it. And whosoever saith that for pity of his neighbour's soul he will have no pity of his body, let him be sure that, as St. John saith, "He that loveth not his neighbour whom he seeth, loveth but little God, whom he seeth not," so he who hath no pity on the pain that he seeth his neighbour feel before him, pitieth little (whatsoever he say) the pain of his soul that he seeth not.

Yet God sendeth us also such tribulation sometimes because it is his pleasure to have us pray unto him for help. And therefore, the scripture telleth that, when St. Peter was in prison, the whole church without intermission prayed incessantly for him, and at their fervent prayer God by miracle delivered him. When the disciples in the tempest stood in fear of drowning, they prayed unto Christ and said, "Save us, Lord, we perish," and then at their prayer he shortly ceased the tempest. And now see we proved often that in sore weather or sickness by general processions God giveth gracious help. And many a man in his great pain and sickness, by calling upon God is marvellously made whole. This is the goodness of God who, because in wealth we remember him not, but forget to pray to him, sendeth us sorrow and sickness to force us to draw toward him, and compelleth us to call upon him and pray for release of our pain. When we learn thereby to know him and to pray to him, we take a good occasion to fall afterward into further grace.

# XVIII

VINCENT: Verily, good uncle, with this good answer I am well content.

ANTHONY: Yea, cousin, but many men are there with whom God is not content! For they abuse this great high goodness of his, whom neither fair treating nor hard handling can cause to remember their maker. But in wealth they are wanton and forget God and follow their pleasure, and when God with tribulation draweth them toward him, then wax they mad and draw back as much as ever they can, and run and seek help at any other hand rather than at his. Some for comfort seek to the flesh, some to the world, and some to the devil himself.

Consider some man who in worldly prosperity is very dull and hath stepped deep into many a sore sin; which sins, when he did them, he counted for part of his pleasure. God, willing of his goodness to call the man to grace, casteth a remorse into his mind, after his first sleep, and maketh him lie a little while and bethink him. Then beginneth he to remember his life, and from that he falleth to think upon his death, and how he must leave all his worldly wealth within a while behind here in this world, and walk hence alone, he knows not whither. Nor knows he how soon he shall take his journey thither, nor can he tell what company he shall meet there. And then beginneth he to think that it would be good to make sure and to be merry, so that he be wise therewith, lest there happen to be indeed such black bugbears as folk call devils, whose torments he was wont to take for poet's tales. Those thoughts, if they sink deep, are a sore tribulation. And surely, if he takes hold of the grace that God therein offereth him, his tribulation is wholesome. And it shall be full comforting to remember that God by this tribulation calleth him and biddeth him come home, out of the country of sin that he was bred and brought up so long in, and come into the land of behest that floweth milk and honey. And then if he follow this calling, as many a one full well doth, joyful shall his sorrow be. And glad shall he be to change his life, to leave his wanton pleasures and do penance for his sins, bestowing his time upon some better business.

But some men, now, when this calling of God causeth them to be sad, they are loth to leave their sinful lusts that hang in their hearts, especially if they have any kind of living such that they must needs leave it off or fall deeper into sin, or if they have done so many great wrongs that they have many amends to make if they follow God, which must diminish much their money. Then are these folk, alas, woefully bewrapped, for God pricketh them of his great goodness still. And the grief of this great pang pincheth them at the heart, and of wickedness they wry away. And from this tribulation they turn to their flesh for help, and labour to shake off this thought. And then they mend their pillow and lay their head softer and essay to sleep. And when that will not be, then they talk a while with those who lie by them. If that cannot be either, then they lie and long for day, and get them forth about their worldly wretchedness, the matter of their prosperity, and the selfsame sinful things with which they displease God most. And at length, when they have many times behaved in this manner, God utterly casteth them off. And then they set naught by either God or devil. "When the sinner cometh even into the depth, then he contemneth," and setteth naught by anything, saving worldly fear that may befall by chance, or that needs must, he knoweth well, befall once by death.

But alas, when death cometh, then cometh again his sorrow. Then will no soft bed serve, nor no company make him merry. Then must he leave his outward worship and comfort of his glory, and lie panting in his bed as it were on a pine bench. Then cometh his fear of his evil life and of his dreadful death. Then cometh his torment, his cumbered conscience and fear of his heavy judgment. Then the devil draweth him to despair with imagination of hell, and suffereth him not then to take it for a fable—and yet, if he do, then the wretch findeth it no fable. Ah, woe worth the time, that folk think not of this in time!

God sometimes sendeth a man great trouble in his mind, and great tribulation about his worldly goods, because he would of his goodness take his delight and confidence from them. And yet the man withdraweth no part of his foolish fancies, but falleth more fervently to them than before, and setteth his whole heart, like a fool, more upon them. And then he betaketh him all to the devices of his worldly counsellors, and without any counsel of God or any trust put in him, maketh many wise ways—or so he thinks, but all turn at length to folly, and one subtle drift driveth another to naught.

Some have I see even in their last sickness, set up in their deathbed, underpropped with pillows, take their playfellows to them and comfort themselves with cards. And this, they said, did ease them well, to put fancies out of their heads. And what fancies, think you? Such as I told you right now, of their own lewd life and peril of their soul, of heaven and of hell, that irked them to think of. And therefore they cast it out with cards, playing as long as ever they might, till the pure pangs of death pulled their heart from their play, and put them in such a case that they could not reckon their game. And then their gamesters left them and slyly slunk away, and it was not long ere they galped up the ghost. And what game they came then to, that God knoweth and not I. I pray God it were good, but I fear it very sore.

Some men are there also that do as did King Saul, and in their tribulation go seek unto the devil. This king had commanded all those to be destroyed who used the false abominable superstition of this ungracious witchcraft and necromancy. And yet fell he to such folly afterwards himself, that ere he went to battle he sought unto a witch and besought her to raise up a dead man to tell him how he should fare. Now God had showed him by Samuel before that he should come to naught, and he went about no amendment, but waxed worse and worse, so that God would not look to him. And when he sought by the prophet to have answer of God, there came no answer to him, which he thought strange. And because he was not heard by God at his pleasure, he made suit to the devil, desiring a woman by witchcraft to raise up the dead Samuel. But he had such success thereof as commonly they have who in their business meddle with such matters. For an evil answer had he, and an evil fortune thereafter—his army discomfited and himself slain. And as it is rehearsed in Paralipomenon, the tenth chapter of the first book, one cause of his fall was for lack of trust in God, for which he left off taking counsel of God and fell to seek counsel of the witch, against God's prohibition in the law and against his own good deed by which he punished and put out all witches so short a time before. Such fortune let them look for, who play the same part! I see many do so, who in a great loss send to seek a conjurer to get their belongings again. And marvellous things there they see, sometimes, but never great of their good. And many a silly fool is there who, when he lies sick, will meddle with no physic in no manner of wise, nor send his urine to no learned man, but will send his cap or his hose to a wisewoman, otherwise called a witch. Then sendeth she word back that she hath spied in his hose where, when he took no heed, he was taken with a spirit between two doors as he went in the twilight. But the spirit would not let him feel it for five days after, and it hath all the while festered in his body, and that is the grief that paineth him so sore. But let him go to no leechcraft nor any manner of physic—other than good meat and strong drink—for medicines would pickle him up. But he shall have five leaves of valerian that she enchanted with a charm and gathered with her left hand. Let him fasten those five leaves to his right thumb by a green thread—not bind it fast, but let it hang loose. He shall never need to change it, provided it fall not away, but let it hang till he be whole and he shall need it no more. In such wise witches, and in such mad medicines, have many fools a great deal more faith than in God.

And thus, cousin, as I tell you, all these folk who in their tribulation call not upon God, but seek for their ease and help elsewhere—to the flesh and the world, and to the flinging fiend—the tribulation that God's goodness sendeth them for good, they themselves by their folly turn into their harm. And those who, on the other hand, seek unto God therein, both comfort and profit they greatly take thereby.

## XIX

VINCENT: I like well, good uncle, all your answers therein. But one doubt yet remaineth there in my mind, which ariseth upon this answer that you make. And when that doubt is solved, I will, mine own good uncle, encumber you no further for this time. For methinketh that I do you very much wrong to give you occasion to labour yourself so much in matter of some study, with long talking at once. I will therefore at this time move you but one thing, and seek some other time at your greater ease for the rest.

My doubt, good uncle, is this: I perceive well by your answers, gathered and considered together, that you will well agree that a man may both have worldly wealth and yet well go to God; and that, on the other hand, a man may be miserable and live in tribulation and yet go to the devil. And as a man may please God by patience in adversity, so may he please God by thanks given in prosperity. Now since you grant these things to be such that either of them both may be matter of virtue or else matter of sin, matter of damnation or matter of salvation, they seem neither good nor bad of their own nature, but things of themselves equal and indifferent, turning to good or to the contrary according as they be taken. And then if this be thus, I can perceive no cause why you should give the pre-eminence unto tribulation, or wherefore you should reckon more cause of comfort in it than in prosperity, but rather a great deal less—in a manner, by half.

For in prosperity a man is well at ease, and may also, by giving thanks to God, get good unto his soul; whereas in tribulation, though he may merit by patience (as the other, in abundance of worldly wealth, may merit by thanks), yet lacketh he much comfort that the wealthy man hath, in that he is sore grieved with heaviness and pain. Besides, a wealthy man, well at ease, may pray to God quietly and merrily with alacrity and great quietness of mind, whereas he who lieth groaning in his grief cannot endure to pray nor can he hardly think upon anything but his pain.

ANTHONY: To begin, cousin, where you leave off: The prayers of him that is in wealth and him that is in woe, if the men be both wicked, are both alike. For neither hath the one desire to pray, nor the other either. And as one is hindered with his pain, so is the other with his pleasure—saving that pain stirreth a man sometimes to call upon God in his grief, though he be right bad, whereas pleasure pulleth his mind another way, though he be good enough.

And this point I think there are few that can, if they say true, say that they find it otherwise. For in tribulation (which cometh, you know, in sundry kinds) any man that is not a dull beast or a desperate wretch calleth upon God, not hoverly but right heartily, and setteth his heart full whole upon his request, so sore he longeth for ease and help of his heaviness. But when we are wealthy and well at our ease, while our tongue pattereth upon our prayers apace—good God, how many mad ways our mind wandereth the while!

Yet I know well that in some tribulation there is such sore sickness or other grievous bodily pain that it would be hard for a man to say a longer prayer of matins. And yet some who lie dying say full devoutly the seven psalms and other prayers with the priest at their anointing. But those who for the grief of their pain cannot endure to do it, or who are more tender and lack that strong heart and stomach that some others have, God requireth no such long prayers of them. But the lifting up of their heart alone, without any words at all, is more acceptable to him from one in such a state, than long service so said as folk usually say it in health. The martyrs in their agony made no long prayers aloud, but one inch of such a prayer, so prayed in that pain, was worth a whole ell or more, even of their own prayers, prayed at some other time.

Great learned men say that Christ, albeit that he was true God, and as God was in eternal equal bliss with his Father, yet as man merited not only for us but for himself too. For proof of this they lay in these words the authority of St. Paul: "Christ hath humbled himself, and became obedient unto the death, and that unto the death of the cross; for which thing God hath also exalted him and given him a name which is above all names, that in the name of Jesus every knee be bowed, both of the celestial creatures and of the terrestrial and of the infernal too, and that every tongue shall confess that our lord Jesus Christ is in the glory of God his Father." Now if it be so as these great learned men say, upon such authorities of holy scripture, that our Saviour merited as man, and as man deserved reward not for us only but for himself also; then were there in his deeds, it seemeth, sundry degrees and differences of deserving. His washing of the disciples' feet was not, then, of like merit as his passion, nor his sleep of like merit as his vigil and his prayer—no, nor his prayers peradventure all of like merit, either. But though there was not, nor could be, in his most blessed person any prayer but was excellent and incomparably surpassing the prayer of any mere creature, yet his own were not all alike, but one far above another. And then if it thus be, of all his holy prayers, the chief seemeth me those that he made in his great agony and pain of his bitter passion. The first was when he thrice fell prostrate in his agony, when the heaviness of his heart with fear of death at hand, so painful and so cruel as he well beheld it, made such a fervent commotion in his blessed body that the bloody sweat of his holy flesh dropped down on the ground. The others were the painful prayers that he made upon the cross, where, for all the torment that he hanged in—of beating, nailing, and stretching out all his limbs, with the wresting of his sinews and breaking of his tender veins, and the sharp crown of thorns so pricking him into the head that his blessed blood streamed down all his face—in all these hideous pains, in all their cruel despites, yet two very devout and fervent prayers he made. One was for the pardon of those who so dispiteously put him to his pain, and the other about his own deliverance, commending his own soul to his holy Father in heaven. These prayers of his, made in his most pain, among all that ever he made, reckon I for the chief. And these prayers of our Saviour at his bitter passion, and of his holy martyrs in the fervour of their torment, shall serve us to see that there is no prayer made at pleasure so strong and effectual as that made in tribulation.

Now come I to the reasoning you make, when you tell me that I grant you that both in wealth and in woe a man may be wicked and offend God, in the one by impatience and in the other by fleshly lust. And on the other hand, both in tribulation and prosperity too, a man may also do very well and deserve thanks of God by thanksgiving to God for his gift of riches, worship, and wealth, as well as for his gift of need and penury, imprisonment, sickness, and pain. And therefore you cannot see why I should give any pre-eminence in comfort unto tribulation, but you would rather allow prosperity for the thing more comforting. And that not a little, but in manner by double, since therein hath the soul comfort and the body too—the soul by thanksgiving unto God for his gifts, and the body by being well at ease—whereas the person pained in tribulation taketh no comfort but in his soul alone.

First, as for your double comfort, cousin, you may cut off the one! For a man in prosperity, though he be bound to thank God for his gifts, wherein he feeleth ease, and may be glad also that he giveth thanks to God; yet hath he little cause of comfort in that he taketh his ease here, unless you wish to call by the name of comfort the sensual feeling of bodily pleasure. I deny not that sometimes men so take it, when they say, "This good drink comforteth well mine heart." But comfort, cousin, is properly taken, by them that take it right, rather for the consolation of good hope that men take in their heart, of some good growing toward them, than for a present pleasure with which the body is delighted and tickled for a while.

Now, though a man without patience can have no reward for his pain, yet when his pain is patiently taken for God's sake and his will conformed to God's pleasure therein, God rewardeth the sufferer in proportion to his pain. And this thing appeareth by many a place in scripture, some of which I have showed you and yet shall I show you more. But never found I any place in scripture that I remember in which, though a rich man thanked God for his gifts, our Lord promised him any reward in heaven for the very reason that he took his ease and his pleasures here. And therefore, since I speak only of such comfort as is true comfort indeed, by which a man hath hope of God's favour and remission of his sins, with diminishing of his pain in purgatory or else reward in heaven; and since such comfort cometh of tribulation well taken, but not of pleasure even though it be well taken, therefore of your comfort that you double by prosperity, you may, as I told you, very well cut away the half.

Now, why I give prerogative in comfort unto tribulation far above prosperity, though a man may do well in both, of this will I show you causes two or three. First, as I before have at length showed you out of all question, continual wealth interrupted with no tribulation is a very discomfortable token of everlasting damnation. Thereupon it followeth that tribulation is one cause of comfort unto a man's heart, in that it dischargeth him of the discomfort that he might of reason take of overlong-lasting wealth. Another is, that the scripture much commendeth tribulation as occasion of more profit than wealth and prosperity, not only to those who are therein but to those who resort unto them too. And therefore saith Ecclesiastes, "Better is it to go to the house of weeping and wailing for some man's death, than to the house of a feast; for in that house of heaviness is a man put in remembrance of the end of every man, and while he liveth he thinketh what shall come after." And after yet he further saith, "The heart of wise men is where heaviness is, and the heart of fools is where there is mirth and gladness." And verily, where you shall hear worldly mirth seem to be commended in scripture, it is either commonly spoken, as in the person of some worldly-disposed people, or else understood of spiritual rejoicing, or else meant of some small moderate refreshing of the mind against a heavy and discomfortable dullness.

Now, prosperity was promised to the children of Israel in the old law as a special gift of God, because of their imperfection at that time, to draw them to God with gay things and pleasant, as men, to make children learn, give them cake-bread and butter. For, as the scripture maketh mention, that people were much after the manner of children in lack of wit and in waywardness. And therefore was their master Moses called Pedagogus, that is, a teacher of children or (as they call such a one in the grammar schools) an "usher" or "master of the petits." For, as St. Paul saith, "the old law brought nothing unto perfection." And God also threateneth folk with tribulation in this world for sin, not because worldly tribulation is evil, but that we should well beware of the sickness of sin for fear of the thing to follow. For that thing, though it be indeed a very good wholesome thing if we take it well, is yet, because it is painful, the thing that we are loth to have. But this I say yet again and again, that the scripture undoubtedly so commandeth tribulation as far the better thing in this world toward the getting of the true good that God giveth in the world to come, that in comparison it utterly discommendeth this worldly wretched wealth and discomfortable comfort. For to what other thing tend the words of Ecclesiastes that I rehearsed to you now, that it is better to be in the house of heaviness than to be at a feast? Whereto tendeth this comparison of his, that the wise man's heart draweth thither where folk are in sadness, and the heart of a fool is where he may find mirth? Whereto tendeth this threat of the wise man, that he who delighteth in wealth shall fall into woe? "Laughter," saith he, "shall be mingled with sorrow, and the end of mirth is taken up with heaviness." And our Saviour saith himself, "Woe be to you that laugh, for you shall weep and wail." But he saith, on the other hand, "Blessed are they that weep and wail, for they shall be comforted." And he saith to his disciples, "The world shall rejoice and you shall be sorry, but your sorrow shall be turned into joy." And so it is now, as you well know, and the mirth of many who then were in joy is now turned all to sorrow. And thus you see plainly by scripture that, in matter of true comfort, tribulation is as far above prosperity as the day is about the night.

Another pre-eminence of tribulation over wealth, in occasion of merit and reward, shall well appear upon certain considerations well marked in them both. Tribulation meriteth in patience and in the obedient conforming of the man's will unto God, and in thanks given to God for his visitation. If you reckon me now, against these, many other good deeds that a wealthy man may do—as, by riches to give alms, or by authority to labour in doing many men justice—or if you find further any other such thing; first, I say that the patient person in tribulation hath, in all these virtues of a wealthy man, an occasion of merit which the wealthy man hath not. For it is easy for the person who is in tribulation to be well willing to do the selfsame thing if he could. And then shall his good will, where the power lacketh, go very near to the merit of the deed. But the wealthy man, now, is not in a like position with regard to the will of patience and conformity and thanks given to God for tribulation. For the wealthy man is not so ready to be content to be in tribulation, which is the occasion of the sufferer's deserving, as the troubled person is to be content to be in prosperity, to do the good deeds that the wealthy man doth. Besides this, all that the wealthy man doth, though he could not do them without those things that are counted for wealth and called by that name—as, not do great alms without great riches, nor do these many men right by his labour without great authority—yet may he do these things being not in wealth indeed. As where he taketh his wealth for no wealth and his riches for no riches, and in heart setteth by neither one, but secretly liveth in a contrite heart and a penitential life, as many times did the prophet David, being a great king, so that worldly wealth was no wealth to him. And therefore worldly wealth is not of necessity the cause of these good deeds, since he may do them (and he doth them best, indeed) to whom the thing that worldly folk call wealth is yet, for his godly-set mind, withdrawn from the delight thereof, no pleasure nor wealth at all.

    Finally, whenever the wealthy man doth those good virtuous deeds, if we rightly consider the nature of them, we shall perceive that in the doing of them he doth ever, for the ratio and proportion of those deeds, diminish the matter of his worldly wealth. In giving great alms, he parteth with a certain amount of his worldly goods, which are in that amount the matter of his wealth. In labouring about the doing of many good deeds, his labour diminisheth his quiet and his rest, and to that extent it diminisheth his wealth, if pain and wealth be each contrary to the other, as I think you will agree that they are. Now, whosoever then will well consider the thing, he shall, I doubt not, perceive and see that in these good deeds that the wealthy man doth, though it be his wealth that maketh him able to do them, yet in so far as he doth them he departeth in that proportion from the nature of wealth toward the nature of some tribulation. And therefore even in those good deeds themselves that prosperity doth, the prerogative in goodness of tribulation above wealth doth appear.

    Now if it happen that some man cannot perceive this point because the wealthy man, for all his alms, abideth rich still, and for all his good labour abideth still in his authority, let him consider that I speak only according to proportion. And because the proportion of all that he giveth of his goods is very little in respect of what he leaveth, therefore is the reason haply with some folk little perceived. But if it were so that he went on giving until he had given out all, and left himself nothing, then would even a blind man see it. For as he would be come from riches to poverty, so would he be willingly fallen from wealth into tribulation. And in respect of labour and rest, the same would be true. Whosoever can consider this, shall see that, in every good deed done by the wealthy man, the matter is proportionately the same.

    Then, since we have somewhat weighed the virtues of prosperity, let us consider on the other hand the afore-named things that are the matter of merit and reward in tribulation—that is, patience, conformity, and thanksgiving. Patience the wealthy man hath not, in so far as he is wealthy.

For if he be pinched in any point in which he taketh patience, to that extent he suffereth some tribulation. And so not by his prosperity but by his tribulation hath he that merit. It is the same if we would say that the wealthy man hath another virtue instead of patience—that is, the keeping of himself from pride and such other sins as wealth would bring him to. For the resisting of such motions is, as I before told you, without any doubt a diminishing of fleshly wealth, and is a very true kind (and one of the most profitable kinds) of tribulation. So all that good merit groweth to the wealthy man not by his wealth but by the diminishing of his wealth with wholesome tribulation.

The most colour of comparison is in the other two; that is, in the conformity of man's will unto God, and in thanks given unto God. For as the good man, in tribulation sent him by God, conformeth his will to God's will in that behalf, and giveth God thanks for it; so doth the wealthy man, in his wealth which God giveth him, conform his will to God in that point, since he is well content to take it as his gift, and giveth God also right hearty thanks for it. And thus, as I said, in these two things can you catch the most colour to compare the wealthy man's merit with the merit of tribulation.

But yet that they be not matches, you may soon see by this: For no one can conform his will unto God's in tribulation and give him thanks for it, but such a man as hath in that point a very specially good disposition. But he that is truly wicked, or hath in his heart but very little good, may well be content to take wealth at God's hand, and say, "Marry, I thank you, sir, for this with all my heart, and I will not fail to love you well—while you let me fare no worse!" Confitebitur tibi, cum benefeceris ei. Now, if the wealthy man be very good, yet, in conformity of his will and thanksgiving to God for his wealth, his virtue is not like to that of him who doth the same in tribulation. For, as the philosophers said very well of old, "virtue standeth in things of hardness and difficulty." And then, as I told you, it is much less hard and less difficult, by a great deal, to be content and conform our will to God's will and to give him thanks, too, for our ease than for our pain, for our wealth and for our woe. And therefore the conforming of our will to God's and the thanks that we give him for our tribulation are more worthy of thanks in return, and merit more reward in the very fast wealth and felicity of heaven, than our conformity and our thanksgiving for our worldly wealth here.

And this thing saw the devil, when he said to our Lord of Job that it was no marvel if Job had a reverent fear unto God—God had done so much for him, and kept him in prosperity. But the devil knew well that it was a hard thing for Job to be so loving, and so to give thanks to God, in tribulation and adversity. And therefore was he glad to get leave of God to put him in tribulation, and trusted thereby to cause him to murmur and grudge against God with impatience. But the devil had there a fall in his own turn, for the patience of Job in the short time of his adversity got him much more favour and thanks of God, and more is he renowned and commended in scripture for that, than for all the goodness of his long prosperous life. Our Saviour saith himself, also, that if we say well by them or yield them thanks who do us good, we do no great thing, and therefore can we with reason look for no great thanks in return.

And thus have I showed you, lo, no little pre-eminence that tribulation hath in merit, and therefore no little pre-eminence of comfort in hope of heavenly reward, above the virtues (the merit and cause of good hope and comfort) that come of wealth and prosperity.

## XX

And therefore, good cousin, to finish our talking for this time, lest I should be too long a hindrance to your other business:

If we lay first, for a sure ground, a very fast faith, whereby we believe to be true all that the scripture saith (understood truly, as the old holy doctors declare it and as the spirit of God instructeth his Catholic church), then shall we consider tribulation as a gracious gift of God, a gift that he specially gave his special friends; a thing that in scripture is highly commended and praised; a thing of which the contrary, long continued, is perilous; a thing which, if God send it not, men have need to put upon themselves and seek by penance; a thing that helpeth to purge our past sins; a thing that preserveth us from sins that otherwise would come; a thing that causeth us to set less by the world; a thing that much diminisheth our pains in purgatory; a thing that much increaseth our final reward in heaven; the thing with which all his apostles followed him thither; the thing to which our Saviour exhorteth all men; the thing without which he saith we be not his disciples; the thing without which no man can get to heaven.

Whosoever thinketh on these things, and remembereth them well, shall in his tribulation neither murmur nor grudge. But first shall he by patience take his pain in worth, and then shall he grow in goodness and think himself well worthy of tribulation. And then shall he consider that God sendeth it for his welfare, and thereby shall be moved to give God thanks for it. Therewith shall his grace increase, and God shall give him such comfort by considering that God is in his trouble evermore near to him—for "God is near," saith the prophet, "to them that have their heart in trouble"—that his joy thereof shall diminish much of his pain. And he shall not seek for vain comfort elsewhere, but shall specially trust in God and seek help of him, submitting his own will wholly to God's pleasure. And he shall pray to God in his heart, and pray his friends pray for him, and especially the priests, as St. James biddeth. And he shall begin first with confession and make him clean to God and ready to depart, and be glad to go to God, putting purgatory to his pleasure. If we thus do, this dare I boldly say, we shall never live here the less by half an hour, but we shall with this comfort find our hearts lightened, and thereby the grief of our tribulation lessened, and the more likelihood to recover and to live the longer.

Now if God will that we shall go hence, then doth he much more for us. For he who taketh this way cannot go but well. For of him who is loth to leave this wretched world, mine heart is much in fear lest he did not well. Hard it is for him to be welcome who cometh against his will, who saith unto God when he cometh to fetch him, "Welcome, my Maker—spite of my teeth!" But he that so loveth him that he longeth to go to him, my heart cannot give me but he shall be welcome, albeit that he come ere he be well purged. For "Charity covereth a multitude of sins," and "He that trusteth in God cannot be confounded." And Christ saith, "He that cometh to me, I will not cast him out." And therefore let us never make our reckoning of long life. Let us keep it while we can, because God hath so commanded, but if God give the occasion that with his good will we may go, let us be glad of it and long to go to him. And then shall hope of heaven comfort our heaviness, and out of our transitory tribulation shall we go to everlasting glory—to which, good cousin, I pray God bring us both!

VINCENT: Mine own good uncle, I pray God reward you, and at this time I will no longer trouble you. I fear I have this day done you much tribulation with my importunate objections, of very little substance. And you have even showed me an example of patience, in bearing my folly so long. And yet I shall be so bold as to seek some time to talk further of the rest of this most profitable matter of tribulation, which you said you reserved to treat of last of all.

ANTHONY: Let that be surely very shortly, cousin, while this is fresh in mind.

VINCENT: I trust, good uncle, so to put this in remembrance that it shall never be forgotten with me. Our Lord send you such comfort as he knoweth to be best!

ANTHONY: This is well said, good cousin, and I pray the same for you and for all our other friends who have need of comfort—for whom, I think, more than for yourself, you needed some counsel.

VINCENT: I shall, with this good counsel that I have heard from you, do them some comfort, I trust in God—to whose keeping I commit you!

ANTHONY: And I you, also. Farewell, mine own good cousin.

# BOOK TWO

VINCENT: It is no little comfort to me, good uncle, that as I came in here I heard from your folk that since my last being here you have had meetly good rest (God be thanked), and your stomach somewhat more come to you. For verily, albeit I had heard before that, in respect of the great pain that for a month's space had held you, you were, a little before my last coming to you, somewhat eased and relieved—for otherwise would I not for any good cause have put you to the pain of talking so much as you then did—yet after my departing from you, remembering how long we tarried together, and that we were all that while talking, and that all the labour was yours, in talking so long together without interpausing between (and that of matter studious and displeasant, all of disease and sickness and other pain and tribulation), I was in good faith very sorry and not a little wroth with myself for mine own oversight, that I had so little considered your pain. And very feared I was, till I heard otherwise, lest you should have waxed weaker and more sick thereafter. But now I thank our Lord, who hath sent the contrary. For a little casting back, in this great age of yours, would be no little danger and peril.

ANTHONY: Nay, nay, good cousin—to talk much, unless some other pain hinder me, is to me little grief. A foolish old man is often as full of words as a woman. It is, you know, as some poets paint us, all the joy of an old fool's life to sit well and warm with a cup and a roasted crabapple, and drivel and drink and talk!

But in earnest, cousin, our talking was to me great comfort, and nothing displeasing at all. For though we commoned of sorrow and heaviness, yet the thing we chiefly thought upon was not the tribulation itself but the comfort that may grow thereon. And therefore am I now very glad that you are come to finish up the rest.

VINCENT: Of truth, my good uncle, it was comforting to me, and hath been since to some other of your friends, to whom, as my poor wit and remembrance would serve me, I did report and rehearse (and not needlessly) your most comforting counsel. And now come I for the rest, and am very joyful that I find you so well refreshed and so ready thereto. But this one thing, good uncle, I beseech you heartily. If I, for delight to hear you speak in the matter, forget myself and you both, and put you to too much pain, remember your own ease. And when you wish to leave off, command me to go my way and seek some other time.

ANTHONY: Forsooth, cousin, if a man were very weak, many words spoken (as you said right now) without interpausing, would peradventure at length somewhat weary him. And therefore wished I the last time, after you were gone (when I felt myself, to say the truth, even a little weary), that I had not so told you a long tale alone, but that we had more often interchanged words, and parted the talking between us, with more often interparling upon your part, in such manner as learned men use between the persons whom they devise, disputing in their feigned dialogues. But yet in that point I soon excused you and laid the lack where I found it, and that was even upon mine own neck.

For I remembered that between you and me it fared as it did once between a nun and her brother. Very virtuous was this lady, and of a very virtuous place and enclosed religion. And therein had she been long, in all which time she had never seen her brother, who was likewise very virtuous too, and had been far off at a university, and had there taken the degree of Doctor of Divinity. When he was come home, he went to see his sister, as one who highly rejoiced in her virtue. So came she to the grate that they call, I believe, the locutory, and after their holy watchword spoken on both sides, after the manner used in that place, each took the other by the tip of the finger, for no hand could be shaken through the grate. And forthwith my lady began to give her brother a sermon of the wretchedness of this world, and frailty of the flesh, and the subtle sleights of the wicked fiend, and gave him surely good counsel (saving somewhat too long) how he should be well wary in his living and master well his body for the saving of his soul. And yet, ere her own tale came to an end, she began to find a little fault with him and said, "In good faith, brother, I do somewhat marvel that you, who have been at learning so long and are a doctor and so learned in the law of God, do not now at our meeting (since we meet so seldom) to me who am your sister and a simple unlearned soul, give of your charity some fruitful exhortation. For I doubt not but you can say some good thing yourself." "By my troth, good sister," quoth her brother, "I cannot, for you! For your tongue hath never ceased, but said enough for us both."

And so, cousin, I remember that when I was once fallen in, I left you little space to say aught between. But now will I therefore take another way with you, for of our talking I shall drive you to the one half.

VINCENT: Now, forsooth, uncle, this was a merry tale! But now, if you make me talk the one half, then shall you be contented far otherwise than was of late a kinswoman of your own—but which one I will not tell you; guess her if you can! Her husband had much pleasure in the manner and behaviour of another honest man, and kept him therefore much company, so that he was at his mealtime the more often away from home. So happed it one time that his wife and he together dined or supped with that neighbour of theirs, and then she made a merry quarrel with him for making her husband so good cheer outside that she could not keep him at home. "Forsooth, mistress," quoth he (for he was a dry merry man), "in my company no thing keepeth him but one. Serve him with the same, and he will never be away from you." "What gay thing may that be?" quoth our cousin then. "Forsooth, mistress," quoth he, "your husband loveth well to talk, and when he sitteth with me, I let him have all the words." "All the words?" quoth she, "marry, than am I content! He shall have all the words with good will, as he hath ever had. But I speak them all myself, and give them all to him, and for aught I care for them, so shall he have them all. But otherwise to say that he shall have them all, you shall keep him still rather than he get the half!"

ANTHONY: Forsooth, cousin, I can soon guess which of our kin she was. I wish we had none, for all her merry words, who would let their husbands talk less!

VINCENT: Forsooth, she is not so merry but what she is equally good. But where you find fault, uncle, that I speak not enough: I was in good faith ashamed that I spoke so much and moved you such questions as (I found upon your answer) might better have been spared, they were of so little worth. But now, since I see you be so well content that I shall not forbear boldly to show my folly, I will be no more so shamefast but will ask you what I like.

# I

And first, good uncle, ere we proceed further, I will be bold to move you one thing more of that which we talked of when I was here before. For when I revolved in my mind again the things that were concluded here by you, methought you would in no wise wish that in any tribulation men should seek for comfort in either worldly things or fleshly. And this opinion of yours, uncle, seemeth somewhat hard, for a merry tale with a friend refresheth a man much, and without any harm delighteth his mind and amendeth his courage and his stomach, so that it seemeth but well done to take such recreation. And Solomon saith, I believe, that men should in heaviness give the sorry man wine, to make him forget his sorrow. And St. Thomas saith that proper pleasant talking, which is called eutrapelia, is a good virtue, serving to refresh the mind and make it quick and eager to labour and study again, whereas continual fatigue would make it dull and deadly.

ANTHONY: Cousin, I forgot not that point, but I longed not much to touch it. For neither might I well utterly forbear it, where it might befall that it should not hurt; and on the other hand, if it should so befall, methought that it should little need to give any man counsel to it—folk are prone enough to such fancies of their own mind! You may see this by ourselves who, coming now together to talk of as earnest sad matter as men can devise, were fallen yet even at the first into wanton idle tales. And of truth, cousin, as you know very well, I myself am by nature even half a gigglot and more. I wish I could as easily mend my fault as I well know it, but scant can I refrain it, as old a fool as I am. Howbeit, I will not be so partial to my fault as to praise it.

But since you ask my mind in the matter, as to whether men in tribulation may not lawfully seek recreation and comfort themselves with some honest mirth (first agreed that our chief comfort must be in God and that with him we must begin and with him continue and with him end also), that a man should take now and then some honest worldly mirth, I dare not be so sore as utterly to forbid it. For good men and well learned have in some cases allowed it, especially for the diversity of divers men's minds. Otherwise, if we were also such as would God we were (and such as natural wisdom would that we should be, and is not clean excusable that we be not indeed), I would then put no doubt but that unto any man the most comforting talking that could be would be to hear of heaven. Whereas now, God help us, our wretchedness is such that in talking a while of it, men wax almost weary. And, as though to hear of heaven were a heavy burden, they must refresh themselves afterward with a foolish tale. Our affection toward heavenly joys waxeth wonderfully cold. If dread of hell were as far gone, very few would fear God, but that yet sticketh a little in our stomachs. Mark me, cousin, at the sermon, and commonly toward the end, somewhat the preacher speaketh of hell and heaven. Now, while he preacheth of the pains of hell, still they stay and give him the hearing. But as soon as he cometh to the joys of heaven, they are busking them backward and flockmeal fall away.

It is in the soul somewhat as it is in the body: There are some who are come, either by nature or by evil custom, to that point where a worse thing sometimes more steadeth them than a better. Some men, if they be sick, can away with no wholesome meat, nor no medicine can go down with them, unless it be tempered for their fancy with something that maketh the meat or the medicine less wholesome than it should be. And yet, while it will be no better, we must let them have it so.

Cassian (that very virtuous man) rehearseth in a certain conference of his that a certain holy father, in making of a sermon, spoke of heaven and heavenly things so celestially that much of his audience, with the sweet sound of it, began to forget all the world and fall asleep. When the father beheld this, he dissembled their sleeping and suddenly said to them, "I shall tell you a merry tale." At that word they lifted up their heads and hearkened unto that, and afterward (their sleep being therewith broken) heard him tell on of heaven again. In what wise that good father rebuked then their untoward minds—so dull to the thing that all our life we labour for, and so quick and eager toward other trifles—I neither bear in mind nor shall here need to rehearse. But thus much of that matter sufficeth for our purpose, that whereas you demand of me whether in tribulation men may not sometimes refresh themselves with worldly mirth and recreation, I can only say that he who cannot long endure to hold up his head and hear talking of heaven unless he be now and then between refreshed (as though heaven were heaviness!) with a merry foolish tale, there is none other remedy but you must let him have it. Better would I wish it, but I cannot help it.

Howbeit, by mine advice, let us at least make those kinds of recreation as short and as seldom as we can. Let them serve us but for sauce, and make themselves not our meat. And let us pray unto God—and all our good friends for us—that we may feel such a savour in the delight of heaven that in respect of the talking of its joys, all worldly recreation may be but a grief to think on. And be sure, cousin, that if we might once purchase the grace to come to that point, we never found of worldly recreation so much comfort in a year as we should find in the bethinking us of heaven for less than half an hour.

VINCENT: In faith, uncle, I can well agree to this, and I pray God bring us once to take such a savour in it. And surely, as you began the other day, by faith must we come to it, and to faith by prayer.

But now, I pray you, good uncle, vouchsafe to proceed in our principal matter.

## II

ANTHONY: Cousin, I have bethought me somewhat upon this matter since we were last together. And I find it a thing that, if we should go some way to work, would require many more days to treat of than we should haply find for it in so few as I myself believe that I have yet to live. For every time is not alike with me. Among them, there are many painful, in which I look every day to depart; my mending days come very seldom and are very shortly done.

For surely, cousin, I cannot liken my life more fitly now than to the snuff of a candle that burneth within the candlestick's nose. For the snuff sometimes burneth down so low that whosoever looketh on it would think it were quite out, and yet suddenly lifteth up a flame half an inch above the nose and giveth a pretty short light again, and thus playeth divers times till at last, ere it be looked for, out it goeth altogether. So have I, cousin, divers such days together as every day of them I look even to die, and yet have I then after that some such few days again as you yourself see me now to have, in which a man would think that I might yet well continue. But I know my lingering not likely to last long, but out will go my snuff suddenly some day within a while. And therefore will I, with God's help, seem I never so well amended, nevertheless reckon every day for my last. For though, to the repressing of the bold courage of blind youth, there is a very true proverb that "as soon cometh a young sheep's skin to the market as an old," yet this difference there is at least between them: that as the young man may hap sometimes to die soon, so the old man can never live long.

And therefore, cousin, in our matter here, leaving out many things that I would otherwise treat of, I shall for this time speak but of very few. Howbeit, if God hereafter send me more such days, then will we, when you wish, further talk of more.

## III

All manner of tribulation, cousin, that any man can have, as far as for this time cometh to my mind, falleth under some one at least of these three kinds: Either it is such as he himself willingly taketh; or, secondly, such as he willingly suffereth; or, finally, such as he cannot put from him.

This third kind I purpose not to speak of now much more, for there shall suffice, for the time, those things that we treated between us the other day. What kind of tribulation this is, I am sure you yourself perceive. For sickness, imprisonment, loss of goods, loss of friends, or such bodily harm as a man hath already caught and can in no wise avoid—these things and such like are the third kind of tribulation that I speak of, which a man neither willingly taketh in the beginning, nor can (though he would) afterward put away.

Now think I that, just as no comfort can serve to the man who lacketh wit and faith, whatsoever counsel be given, so to those who have both I have, as for this kind, said in manner enough already. And considering that suffer it he must, since he can by no manner of means put it from him, the very necessity is half counsel enough to take it in good worth and bear it patiently, and rather of his patience to take both ease and thanks than by fretting and fuming to increase his present pain, and afterward by murmur and grudge to fall in further danger of displeasing God with his froward behaviour.

And yet, albeit that I think that what has been said sufficeth, yet here and there I shall in the second kind show some such comfort as shall well serve unto this last kind too.

## IV

The first kind also will I shortly pass over, too. For the tribulation that a man willingly taketh himself, which no man putteth upon him against his own will, is, you know as well as I (for it was somewhat touched the last day), such affliction of the flesh or expense of his goods as a man taketh himself or willingly bestoweth in punishment of his own sin and for devotion to God.

Now, in this tribulation needeth he no man to comfort him. For no man troubleth him but himself, who feeleth how far forth he may conveniently bear, and of reason and good discretion shall not pass that—and if any doubt arise therein, it is counsel that he needeth and not comfort. And so the courage that kindleth his heart and enflameth it for God's sake and his soul's health shall, by the same grace that put it in his mind, give him such comfort and joy therein that the pleasure of his soul shall surpass the pain of his body.

Yea, and while he hath in heart also some great heaviness for his sin, yet when he considereth the joy that shall come of it, his soul shall not fail to feel then that strange state which my body felt once in a great fever.

VINCENT: What strange state was that, uncle?

ANTHONY: Forsooth, cousin, even in this same bed, it is now more than fifteen years ago, I lay in a tertian fever. And I had passed, I believe, three or four fits, when afterward there fell on me one fit out of course, so strange and so marvellous that I would in good faith have thought it impossible. For I suddenly felt myself verily both hot and cold throughout all my body; not in one part the one and in another part the other—for it would have been, you know, no very strange thing to feel the head hot while the hands were cold—but the selfsame parts, I say, so God save my soul, I sensibly felt (and right painfully, too) all in one instant both hot and cold at once.

VINCENT: By my faith, uncle, this was a wonderful thing, and such as I never heard happen to any other man in my days. And few men are there out of whose mouths I could have believed it.

ANTHONY: Courtesy, cousin, peradventure hindereth you from saying that you believe it not yet of my mouth, neither! And surely, for fear of that, you should not have heard it of me neither, had there not another thing happed me soon thereafter.

VINCENT: I pray you, what was that, good uncle?

ANTHONY: Forsooth, cousin, this: I asked a physician or twain, who then considered how this should be possible, and they both twain told me that it could not be so, but that I was fallen into some slumber and dreamed that I felt it so.

VINCENT: This hap, hold I, little caused you to tell that tale more boldly!

ANTHONY: No, cousin, that is true, lo. But then happed there another: A young girl here in this town, whom a kinsman of hers had begun to teach physic, told me that there was such a kind of fever indeed.

VINCENT: By our Lady, uncle, save for the credence of you, the tale would I not yet tell again upon that hap of the maid! For though I know her now for such that I durst well believe her, it might hap her very well at that time to lie, because she would that you should take her for learned.

ANTHONY: Yea, but then happed there yet another hap thereon, cousin, that a work of Galen, "De differentiis febrium," is ready to be sold in the booksellers' shops, in which work she showed me then the chapter where Galen saith the same.

VINCENT: Marry, uncle, as you say, that hap happed well. And that maid had, as hap was, in that one point more learning than had both your physicians besides—and hath, I believe, at this day in many points more.

ANTHONY: In faith, so believe I too. She is very wise and well learned, and very virtuous too.

But see now what age is: lo, I have been so long in my tale that I have almost forgotten for what purpose I told it. Oh, now I remember me: As I say, just as I myself felt my body then both hot and cold at once, so he who is contrite and heavy for his sin shall have cause to be both glad and sad, and shall indeed be both twain at once. And he shall do as I remember holy St. Jerome biddeth—"Both be thou sorry," saith he, "and be thou also of thy sorrow joyful."

And thus, as I began to say, to him that is in this tribulation—that is, in fruitful heaviness and penance for his sin—shall we need to give none other comfort than only to remember and consider well the goodness of God's excellent mercy, that infinitely surpasseth the malice of all men's sins. By that mercy he is ready to receive every man, and did spread his arms abroad upon the cross, lovingly to embrace all those who will come. And by that mercy he even there accepted the thief at his last end, who turned not to God till he might steal no longer, and yet maketh more feast in heaven for one who turneth from sin than for ninety-nine good men who sinned not at all.

And therefore of that first kind of tribulation will I make no longer tale.

## V

VINCENT: Forsooth, uncle, this is very great comfort unto that kind of tribulation. And so great, also, that it may make many a man bold to abide in his sin even unto his end, trusting to be then saved as that thief was.

ANTHONY: Very sooth you say, cousin, that some wretches are there who so abuse the great goodness of God that the better he is the worse in return are they. But, cousin, though there be more joy made of his turning who from the point of perdition cometh to salvation, for pity that God had and all his saints of the peril of perishing that the man stood in, yet is he not set in like state in heaven as he should have been if he had lived better before. Unless it so befall that he live so well afterward and do so much good that he outrun, in the shorter time, those good folk that yet did so much in much longer. This is proved in the blessed apostle St. Paul, who of a persecutor became an apostle, and last of all came in unto that office, and yet in the labour of sowing the seed of Christ's faith outran all the rest so far that he forbore not to say of himself, "I have laboured more than all the rest have."

But yet, my cousin, though I doubt not that God be so merciful unto those who, at any time of their life, turn and ask his mercy and trust in it, though it be at the last end of a man's life; and that he hireth him as well for heaven who cometh to work in his vineyard toward night at such time as workmen leave work, and goeth home, being then willing to work if time should serve, as he hireth him who cometh in the morning; yet may no man upon the trust of this parable be bold all his life to lie still in sin. For let him remember that no man goeth into God's vineyard but he who is called thither. Now he who, in hope to be called toward the night, will sleep out the morning and drink out the day, is full likely to pass at night unspoken to. And then shall he with ill rest go supperless to bed!

They tell of one who was wont always to say that all the while he lived he would do what he pleased, for three words when he died should make all safe enough. But then it so happed that long ere he was old his horse once stumbled upon a broken bridge. And as he laboured to recover him, when he saw that it would not be, but that down into the flood headlong he must go, in sudden dismay he cried out in the falling, "Have all to the devil!" And there was he drowned with his three words ere he died, whereon his hope hung all his wretched life.

And therefore let no man sin in hope of grace, for grace cometh but at God's will, and that state of mind may be the hindrance that grace of fruitful repenting shall never after be offered him, but that he shall either graceless go linger on careless, or with a care that is fruitless shall fall into despair.

## VI

VINCENT: Forsooth, uncle, in this point methinketh you say very well. But then are there some again who say on the other hand that we shall need no heaviness for our sins at all, but need only change our intent and purpose to do better, and for all that is passed take no thought at all. And as for fasting and other affliction of the body, they say we should not do it save only to tame the flesh when we feel it wax wanton and begin to rebel. For fasting, they say, serveth to keep the body in temperance, but to fast for penance or to do any other good work, almsdeed or other, toward satisfaction for our own sins—this thing they call plain injury to the passion of Christ, by which alone our sins are forgiven freely without any recompense of our own. And they say that those who would do penance for their own sins look to be their own Christs, and pay their own ransoms, and save their souls themselves. And with these reasons in Saxony many cast fasting off, and all other bodily affliction, save only where need requireth to bring the body to temperance. For no other good, they say, can it do to ourselves, and then to our neighbour can it do none at all. And therefore they condemn it for superstitious folly. Now, heaviness of heart and weeping for our sins, this they reckon shame almost, and womanish childishness—howbeit, God be thanked, their women wax there now so mannish that they are not so childish, nor so poor of spirit, but what they can sin on as men do and be neither afraid nor ashamed nor weep for their sins at all.

And surely, mine uncle, I have marvelled the less ever since I heard the manner of their preachers there. For, as you remember, when I was in Saxony these matters were (in a manner) but in a mammering. Luther was not then wedded yet, nor religious men out of their habits, but those that would be of the sect were suffered freely to preach what they would unto the people. And forsooth I heard a religious man there myself—one that had been reputed and taken for very good, and who, as far as the folk perceived, was of his own living somewhat austere and sharp. But his preaching was wonderful! Methinketh I hear him yet, his voice so loud and shrill, his learning less than mean. But whereas his matter was much part against fasting and all affliction for any penance, which he called men's inventions, he ever cried out upon them to keep well the laws of Christ, let go their childish penance, and purpose then to mend and seek nothing to salvation but the death of Christ. "For he is our justice, and he is our Saviour and our whole satisfaction for all our deadly sins. He did full penance for us all upon his painful cross, he washed us there all clean with the water of his sweet side, and brought us out of the devil's danger with his dear precious blood. Leave therefore, leave, I beseech you, these inventions of men, your foolish Lenten fasts and your childish penance! Diminish never Christ's thanks nor look to save yourselves! It is Christ's death, I tell you, that must save us all—Christ's death, I tell you yet again, and not our own deeds. Leave your own fasting, therefore, and lean to Christ alone, good Christian people, for Christ's dear bitter passion!" Now, so loud and shrill he cried "Christ" in their ears, and so thick he came forth with Christ's bitter passion, and that so bitterly spoken with the sweat dropping down his cheeks, that I marvelled not that I saw the poor women weep. For he made my own hair stand up upon my head.

And with such preaching were the people so taken in that some fell to break their fast on the fasting days, not of frailty or of malice first, but almost of devotion, lest they should take from Christ the thanks of his bitter passion. But when they were awhile nursled in that point first, they could afterward abide and endure many things more, for which, if he had begun with them, they would have pulled him down.

ANTHONY: Cousin, God amend that man, whatsoever he be, and God keep all good folk from such manner of preachers! One such preacher much more abuseth the name of Christ and of his bitter passion than do five hundred gamblers who in their idle business swear and foreswear themselves by his holy bitter passion at dice. They carry the minds of the people from perceiving their craft by the continual naming of the name of Christ, and crying his passion so shrill into their ears that they forget that the Church hath ever taught them that all our penance without Christ's passion would not be worth a pea. And they make the people think that we wish to be saved by our own deeds, without Christ's death; whereas we confess that his passion alone meriteth incomparably more for us than all our own deeds do, but that it is his pleasure that we shall also take pain ourselves with him. And therefore he biddeth all who will be his disciples to take their crosses on their backs as he did, and with their crosses follow him.

And where they say that fasting serveth but for temperance to tame the flesh and keep it from wantonness, I would in good faith have thought that Moses had not been so wild that for the taming of his flesh he should have need to fast whole forty days together. No, not Hely neither. Nor yet our Saviour himself, who began the Lenten forty-days fast—and the apostles followed, and all Christendom hath kept it—that these folk call now so foolish. King Achab was not disposed to be wanton in his flesh, when he fasted and went clothed in sackcloth and all besprent with ashes. No more was the king in Nineveh and all the city, but they wailed and did painful penance for their sin to procure God to pity them and withdraw his indignation. Anna, who in her widowhood abode so many years with fasting and praying in the temple till the birth of Christ, was not, I suppose, in her old age so sore disposed to the wantonness of the flesh that she fasted for all that. Nor St. Paul, who fasted so much, fasted not all for that, neither. The scripture is full of places that prove fasting to be not the invention of man but the institution of God, and to have many more profits than one. And that the fasting of one man may do good unto another, our Saviour showeth himself where he saith that some kind of devils cannot be cast out of one man by another "without prayer and fasting." And therefore I marvel that they take this way against fasting and other bodily penance.

And yet much more I marvel that they mislike the sorrow and heaviness and displeasure of mind that a man should take in thinking of his sin. The prophet saith, "Tear your hearts and not your clothes." And the prophet David saith, "A contrite heart and an humbled"—that is to say, a heart broken, torn, and laid low under foot with tribulation of heaviness for his sins—"shalt thou not, good Lord, despise." He saith also of his own contrition, "I have laboured in my wailing; I shall every night wash my bed with my tears, my couch will I water."

But why should I need in this matter to lay forth one place or twain? The scripture is full of those places, by which it plainly appeareth that God looketh of duty, not only that we should amend and be better in the time to come, but also that we should be sorry and weep and bewail our sins committed before. And all the old holy doctors be full and whole of that opinion, that men must have for their sins contrition and sorrow in heart.

## VII

VINCENT: Forsooth, uncle, this thing yet seemeth to me a somewhat sore sentence, not because I think otherwise but that there is good cause and great wherefore a man should so sorrow, but because of truth sometimes a man cannot be sorry and heavy for his sin that he hath done, though he never so fain would. But though he can be content for God's sake to forbear it thenceforth, yet not only can he not weep for every sin that is past, but some were haply so wanton that when he happeth to remember them he can scantly forbear to laugh.

Now, if contrition and sorrow of heart be so requisite of necessity to remission, many a man should stand, it seemeth, in a very perilous state.

ANTHONY: Many so should indeed, cousin, and indeed many do so. And the old saints write very sore on this point. Howbeit, "the mercy of God is above all his works," and he standeth bound to no common rule. "And he knoweth the frailty of this earthen vessel that is of his own making, and is merciful and hath pity and compassion upon our feeble infirmities," and shall not exact of us above the thing that we can do.

And yet, cousin, he who findeth himself in that state, let him give God thanks that he is no worse, in that he is minded to do well hereafter. But in that he cannot be sorry for his sin passed, let him be sorry at least that he is no better. And as St. Jerome biddeth him who sorroweth in his heart for sin to be glad and rejoice in his sorrow, so would I counsel him who cannot be sad for his sin to be sorry at least that he cannot be sorry!

Besides this, though I would in no wise that any man should despair, yet would I counsel such a man while that affection lasteth not to be bold of courage, but to live in double fear: First, because it is a token either of faint faith or of a dull diligence. For surely if we believe in God, and therewith deeply consider his high majesty, with the peril of our sin and the great goodness of God also, then either dread should make us tremble and break our stony heart, or love should for sorrow relent it into tears. Besides this, because, since so little misliking of our old sin is an affection not very pure and clean, and since no unclean thing shall enter into heaven, I can scantly believe but it shall be cleansed and purified before we come there. And therefore would I further give one in that state the counsel which Master Gerson giveth every man: that since the body and the soul together make the whole man, the less affliction he feeleth in his soul, the more pain in recompense let him put upon his body, and purge the spirit by the affliction of the flesh. And he who so doth, I dare lay my life, shall have his hard heart afterward relent into tears, and his soul in a wholesome heaviness and heavenly gladness too—especially if he join therewith faithful prayer, which must be joined with every good thing.

But, cousin, as I told you the other day, in these matters with these new men I will not dispute, but surely for mine own part I cannot well hold with them. For as far as mine own poor wit can perceive, the holy scripture of God is very plain against them, and the whole corps of Christendom in every Christan region. And the very places in which they dwell themselves have ever unto their own days clearly believed against them and all the old holy doctors have evermore taught against them, and all the old holy interpreters have construed against them. And therefore if these men have now perceived so late that the scripture hath been misunderstood all this while, and that of all those old holy doctors no man could understand it, then am I too old at this age to begin to study it now! And I dare not in no wise trust these men's learning, cousin, since I cannot see nor perceive any cause wherefore I should think that these men might not now in the understanding of scripture as well be deceived themselves as they would have us believe all those others have been, all this while before.

Howbeit, cousin, if it so be that their way be not wrong, but that they have found out so easy a way to heaven as to take no thought, but make merry, nor take no penance at all, but sit them down and drink well for our Saviour's sake—set cockahoop and fill all the cups at once, and then let Christ's passion pay for all the scot—I am not he who will envy their good hap. But surely, counsel dare I give no man to adventure that way with them. But those who fear lest that way be not sure, and take upon themselves willingly tribulation of penance—what comfort they do take, and well may take therein, that have I somewhat told you already. And since these other folk sit so merry with such tribulation, we need talk to them, you know, of no such manner of comfort.

And therefore of this kind of tribulation will I make an end.

## VIII

VINCENT: Verily, good uncle, so may you well do, for you have brought it unto a very good pass.

And now, I pray you, come to the other kind, of which you purposed always to treat last.

ANTHONY: That shall I, cousin, very gladly do. The other kind is the one which I rehearsed second, and (sorting out the other two) have kept for the last. This second kind of tribulation is, you know, of those who willingly suffer tribulation, though of their own choice they took it not at first.

This kind, cousin, we shall divide into twain; the first we might call temptation, the second persecution. But here must you consider that I mean not every kind of persecution, but only that kind which, though the sufferer would be loth to fall in, yet will he rather abide it and suffer than, by flying from it, fall into the displeasure of God or leave God's pleasure unprocured. Howbeit, if we well consider these two things, temptation and persecution, we may find that either of them is incident into the other. For both by temptation the devil persecuteth us, and by persecution the devil also tempteth us. And as persecution is tribulation to every man, so is temptation tribulation to a good man. Now, though the devil, our spiritual enemy, fight against man in both, yet this difference hath the common temptation from the persecution: Temptation is, as it were, the fiend's snare, and persecution his plain open fight. And therefore will I now call all this kind of tribulation here by the name of temptation, and that shall I divide into two parts. The first shall I call the devil's snares, the other his open fight.

## IX

To speak of every kind of temptation particularly, by itself, would be, you know, in a manner an infinite thing. For under that, as I told you, fall persecutions and all. And the devil hath a thousand subtle ways of his snares, and of his open fight as many sundry poisoned darts. He tempteth us by the world, he tempteth us by our own flesh; he tempteth us by pleasure, he tempteth us by pain; he tempteth us by our foes, he tempteth us by our own friends—and, under colour of kindred, he maketh many times our nearest friends our most foes. For, as our Saviour said, "Inimici hominis domestici eius."

But in all manner of so diverse temptations, one marvellous comfort is that, the more we be tempted, the gladder have we cause to be. For, as St. James saith, "Esteem and take it, my brethren, for a thing of all joy when you fall into diverse and sundry manner of temptations." And no marvel, for there is in this world set up (as it were) a game of wrestling, in which the people of God come in on the one side, and on the other side come mighty strong wrestlers and wily—that is, the devils, the cursed proud damned spirits. For it is not our flesh alone that we must wrestle with, but with the devil too. "Our wrestling is not here," saith St. Paul, "against flesh and blood, but against the princes and potentates of these dark regions, against the spiritual wicked ghosts of the air."

But as God hath prepared a crown for those who on his side give his adversary the fall, so he who will not wrestle shall have none. For, as St. Paul saith, "There shall no man have the crown but he who contendeth for it according to the law of the game." And then, as holy St. Bernard saith, how couldst thou fight or wrestle for it, if there were no challenger against thee who would provoke thee thereto? And therefore may it be a great comfort, as St. James saith, to every man who feeleth himself challenged and provoked by temptation. For thereby perceiveth he that it cometh to his course to wrestle, which shall be, unless he willingly play the coward or the fool, the matter of his eternal reward.

## X

But now must this needs be to man an inestimable comfort in all temptation if his faith fail him not: that is, that he may be sure that God is always ready to give him strength against the devil's might and wisdom against the devil's snares.

For, as the prophet saith, "My strength and my praise is our Lord, he hath been my safeguard." And the scripture saith, "Ask wisdom of God and he shall give it thee," in order "that you may espy," as St. Paul saith, "and perceive all the crafts." A great comfort may this be in all kinds of temptation, that God hath so his hand upon him who is willing to stand and will trust in him and call upon him, that he hath made him sure by many faithful promises in holy scripture that either he shall not fall or, if he sometimes through faintness of faith stagger and hap to fall, yet if he call upon God betimes his fall shall be no sore bruising to him. But as the scripture saith, "The just man, though he fall, shall not be bruised, for our Lord holdeth under his hand."

The prophet expresseth a plain comfortable promise of God against all temptations where he saith, "Whoso dwelleth in the help of the highest God, he shall abide in the protection or defence of the God of heaven." Who dwelleth, now, good cousin, in the help of the high God? Surely, he who through a good faith abideth in the trust and confidence of God's help, and neither, for lack of that faith and trust in his help, falleth desperate of all help, nor departeth from the hope of his help to seek himself help (as I told you the other day) from the flesh, the world, or the devil.

Now he then who by fast faith and sure hope dwelleth in God's help, and hangeth always upon that hope, never falling from it, he shall, saith the prophet, ever dwell and abide in God's defence and protection. That is to say, while he faileth not to believe well and hope well, God will never fail in all temptation to defend him. For unto such a faithful well-hoping man the prophet in the same psalm saith further, "With his shoulders shall he shadow thee, and under his feathers shalt thou trust." Lo, here hath every faithful man a sure promise that in the fervent heat of temptation or tribulation—for, as I have said divers times before, each is in such wise incident to the other that the devil useth every tribulation for temptation to bring us to impatience, and thereby to murmur and grudge and blasphemy; and every kind of temptation, to a good man who fighteth against it and will not follow it, is a very painful tribulation. In the fervent heat, I say therefore, of every temptation, God giveth the faithful man who hopeth in him the shadow of his holy shoulders. His shoulders are broad and large enough to cool and refresh the man in that heat, and in every tribulation he putteth them for a defence between. And then what weapon of the devil may give us any deadly wound, while that impenetrable shield of the shoulder of God standeth always between?

Then goeth the verse further, and saith unto such a faithful man, "Thine hope shall be under his feathers." That is, for the good hope thou hast in his help, he will take thee so near him into his protection that, as the hen, to keep her young chickens from the kite, nestled them together under her wings, so from the devil's claws—the ravenous kite of this dark air—will the God of heaven gather the faithful trusting folk near unto his own sides, and set them in surety, very well and warm, under the covering of his heavenly wings. And of this defence and protection, our Saviour spoke himself unto the Jews, as mention is made in the twenty-third chapter of St. Matthew, to whom he said in this wise: "Jerusalem, Jerusalem, that killest the prophets and stonest unto death them that are sent to thee, how often would I have gathered thee together, as the hen gathereth her chickens under her wings, and thou wouldst not."

Here are, cousin Vincent, words of no little comfort unto every Christian man. For by them we may see with what tender affection God of his great goodness longeth to gather us under the protection of his wings, and how often like a loving hen he clucketh home unto him even those chickens of his that wilfully walk abroad into the kite's danger and will not come at his clucking, but ever, the more he clucketh for them, the farther they go from him. And therefore can we not doubt that, if we will follow him and with faithful hope come running to him, he shall in all matter of temptation take us near unto him and set us even under his wing. And then are we safe, if we will tarry there, for against our will no power can pull us thence, nor hurt our souls there. "Set me near unto thee," saith the prophet, "and fight against me whose hand that will." And to show the great safeguard and surety that we shall have while we sit under his heavenly feathers, the prophet saith yet a great deal further, "In velamento alarum tuarum exaltabo." That is, that we shall not only sit in safeguard when we sit by his sweet side under his holy wing, but we shall also under the covering of his heavenly wings with great exultation rejoice.

## XI

Now, in the two next verses following, the prophet briefly comprehendeth four kinds of temptations, and therein all the tribulation that we shall now speak of, and also some part of that which we have spoken of before. And therefore I shall peradventure (unless any further thing fall in our way) with treating of those two verses, finish and end all our matter.

The prophet saith in the ninetieth psalm, "Scuto circumdabit te veritas eius; non timebis a timore nocturno, a sagitta volante in die, a negotio perambulante in tenebris, ab incurso et demonio meridiano. The truth of God shall compass thee about with a shield, you shall not be afraid of the night's fear, nor of the arrow flying in the day, nor of business walking about in the darknesses, nor of the incursion or invasion of the devil in the midday."

First, cousin, in these words "the truth of God shall compass thee about with a shield," the prophet for the comfort of every good man in all temptation and in all tribulation, besides those other things that he said before—that the shoulders of God should shadow them and that also they should sit under his wing—here saith he further that the truth of God shall compass thee with a shield. That is, as God hath faithfully promised to protect and defend those that faithfully will dwell in the trust of his help, so will he truly perform it. And thou who art such a one, the truth of his promise will defend thee not with a little round buckler that scantly can cover the head, but with a long large shield that covereth all along the body. This shield is made (as holy St. Bernard saith) broad above with the Godhead and narrow beneath with the Manhood, so that it is our Saviour Christ himself. And yet is this shield not like other shields of the world, which are so made that while they defend one part the man may be wounded upon another. But this shield is such that, as the prophet saith, it shall round about enclose and compass thee, so that thine enemy shall hurt thy soul on no side. For "with a shield," saith he, "shall his truth environ and compass thee round about."

And then incontinently following, to the intent that we should see that it is not without necessity that the shield of God should compass us about upon every side, he showeth in what wise we are environed by the devil upon every side with snares and assaults, by four kinds of temptations and tribulations. Against all this compass of temptations and tribulations that round-compassing shield of God's truth shall so defend us and keep us safe that we shall need to dread none of them at all.

## XII

First, he saith, "thou shalt not be afraid of the fear of the night." By the night is there in scripture sometimes understood tribulation, as appeareth in the thirty-fourth chapter of Job: "God hath known the works of them, and therefore shall he bring night upon them," that is, tribulation for their wickedness. And well you know that the night is of its own nature discomfortable and full of fear. And therefore by the night's fear here I understand the tribulation by which the devil, through the sufferance of God, either by himself or by others who are his instruments, tempteth good folk to impatience as he did Job. But he who, as the prophet saith, dwelleth and continueth faithfully in the hope of God's help, shall so be clipped in on every side with the shield of God that he shall have no need to be afraid of such tribulation as is here called the night's fear. And it may be also fittingly called the night's fear for two causes: One, because many times, unto him who suffereth, the cause of his tribulation is dark and unknown. And therein it varieth and differeth from that tribulation by which the devil tempteth a man with open fight and assault for a known good thing from which he would withdraw him, or for some known evil thing into which he would drive him by force of such persecution. Another cause for which it is called the night's fear may be because the night is so far out of courage, and naturally so casteth folk into fear, that their fancy doubleth their fear of everything of which they perceive any manner of dread, and maketh them often think that it were much worse than indeed it is.

The prophet saith in the psalter, "Thou hast, good Lord, set the darkness and made was the night, and in the night walk all the beasts of the woods, the whelps of the lions roaring and calling unto God for their meat." Now, though the lions' whelps walk about roaring in the night and seek for their prey, yet can they not get such meat as they would always, but must hold themselves content with such as God suffereth to fall in their way. And though they be not aware of it, yet of God they ask it and of him they have it. And this may be comfort to all good men in their night's fear, that though they fall in their dark tribulation into the claws of the devil or the teeth of those lions' whelps, yet all that they can do shall not pass beyond the body, which is but as the garment of the soul. For the soul itself, which is the substance of the man, is so surely fenced in round about with the shield of God, that as long as he will abide faithfully in the hope of God's help the lions' whelp shall not be able to hurt it. For the great Lion himself could never be suffered to go further in the tribulation of Job than God from time to time gave him leave.

And therefore the deep darkness of the midnight maketh men who stand out of faith and out of good hope in God to be in far the greater fear in their tribulation, for lack of the light of faith, by which they might perceive that the uttermost of their peril is a far less thing than they take it for. But we are so wont to set so much by our body, which we see and feel, and in the feeding and fostering of which we set out delight and our wealth; and so little (alas) and so seldom we think upon our soul, because we cannot see that but by spiritual understanding, and most especially by the eye of our faith (in the meditation of which we bestow, God knows, little time), that the loss of our body we take for a sorer thing and for a great deal greater tribulation than we do the loss of our soul. Our Saviour biddeth us not fear those lions' whelps that can but kill our bodies and when that is done have no further thing in their power with which they can do us harm, but he biddeth us stand in dread of him who when he hath slain the body is able then beside to cast the soul into everlasting fire. Yet are we so blind in the dark night of tribulation, for lack of full and fast belief of God's word, that, whereas in the day of prosperity we very little fear God for our soul, our night's fear of adversity maketh us very sore to fear the lion and his whelps for dread of loss of our bodies. And whereas St. Paul in sundry places telleth us that our body is but the garment of the soul, yet the faintness of our faith in the scripture of God maketh us, with the night's fear of tribulation, not only to dread the loss of our body more than that of our soul—that is, of the clothing more than of the substance that is clothed therewith—but also of the very outward goods that serve for the clothing of the body. And much more foolish are we in that dark night's fear than would be a man who would forget the saving of his body for fear of losing his old rain-beaten cloak, that is but the covering of his gown or his coat. Now, consider further yet, that the prophet in the afore-remembered verses saith that in the night there walk not only the lions' whelps but also "all the beasts of the wood." Now, you know that if a man walk through the wood in the night, many things can make him afraid of which in the day he would not be afraid a whit. For in the night every bush, to him that waxeth once afraid, seemeth a thief.

I remember that when I was a young man, I was once in the war with the king then my master (God absolve his soul) and we were camped within the Turk's ground many a mile beyond Belgrade—would God it were ours now as it was then! But so happed it that in our camp about midnight there suddenly rose a rumour and a cry that the Turk's whole army was secretly stealing upon us. Therewith our whole host was warned to arm them in haste and set themselves in array to fight. And then were runners of ours, who had brought those sudden tidings, examined more leisurely by the council, as to what surety or what likelihood they had perceived. And one of them said that by the glimmering of the moon he had espied and perceived and seen them himself, coming on softly and soberly in a long range, all in good order, not one farther forth than the other in the forefront, but as even as a third, and in breadth farther than he could see the length. His fellows, being examined, said that he had somewhat pricked forth before them, and came back so fast to tell it to them that they thought it rather time to make haste and giving warning to the camp than to go nearer unto them. For they were not so far off but what they had yet themselves somewhat an imperfect sight of them, too. Thus stood we on watch all the rest of the night, evermore hearkening when we should hear them come, but "Hush, stand still! Methink I hear a trampling," so that at last many of us thought we heard them ourselves too. But when the day was sprung, and we saw no one, out was our runner sent again, and some of our captains with him, to show whereabout was the place in which he had perceived them. And when they came thither, they found that the great fearful army of the Turks, so soberly coming on, turned (God be thanked) into a fair long hedge standing even stone-still.

And thus fareth it in the night's fear of tribulation, in which the devil, to bear down and overwhelm with dread the faithful hope that we should have in God, casteth in our imagination much more fear than cause. For since there walk in that night not only the lion's whelps but all the beasts of the wood beside, the beast that we hear roar in the dark night of tribulation, and fear for a lion, we sometimes find well afterward in the way that it was no lion at all, but a silly rude roaring ass. And sometimes the thing that on the sea seemeth a rock is indeed nothing else but a mist. Howbeit, as the prophet saith, he that faithfully dwelleth in the hope of God's help, the shield of his truth shall so fence him round about that, be it an ass or a colt or a lion's whelp, or a rock of stone or a mist, the night's fear thereof shall be nothing to dread.

## XIII

Therefore find I that in the night's fear one great part is the fault of pusillanimity; that is, of faint and feeble stomach, by which a man for faint heart is afraid where he needeth not. By reason of this, he flieth oftentime for fear of something of which, if he fled not, he should take no harm. And a man doth sometimes by his fleeing make an enemy bold on him, who would, if he fled not but dared abide, give over and fly from him.

This fault of pusillanimity maketh a man in his tribulation first, for feeble heart, impatient. And afterward oftentimes it driveth him by impatience into a contrary affection, making him frowardly stubborn and angry against God, and thereby to fall into blasphemy, as do the damned souls in hell. This fault of pusillanimity and timorous mind hindereth a man also many times from doing many good things which, if he took a good stomach to him in the trust of God's help, he would be well able to do. But the devil casteth him in a cowardice and maketh him take it for humility to think himself unfit and unable to do them. And therefore he leaveth undone the good thing of which God offereth him occasion and to which he had made him fit.

But such folk have need to lift up their hearts and call upon God, and by the counsel of other good spiritual folk to cast away the cowardice of their own conceiving which the night's fear by the devil hath framed in their fancy. And they have need to look in the gospel upon him who laid up his talent and left it unoccupied and therefore utterly lost it, with a great reproach of his pusillanimity, but which he had thought to have excused himself, in that he was afraid to put it forth into use and occupy it.

And all this fear cometh by the devil's drift, wherein he taketh occasion of the faintness of our good and sure trust in God. And therefore let us faithfully dwell in the good hope of his help, and then shall the shield of his truth so compass us about that of this night's fear we shall have no fear at all.

## XIV

This pusillanimity bringeth forth, by the night's fear, a very timorous daughter, a silly wretched girl and ever whining, who is called Scrupulosity, or a scrupulous conscience.

This girl is a good enough maidservant in a house, never idle but ever occupied and busy. But albeit she hath a very gentle mistress who loveth her well and is well content with what she doth—or, if all be not well (as all cannot always be well), is content to pardon her as she doth others of her fellows, and letteth her know that she will do so—yet can this peevish girl never cease whining and puling for fear lest her mistress be always angry with her and she shall severely be chidden. Would her mistress, think you, be likely to be content with this condition? Nay, surely not.

I knew such a one myself, whose mistress was a very wise woman and (a thing which is in women very rare) very mild also and meek, and liked very well such service as she did her in the house. But she so much misliked this continual discomfortable fashion of hers that she would sometimes say, "Eh, what aileth this girl? The elvish urchin thinketh I were a devil, I do believe. Surely if she did me ten times better service than she doth, yet with this fantastical fear of hers I would be loth to have her in mine house."

Thus fareth, lo, the scrupulous person, who frameth himself many times double the fear that he hath cause, and many times a great fear where there is no cause at all. And of that which is indeed no sin, he maketh a venial one. And that which is venial, he imagineth to be deadly—and yet, for all that, he falleth into them, since they are of their nature such as no man long liveth without. And then he feareth that he is never fully confessed nor fully contrite, and then that his sins be never fully forgiven him. And then he confesseth and confesseth again, and cumbereth himself and his confessor both. And then every prayer that he saith, though he say it as well as the frail infirmity of the man will suffer, yet he is not satisfied unless he say it again, and yet after that again. And when he hath said the same thing thrice, as little is he satisfied with the last time as the first. And then is his heart evermore in heaviness, unquiet, and fear, full of doubt and dullness, without comfort or spiritual consolation.

With this night's fear the devil sore troubleth the mind of many a right good man, and that doth he to bring him to some great evil. For he will, if he can, drive him so much to the fearful minding of God's rigorous justice, that he will keep him from the comfortable remembrance of God's great mighty mercy, and so make him do all his good works wearily and without consolation or quickness.

Moreover, he maketh him take for a sin something that is not one, and for a deadly sin one that is but venial, to the intent that when he shall fall into them he shall, by reason of his scruple, sin where otherwise he would not, or sin mortally (because his conscience, in doing the deed, so told him) where otherwise indeed he would have offended only venially.

Yes, and further, the devil longeth to make all his good works and spiritual exercises so painful and so tedious to him, that, with some other subtle suggestion or false wily doctrine of a false spiritual liberty, he should be easily conveyed from that evil fault into one much worse, for the false ease and pleasure that he should suddenly find therein. And then should he have his conscience as wide and large afterward as ever it was narrow and straight before. For better is yet, of truth, a conscience a little too narrow than a little too large.

My mother had, when I was a little boy, a good old woman who took care of her children. They called her Mother Maud—I daresay you have heard of her?

VINCENT: Yea, yea, very much.

ANTHONY: She was wont, when she sat by the fire with us, to tell us who were children many childish tales. But as Pliny saith that there is no book lightly so bad but that a man may pick some good thing out of it, so think I that there is almost no tale so foolish but that yet in one matter or another, it may hap to serve to some purpose.

For I remember me that among others of her foolish tales, she told us once that the ass and the wolf came upon a time to confession to the fox. The poor ass came to shrift in Shrovetide, a day or two before Ash Wednesday. But the wolf would not come to confession till he saw first Palm Sunday past, and then he put it off yet further until Good Friday.

The fox asked the ass, before he began "Benedicite," wherefore he came to confession so soon, before Lent began. The poor beast answered him that it was for fear of deadly sin, if he should lose his part of any of those prayers that the priests in the cleansing days pray for them who are then confessed already. Then in his shrift he had a marvellous grudge in his inward conscience, that he had one day given his master a cause of anger in that, with his rude roaring before his master arose, he had wakened him out of his sleep and bereaved him of his rest. The fox, for that fault, like a good discreet confessor, charged him to do so no more, but to lie still and sleep like a good son himself until his master were up and ready to go to work, and so should he be sure that he should wake him no more.

To tell you all the poor ass's confession, it would be a long work. For everything that he did was deadly sin with him, the poor soul was so scrupulous. But his wise wily confessor accounted them for trifles (as they were) and swore afterward to the badger that he was so weary to sit so long and hear him that, saving for the sake of manners, he had rather have sat all that time at breakfast with a good fat goose. But when it came to the giving of the penance, the fox found that the most weighty sin in all his shrift was gluttony. And therefore he discreetly gave him in penance that he should never for greediness of his food do any other beast any harm or hindrance. And then he should eat his food and worry no more.

Now, as good Mother Maud told us, when the wolf came to Father Reynard (that was, she said, the fox's name) to confession upon Good Friday, his confessor shook his great pair of beads at him, almost as big as bowling balls, and asked him wherefore he came so late. "Forsooth, Father Reynard," quoth he, "I must needs tell you the truth—I come, you know, for that. I dared not come sooner for fear lest you would, for my gluttony, have given me in penance to fast some part of this Lent." "Nay, nay," quoth Father Fox, "I am not so unreasonable, for I fast none of it myself. For I may say to thee, son, between us twain here in confession, it is no commandment of God, this fasting, but an invention of man. The priests make folk fast, and then put them to trouble about the moonshine in the water, and do but make folk fools. But they shall make me no such fool, I warrant thee, son, for I ate flesh all this Lent, myself. Howbeit indeed, because I will not be occasion of slander, I ate it secretly in my chamber, out of sight of all such foolish brethren as for their weak scrupulous conscience would wax offended by it. And so would I counsel you to do." "Forsooth, Father Fox," quoth the wolf, "and so, thank God, I do, as near as I can. For when I go to my meal, I take no other company with me but such sure brethren as are of mine own nature, whose consciences are not weak, I warrant you, but their stomachs are as strong as mine." "Well, then, no matter," quoth Father Fox. But when he heard afterward, by his confession, that he was so great a ravener that he devoured and spent sometimes so much victuals at a meal that the price of them would well keep some poor man with his wife and children almost all the week, then he prudently reproved that point in him, and preached him a sermon of his own temperance. For he never used, he said, to pass the value of sixpence at a meal—no, nor even that much, "For when I bring home a goose," quoth he, "it is not out of the poulterer's shop, where folk find them with their feathers ready plucked and see which is the fattest, and yet for sixpence buy and choose the best; but out of the housewife's house, at first hand, which can supply them somewhat cheaper, you know, than the poulterer can. Nor yet can I be suffered to see them plucked, and stand and choose them by day, but am fain by night to take one at adventure. And when I come home, I am fain to do the labour to pluck it myself too. Yet, for all this, though it be but lean and, I know, not well worth a groat, it serveth me sometimes both for dinner and for supper too. As for the fact that you live of ravine, I can find no fault in that. You have used it so long that I think you can do no otherwise, and therefore it would be folly to forbid it to you—and, to say the truth, against good conscience too. For live you must, I know, and other craft know you none, and therefore, as reason is, must you live by that. But yet, you know, too much is too much, and measure is a merry mean, which I perceive by your shrift you have never used to keep. And therefore surely this shall be your penance, that you shall all this year never pass the price of sixpence at a meal, as near as your conscience can guess the price."

Their shrift have I told you, as Mother Maud told it to us. But now serveth for our matter the conscience of them both in the true performing of their penance. The poor ass after his shrift, when he waxed anhungered, saw a sow lie with her pigs, well lapped in new straw. And he drew near and thought to have eaten of the straw, but anon his scrupulous conscience began therein to grudge him. For since his penance was that, for greediness of his good, he should do nobody else any harm, he thought he might not eat one straw there lest, for lack of that straw, some of those pigs might hap to die for cold. So he held still his hunger until someone brought him food. But when he was about to fall to it, then fell he yet into a far further scruple. For then it came in his mind that he should yet break his penance if he should eat any of that either, since he was commanded by his ghostly father that he should not, for his own food, hinder any other beast. For he thought that if he ate not that food, some other beast might hap to have it. And so should he, by the eating of it, peradventure hinder another. And thus stayed he still fasting till, when he told the cause, his ghostly father came and informed him better, and then he cast off that scruple and fell mannerly to his meal, and was a right honest ass many a fair day after.

The wolf now, coming from shrift clean absolved from his sins, went about to do as a certain shrewish wife once told her husband that she would do, when she came from shrift. "Be merry, man," quoth she now, "for this day, I thank God, I was well shriven. And I purpose now therefore to leave off all mine old shrewishness and begin even afresh!"

VINCENT: Ah, well, uncle, can you report her so? That word I heard her speak, but she said it in sport to make her goodman laugh.

ANTHONY: Indeed, it seemed she spoke it half in sport. For in that she said she would cast away all her old shrewishness, therein I daresay she sported. But in that she said she would begin it all afresh, her husband found that in good earnest!

VINCENT: Well, I shall tell her what you say, I warrant you.

ANTHONY: Then will you make me make my word good!
But whatsoever she did, at least so fared now this wolf, who had cast out in confession all his old ravine. For then hunger pricked him forward so that, as the shrewish wife said, he should begin all afresh. But yet the prick of conscience withdrew him and held him back, because he would not, for breaking of his penance, take any prey for his mealtide that should pass the price of sixpence.

It happed him then, as he walked prowling for his gear about, that he came where a man had, a few days before, cast off two old lean and lame horses, so sick that no flesh was there left upon them. And the one, when the wolf came by, could scant stand on his legs, and the other was already dead and his skin ripped off and carried away. And as he looked upon them suddenly, he was first about to feed upon them and whet his teeth upon their bones. But as he looked aside, he spied a fair cow in an enclosure, walking with her young calf by her side. And as soon as he saw them, his conscience began to grudge him against both those two horses. And then he sighed and said to himself, "Alas, wicked wretch that I am, I had almost broken my penance ere I was aware! For yonder dead horse, because I never sad a dead horse sold in the market, even if I should die for it, I cannot guess, to save my sinful soul, what price I should set on him. But in my conscience I set him far above sixpence, and therefore I dare not meddle with him. Now, then, yonder live horse is in all likelihood worth a great deal of money. For horses are dear in this country—especially such soft amblers, for I see by his pace he trotteth not, nor can scant shift a foot. And therefore I may not meddle with him, for he very far passeth my sixpence. But cows this country hath enough, while money have they very little. And therefore, considering the plenty of the cows and the scarcity of the money, yonder foolish cow seemeth unto me, in my conscience, worth not past a groat, if she be worth so much. Now then, her calf is not so much as she, by half. And therefore, since the cow is in my conscience worth but fourpence, my conscience cannot serve me, for sin of my soul, to appraise her calf above twopence. And so pass they not sixpence between them both. And therefore may I well eat them twain at this one meal and break not my penance at all." And so thereupon he did, without any scruple of conscience.

If such beasts could speak now, as Mother Maud said they could then, some of them would, I daresay, tell a tale almost as wise as this! Save for the diminishing of old Mother Maud's tale, a shorter sermon would have served. But yet, as childish as the parable is, in this it serveth for our purpose: that the night's fear of a somewhat scrupulous conscience, though it be painful and troublous to him who hath it, as this poor ass had here, is yet less harm than a conscience that is over-large. And less harm is it than a conscience such as a man pleases to frame himself for his own fancy— now drawing it narrow, now stretching it in breadth, after the manner of a leather thong—to serve on every side for his own commodity, as did here the wily wolf.

But such folk are out of tribulation, and comfort need they none, and therefore are they out of our matter. But he who is in the night's fear of his own scrupulous conscience, let him well beware, as I said, that the devil draw him not, for weariness of the one, into the other, and while he would fly from Scilla draw him into Charibdis. He must do as doth a ship coming into a haven in the mouth of which lie secret rocks under the water on both sides. If by mishap he be entered in among them that are on the one side, and cannot tell how to get out, he must get a substantial clever pilot who can so conduct him from the rocks on that side that yet he bring him not into those that are on the other side, but can guide him in the mid way. Let them, I say therefore, who are in the troublous fear of heir own scrupulous conscience, submit the rule of their conscience to the counsel of some other good man, who after the variety and the nature of the scruples may temper his advice.

Yea, although a man be very well learned himself, yet if he be in this state let him learn the custom used among physicians. For if one of them be never so learned, yet in his own disease and sickness he never useth to trust all to himself, but sendeth for such of his fellows as he knoweth to be able, and putteth himself in their hands. This he doth for many considerations, and one of the causes is fear. For upon some tokens in his own sickness he may conceive a great deal more fear than needeth, and then it would be good for his health if for the time he knew no such thing at all.

I knew once in this town one of the most learned men in that profession and the most expert, and the most famous too, and him who did the greatest cures upon other men. And yet when he was himself once very sore sick, I heard his fellows who then took care of him—every one of whom would, in his own disease, have used his help before that of any other man—wish that yet, while his own sickness was so sore, he had known no physic at all. He took so great heed unto every suspicious token, and feared so far the worst, that his fear did him sometimes much more harm than the sickness gave him cause.

And therefore, as I say, whosoever hath such a trouble of his scrupulous conscience, let him for a while forbear the judgment of himself, and follow the counsel of some other man whom he knoweth for well learned and virtuous. And especially in the place of confession, for these is God specially present with his grace assisting the sacrament. And let him not doubt to quiet his mind and follow what he is there bidden, and think for a while less of the fear of God's justice, and be more merry in remembrance of his mercy, and persevere in prayer for grace, and abide and dwell faithfully in the sure hope of his help. And then shall he find, without any doubt, that the shield of God's truth shall, as the prophet saith, so compass him about, that he shall not dread this night's fear of scrupulosity, but shall have afterward his conscience established in good quiet and rest.

# XV

VINCENT: Verily, good uncle, you have in my mind well declared these kinds of the night's fear.

ANTHONY: Surely, cousin, but yet are there many more than I can either remember or find. Howbeit, one yet cometh now to my mind, of which I thought not before, and which is yet in mine opinion. That is, cousin, where the devil tempteth a man to kill and destroy himself.

VINCENT: Undoubtedly this kind of tribulation is marvellous and strange. And the temptation is of such a sort that some men have the opinion that those who once fall into that fantasy can never fully cast it off.

ANTHONY: Yes, yes, cousin, many a hundred, and else God forbid. But the thing that maketh men so to say is that, of those who finally do destroy themselves, there is much speech and much wondering, as it is well worthy. But many a good man and woman hath sometime—yea, for some years, once after another—continually been tempted to do it, and yet hath, by grace and good counsel, well and virtuously withstood that temptation, and been in conclusion clearly delivered of it. And their tribulation is not known abroad and therefore not talked of.

But surely, cousin, a horrible sore trouble it is to any man or woman whom the devil tempteth with that temptation. Many have I heard of, and with some have I talked myself, who have been sore cumbered with it, and I have marked not a little the manner of them.

VINCENT: I pray you, good uncle, show me somewhat of such things as you perceive therein. For first, whereas you call the kind of temptation the daughter of pusillanimity and thereby so near of kin to the night's fear, methinketh on the other hand that it is rather a thing that cometh of a great courage and boldness. For they dare with their own hands to put themselves to death, from which we see almost every man shrink and flee, and many of them we know by good proof and plain experience for men of great heart and excellent bold courage.

ANTHONY: I said, Cousin Vincent, that of pusillanimity cometh this temptation, and very truth it is that indeed so it doth. But yet I meant not that only of faint heart and fear it cometh and growth always. For the devil tempteth sundry folk by sundry ways.

But I spoke of no other kind of that temptation save only that one which is the daughter that the devil begetteth upon pusillanimity, because those other kinds of temptation fall not under the nature of tribulation and fear, and therefore fall they far out of our matter here. They are such temptations as need only counsel, and not comfort or consolation, because the persons tempted with them are not troubled in their mind with that kind of temptation. but are very well content both in the tempting and in the following. For some have there been, cousin, such that they have been tempted to do it by means of a foolish pride, and some by means of anger, without any fear at all—and very glad to go thereto, I deny not. But if you think that none fall into it by fear, but that they have all a mighty strong stomach, that shall you well see to be the contrary. And that peradventure in those of whom you would think the stomach more strong and their heart and courage most bold.

VINCENT: Yet is it marvel to me, uncle, that it should be as you say it is—that this temptation is unto them that do it for pride or anger no tribulation, or that they should not need, in so great a distress and peril, both of body and soul to be lost, no manner of good ghostly comfort.

ANTHONY: Let us therefore, cousin, consider an example or two, for thereby shall we better perceive it.
There was here in Buda in King Ladilaus' days, a good poor honest man's wife. This woman was so fiendish that the devil, perceiving her nature, put her in the mind that she should anger her husband so sore that she might give him occasion to kill her, and then should he be hanged because of her.

VINCENT: This was a strange temptation indeed! What the devil should she be the better then?

ANTHONY: Nothing, but that it eased her shrewish stomach beforehand, to think that her husband should be hanged afterward. And peradventure, if you look about the world and consider it well, you shall find more such stomachs than a few. Have you never heard a furious body plainly say that, to see such-and-such man have a mischief, he would with good will be content to lie as long in hell as God liveth in heaven?

VINCENT: Forsooth, and some such have I heard.

ANTHONY: This mind of his was not much less mad than hers, but rather perhaps the more mad of the twain. For the woman peradventure did not cast so far peril therein.
But to tell you now to what good pass her charitable purpose came: As her husband (the man was a carpenter) stood hewing with his chip axe upon a piece of timber, she began after her old guise to revile him so that he waxed wroth at last, and bade her get herself in or he would lay the helm of his axe about her back. And he said also that it would be little sin even with that axe head to chop off the unhappy head of hers that carried such an ungracious tongue in it. At that word the devil took his time and whetted her tongue against her teeth. And when it was well sharpened she swore to him in very fierce anger, "By the mass, whoreson husband, I wish thou wouldst! Here lieth my head, lo," and with that down she laid her head upon the same timber log. "If thou smite it not off, I beshrew thine

whoreson's heart!" With that, likewise as the devil stood at her elbow, so stood (as I heard say) his good angel at his, and gave him ghostly courage and bade him be bold and do it. And so the good man up with his chip axe and at a chop he chopped off her head indeed.

There were other folk standing by, who had a good sport to hear her chide, but little they looked for this chance, till it was done ere they could stop it. They said they heard her tongue babble in her head, and call, "Whoreson, whoreson!" twice after the head was off the body. At least, thus they all reported afterward unto the king, except only one, and that was a woman, and she said that she heard it not.

VINCENT: Forsooth, this was a wonderful work! What became, uncle, of the man?

ANTHONY: The king gave him his pardon.

VINCENT: Verily, he might in conscience do no less.

ANTHONY: But then was there almost made a statute that in such a case there should never after be granted a pardon, but (if the truth were able to be proved) no husband should need any pardon, but should have leave by the law to follow the example of that carpenter, and do the same.

VINCENT: How happed it, uncle, that that good law was left unmade?

ANTHONY: How happed it? As it happeth, cousin, that many more be left unmade as well as that one, and almost as good as it too, both here and in other countries—and sometimes some that are worse be made in their stead. But they say that the hindrance of that law was the queen's grace, God forgive her soul! It was the greatest thing, I daresay, that she had to answer for, good lady, when she died. For surely, save for that one thing, she was a full blessed woman.

But letting now that law pass, this temptation in procuring her own death was unto this carpenter's wife no tribulation at all, as far as men could ever perceive. For she liked well to think upon it, and she even longed for it. And therefore if she had before told you or me her intent, and that she would so fain bring it so to pass, we could have had no occasion to comfort her, as one that were in tribulation. But marry, counsel her we might, as I told you before, to refrain and amend that malicious devilish intent.

VINCENT: Verily, that is truth. But such as are well willing to do any purpose that is so shameful, they will never tell their intent to nobody, for very shame.

ANTHONY: Some will not, indeed. And yet are there some again who, be their intent never so shameful, find some yet whom their heart serveth them to make of their counsel therein.

Some of my folk here can tell you that no longer ago than even yesterday, someone who came out of Vienna told us, among other talking, that a rich widow (but I forgot to ask him where it happened), having all her life a high proud mind and a malicious one—as those two virtues are wont always to keep company together—was at dispute with another neighbour of hers in the town. And on a time she made of her counsel a poor neighbour of hers, whom she thought she might induce, for money, to follow her intent. With him she secretly spoke, and offered him ten ducats for his labour, to do so much for her as in a morning early to come to her house and with an axe unknown privily strike off her head. And when he had done so, he was to convey the bloody axe into the house of him with whom she was at dispute, in such manner as it might be thought that he had murdered her for malice. And then she thought she should be taken for a martyr. And yet had she farther devised that another sum of money should afterward be sent to Rome, and there should be measures made to the Pope that she might in all haste be canonized!

This poor man promised, but intended not to perform it. Howbeit, when he deferred it, she provided the axe herself. And he appointed with her the morning when he should come and do it, and thereupon into her house he came. But then set he such other folk as he wished should know of her mad fancy, in such place appointed as they might well hear her and him talk together. And after he had talked with her so much as he thought was enough, he made her lie down, and took up the axe in his own hand. And with the other hand he felt the edge, and found a fault that it was not sharp, and that therefore he would in no wise do it, till he had ground it sharp. He could not otherwise, he said, for pity, it would put her to so much pain. And so, full sore against her will, for that time she kept her head still. But because she would no more suffer any more to deceive her and put her off with delays, ere it was very long thereafter, she hung herself with her own hands.

VINCENT: Forsooth, here was a tragical story, whereof I never heard the like.

ANTHONY: Forsooth, the party who told it to me swore that he knew it for a truth. And he is, I promise you, such as I reckon for right honest and of substantial truth.

Now, here she forbore not, as shameful an intent as she had, to make someone of her counsel—and yet, I remember, another too, whom she trusted with the money that should procure her canonization. And here I believe that her temptation came not of fear but of high malice and pride. And then was she so glad in that pleasant device that, as I told you, she took it for no tribulation. And therefore comforting of her could have no place. But if men should give her anything toward her help, it must have been, as I told you, good counsel.

And therefore, as I said, this kind of temptation to a man's own destruction, which requireth counsel, and is outside tribulation, was outside of our matter, which is to treat of comfort in tribulation.

## XVI

But lest you might reject both these examples, thinking they were but feigned tales, I shall put you in remembrance of one which I reckon you yourself have read in the Conferences of Cassian. And if you have not, there you may soon find it. For I myself have half forgotten the thing, it is so long since I read it.

But thus much I remember: He telleth there of one who was many days a very special holy man in his living, and, among the other virtuous monks and anchorites that lived there in the wilderness, was marvellously much esteemed. Yet some were not all out of fear lest his revelations (of which he told many himself) would prove illusions of the devil. And so it proved afterwards indeed, for the man was by the devil's subtle suggestions brought into such a high spiritual pride that in conclusion the devil brought him to that horrible point that he made him go kill himself.

And, as far as my mind giveth me now, without new sight of the book, he brought him to it by this persuasion: He made him believe that it was God's will that he should do so, and that thereby he should go straight to heaven. And if it were by that persuasion, with which he took very great comfort in his own mind himself, then was it, as I said, out of our case, and he needed not comfort but counsel against giving credence to the devil's persuasion. But marry, if he made him first perceive how he had been deluded and then tempted him to his own death by shame and despair, then it was within our matter. For then was his temptation fallen down from pride to pusillanimity, and was waxed that kind of the night's fear that I spoke of. And in such fear a good part of the counsel to be given him should have need to stand in good comforting, for then was he brought into right sore tribulation.

But, as I was about to tell you, strength of heart and courage are there none in that deed, not only because true strength (as it hath the name of virtue in a reasonable creature) can never be without prudence, but also because, as I said, even in them that seem men of most courage, it shall well appear to them that well weigh the matter that the mind whereby they be led to destroy themselves groweth of pusillanimity and very foolish fear.

Take for example Cato of Utica, who in Africa killed himself after the great victory that Julius Caesar had. St. Austine well declareth in his work De civitate Dei that there was no strength nor magnanimity in his destruction of himself, but plain pusillanimity and impotency of stomach. For he was forced to do it because his heart was too feeble to bear the beholding of another man's glory or the suffering of other worldly calamities that he feared should fall on himself. So that, as St. Austine well proveth, that horrible deed is no act of strength, but an act of a mind either drawn from the consideration of itself with some fiendish fancy, in which the man hath need to be called home with good counsel; or else oppressed by faint heart and fear, in which a good part of the counsel must stand in lifting up his courage with good consolation and comfort.

And therefore if we found any such religious person as was that father whom Cassian writeth of, who were of such austerity and apparent ghostly living as he was, and reputed by those who well knew him for a man of singular virtue; and if it were perceived that he had many strange visions appearing unto him; and if after that it should now be perceived that the man went about secretly to destroy himself—whosoever should hap to come to the knowledge of it and intended to do his best to hinder it, he must first find the means to search and find out the manner and countenance of the man. He must see whether he be lightsome, glad, and joyful or dumpish, heavy, and sad, and whether he go about it as one that were full of the glad hope of heaven, or as one who had his breast stuffed full of tediousness and weariness of the world. If he were found to be of the first fashion, it would be a token that the devil had, by his fantastical apparitions, puffed him up in such a childish pride that he hath finally persuaded him, by some illusion showed him for the proof, that God's pleasure is that he shall for his sake with his own hands kill himself.

VINCENT: Now, if a man so found it, uncle, what counsel should he give him then?

ANTHONY: That would be somewhat out of our purpose, cousin, since (as I told you before) the man would not be in sorrow and tribulation, of which our matter speaketh, but in a perilous merry mortal temptation. So that if we should, beside our matter that we have in hand, enter into that too, we might make a longer work between both than we could well finish this day. Howbeit, to be short, it is soon seen that in such a case the sum and effect of the counsel must (in a manner) rest in giving him warning of the devil's sleights. And that must be done under such a sweet pleasant manner that the man should not abhor to hear it. For while it could not lightly be otherwise that the man were rocked and sung asleep by the devil's craft, and his mind occupied as it were in a delectable dream, he should never have good audience of him who would rudely and boisterously shog him and wake him, and so shake him out of it. Therefore must you fair and easily touch him, and with some pleasant speech awake him, so that he wax not wayward, as children do who are waked ere they wish to rise.

But when a man hath first begun with his praise (for if he be proud you shall much better please him with a commendation than with a dirge) then, after favour won therewith, a man may little by little insinuate the doubt of such revelations—not at first as though it were for any doubt of his, but of some other man's, that men in some other places talk of. And peradventure it shall not miscontent him to say that great perils may fall therein, in another man's case than his own, and he shall begin to preach upon it. Or, if you were a man that had not so very great scrupulous conscience of a harmless lie devised to do good with (the kind which St. Austine, though he take it always for sin, yet he taketh but for venial; and St. Jerome, as by divers places in his books appeareth, taketh not fully for that much), then may you feign some secret friend of yours to be in such a state. And you may say that you yourself somewhat fear his peril, and have made of charity this voyage for his sake, to ask this good father's counsel.

And in the communication, upon these words of St. John, "Give not credence to every spirit, but prove the spirits whether they be of God," and these words of St. Paul, "The angel of Satan transfigureth himself into the angel of light," you shall take occasion (the better if they hap to come in on his side), but yet not lack occasion neither if those texts, for lack of his offer, come in upon your own—occasion, I say, you shall not lack to enquire by what sure and undeceivable tokens a man may discern the true revelations from the false illusions. A man shall find many such tokens both here and there in divers other authors and all together in divers goodly treatises of that good godly doctor, Master John Gerson, entitled De probatione spirituum. As, whether the party be natural in manner or seem anything fantastical. Or, whether the party be poor-spirited or proud. The pride will somewhat appear by his delight in his own praise; or if, of wiliness, or of another pride for to be praised of humility, he refused to hear of that, yet any little fault found in himself, or diffidence declared and mistrust of his own revelations and doubtful tokens told, wherefore he himself should fear lest they be the devil's illusion—such things, as Master Gerson saith, will make him spit out somewhat of his spirit, if the devil lie in his breast. Or if the devil be yet so subtle that he keep himself close in his warm den and blow out never a hot word, yet it is to be considered what end his revelations tend to—whether to any spiritual profit to himself or other folk, or only to vain marvels and wonders. Also, whether they withdraw him from such other good virtuous business as, by the common rule of Christendom or any of the rules of his profession, he was wont to use or bound to be occupied in. Or whether he fall into any singularity of opinions against the scripture of God, or against the common faith of Christ's Catholic Church. Many other tokens are spoken of in the work of Master Gerson, by which to consider whether the person, neither having revelations of God nor illusions from the devil, do feign his revelations himself, either for winning of money or worldly favour, and delude the people withal.

But now for our purpose: If, among any of the marks by which the true revelations may be known from false illusions, that man himself bring forth, for one mark, the doing or teaching of anything against the scripture of God or the common faith of the church, you may enter into the special matter, in which he can never well flee from you. Or else may you yet, if you wish, feign that your secret friend, for whose sake you come to him for counsel, is brought to that mind by a certain apparition showed unto him, as he himself saith, by an angel—as you fear, by the devil. And that he cannot as yet be otherwise persuaded by you but that the pleasure of God is that he shall go kill himself. And that he believeth if he do so he shall then be thereby so specially participant of Christ's passion that he shall forthwith be carried up with angels into heaven. And that he is so joyful for this that he firmly purposeth upon it, no less glad to do it than another man would be glad to avoid it. And therefore may you desire his good counsel to instruct you with some substantial good advice, with which you may turn him from this error, that he be not, under hope of God's true revelation, destroyed in body and soul by the devil's false illusion.

If he will in this thing study and labour to instruct you, the things that he himself shall find, of his own invention, though they be less effectual, shall peradventure more work with him toward his own amendment (since he shall, of likelihood, better like them) than shall things double so substantial that were told him by another man. If he be loth to think upon that side, and therefore shrink from the matter, then is there no other way but to venture to fall into the matter after the plain fashion, and tell what you hear, and give him counsel and exhortation to the contrary. Unless you wish to say that thus and thus hath the matter been reasoned already between your friend and you. And therein may you rehearse such things as should prove that the vision which moveth him is no true revelation, but a very false illusion.

VINCENT: Verily, uncle, I well allow that a man should, in this thing as well as in every other in which he longeth to do another man good, seek such a pleasant way that the party should be likely to like his communication, or at least to take it well in worth. And he should not enter in unto it in such a way that he whom he would help should abhor him and be loth to hear him, and therefore take no profit by him.

But now, uncle, if it come, by the one way or the other, to the point where he will or shall hear me; what be the effectual means with which I should by my counsel convert him?

ANTHONY: All those by which you may make him perceive that he is deceived, and that his visions are no godly revelations but very devilish illusion. And those reasons must you gather of the man, of the matter, and of the law of God, or of some one of these.

Of the man may you gather them, if you can peradventure show him that in such-and-such a point he is waxed worse since such revelations have haunted him than he was before—as, in those who are deluded, whosoever be well acquainted with them shall well mark and perceive. For they wax more proud, more wayward, more envious, suspicious, misjudging and depraving other men, with the delight of their own praise, and such other spiritual vices of the soul.

Of the matter may you gather, if it has happened that his revelations before have proved false, or if they be strange things rather than profitable ones. For that is a good mark between God's miracles and the devil's wonders. For Christ and his saints have their miracles always tending to fruit and profit. The devil and his witches and necromancers, all their wonderful works tend to no fruitful end, but to a fruitless ostentation and show, as it were a juggler who would for a show before the people play feats of skill at a feast.

Of the law of God you must draw your reasons in showing by the scripture that the thing which he thinketh God biddeth by his angel, God hath by his own mouth forbidden. And that is, you know well, in the case that we speak of, so easy to find that I need not to rehearse it to you. For among the Ten Commandments there is plainly forbidden the unlawful killing of any man, and therefore of himself, as (St. Austine saith) all the church teacheth, unless he himself be no man.

VINCENT: This is very true, good uncle, nor will I dispute upon any glossing of that prohibition. But since we find not the contrary but that God may dispense with that commandment himself, and both license and command also, if he himself wish, any man to go kill either another man or himself, this man who is now by such a marvellous vision induced to believe that God so biddeth him, and therefore thinketh himself in that case discharged of that prohibition and charged with the contrary commandment—with what reason can we make him perceive that his vision is but an illusion and not a true revelation?

ANTHONY: Nay, Cousin Vincent, you shall in this case not need to ask those reasons of me. But taking the scripture of God for a ground for this matter, you know very well yourself that you shall go somewhat a shorter way to work if you ask this question of him: Since God hath forbidden once the thing himself, though he may dispense with it if he will, yet since the devil may feign himself God and with a marvellous vision delude one, and make as though God did it; and since the devil is also more likely to speak against God's commandment than God against his own; you shall have good cause, I say, to demand of the man himself whereby he knoweth that his vision is God's true revelation and not the devil's false delusion.

VINCENT: Indeed, uncle, I think that would be a hard question to him. Can a man, uncle, have in such a thing even a very sure knowledge of his own mind?

ANTHONY: Yea, cousin, God may cast into the mind of a man, I suppose, such an inward light of understanding that he cannot fail but be sure thereof. And yet he who is deluded by the devil may think himself as sure and yet be deceived indeed. And such a difference is there in a manner between them, as between the sight of a thing while we are awake and look thereon, and the sight with which we see a thing in our sleep while we dream thereof.

VINCENT: This is a pretty similitude, uncle, in this thing! And then is it easy for the monk that we speak of to declare that he knoweth his vision for a true revelation and not a false delusion, if there be so great a difference between them.

ANTHONY: Not so easy yet, cousin, as you think it would be. For how can you prove to me that you are awake?

VINCENT: Marry, lo, do I not now wag my hand, shake my head, and stamp with my foot here on the floor?

ANTHONY: Have you never dreamed ere this that you have done the same?

VINCENT: Yes, that have I, and more too than that. For I have ere this in my sleep dreamed that I doubted whether I were asleep or awake, and have in good faith thought that I did thereupon even the same things that I do now indeed, and thereby determined that I was not asleep. And yet have I dreamed in good faith further, that I have been afterward at dinner and there, making merry with good company, have told the same dream at the table and laughed well at it, to think that while I was asleep I had by such means of moving the parts of my body and considering thereof, so verily thought myself awake!

ANTHONY: And will you not now soon, think you, when you wake and rise, laugh as well at yourself when you see that you lie now in your warm bed asleep again, and dream all this time, while you believe so verily that you are awake and talking of these matters with me?

VINCENT: God's Lord, uncle, you go now merrily to work with me indeed, when you look and speak so seriously and would make me think I were asleep!

ANTHONY: It may be that you are, for anything that you can say or do whereby you can, with any reason that you make, drive me to confess that you yourself be sure of the contrary. For you cannot do or say anything now whereby you are sure to be awake but what you have ere this, or hereafter may, think yourself as surely to do the selfsame thing indeed while you be all the while asleep and do nothing but lie dreaming.

VINCENT: Well, well, uncle, though I have ere this thought myself awake while I was indeed asleep, yet for all this I know well enough that I am awake now. And so do you too, though I cannot find the words by which I may with reason force you to confess it, without your always driving me off by the example of my dream.

ANTHONY: Meseemeth, cousin, this is very true. And likewise

meseemeth the manner and difference between some kind of true revelations and some kind of false illusions is like that which standeth between the things that are done awake and the things that in our dreams seem to be done when we are sleeping. That is, he who hath that kind of revelation from God is as sure of the truth as we are of our own deeds while we are awake. And he who is deluded by the devil is in such wise deceived as they are by their dream, and worse, too. And yet he reckoneth himself for the time as sure as the other, saving that one believeth falsely, the other truly knoweth. But I say not, cousin, that this kind of sure knowledge cometh in every kind of revelation. For there are many kinds, of which it would be too long to talk now. But I say that God doth certainly send some such to a man in some thing, or may.

VINCENT: Yet then this religious man of whom we speak, when I show him the scripture against his revelation and therefore call it an illusion, may bid me with reason go mind my own affairs. For he knoweth well and surely himself that his revelation is very good and true and not any false illusion, since for all the general commandment of God in the scripture, God may dispense where he will and when he will, and may command him to do the contrary. For he commanded Abraham to kill his own son, and Sampson had, by inspiration of God, commandment to kill himself by pulling down the house upon his own head at the feast of the Philistines.

Now, if I would then do as you bade me right now, tell him that such apparitions may be illusions, and since God's word is in the scripture against him plain for the prohibition, he must perceive the truth of his revelation whereby I may know it is not a false illusion; then shall he in turn bid me tell him whereby I can prove myself to be awake and talk with him and not be asleep and dream so, since in my dream I may as surely think so as I know that I do so. And thus shall he drive me to the same bay to which I would bring him.

ANTHONY: This is well said, cousin, but yet could he not escape you so. For the dispensation of God's common precept, which dispensation he must say that he hath by his private revelation, is a thing of such sort as showeth itself naught and false. For it never hath any example like, since the world began until now, that ever man hath read or heard of, among faithful people commended.

First, as for Abraham, concerning the death of his son: God intended it not, but only tempted the towardness of the father's obedience. As for Sampson, all men make not the matter very sure whether he be saved or not, but yet therein some matter and cause appeareth. For the Philistines being enemies of God and using Sampson for their mocking-stock in scorn of God, it is well likely that God gave him the mind to bestow his own life upon the revenging of the displeasure that those blasphemous Philistines did unto God. And that appeareth clear enough by this: that though his strength failed him when he lacked his hair, yet had he not, it seemeth, that strength evermore at hand while he had his hair, but only at such times as it pleased God to give it to him. This thing appeareth by these words, that the scripture in some place of that matter saith, "The power or might of God rushed into Sampson." And so therefore, since this thing that he did in the pulling down of the house was done by the special gift of strength then at that point given him by God, it well declareth that the strength of God, and with it the spirit of God, entered into him for it.

St. Austine also rehearseth that certain holy virtuous virgins, in time of persecution, being pursued by God's enemies the infidels to be deflowered by force, ran into a water and drowned themselves rather than be bereaved of their virginity. And, albeit that he thinketh it is not lawful for any other maid to follow their example, but that she should suffer another to do her any manner of violence by force and commit sin of his own upon her against her will, rather than willingly and thereby sinfully herself to become a homicide of herself; yet he thinketh that in them it happened by the special instinct of the spirit of God, who, for causes seen to himself, would rather that they should avoid it with their own temporal death than abide the defiling and violation of their chastity.

But now this good man neither hath any of God's enemies to be revenged on by his own death, nor any woman who violently pursues him to bereave him by force of his virginity! And we never find that God proved any man's obedient mind by the commandment of his own slaughter of himself. Therefore is both his case plainly against God's open precept, and the dispensation strange and without example, no cause appearing nor well imaginable. Unless he would think that God could neither any longer live without him, nor could take him to him in such wise as he doth other men, but must command him to come by a forbidden way, by which, without other cause, we never heard that ever he bade any man else before.

Now, you think that, if you should after this bid him tell you by what way he knoweth that his intent riseth upon a true revelation and not upon a false illusion, he in turn would bid you tell him by what means you know that you are talking with him well awake and not dreaming it asleep. You may answer him that for men thus to talk together as you do and to prove and perceive that they do so, by the moving of themselves, with putting the question unto themselves for their pleasure, and marking and considering it, is in waking a daily common thing that every man doth or can do when he will, and when they do it, they do it but for pleasure. But in sleep it happeneth very seldom that men dream that they do so, and in the dream they never put the question except for doubt. And you may tell him that, since this revelation is such also as happeneth so seldom and oftener happeneth that men dream of such than have such indeed, therefore it is more reasonable that he show you how he knoweth, in such a rare thing and a thing more like a dream, that he himself is not asleep, than that you, in such a common thing among folk that are awake and so seldom happening in a dream, should need to show him whereby you know that you be not asleep.

Besides this, he to whom you should show it seeth himself and perceiveth the thing that he would bid you prove. But the thing that he would make you believe—the truth of his revelation which you bid him prove—you see not that he knoweth it well himself. And therefore, ere you believe it against the scripture, it would be well consonant unto reason that he should show you how he knoweth it for a true waking revelation and not a false dreaming delusion.

VINCENT: Then shall he peradventure answer me that whether I believe him or not maketh to him no matter; the thing toucheth himself and not me, and he himself is in himself as sure that it is a true revelation as that he can tell that he dreameth not but talketh with me awake.

ANTHONY: Without doubt, cousin, if he abide at that point and can by no reason be brought to do so much as doubt, nor can by no means be shogged out of his dead sleep, but will needs take his dream for a very truth, and—as some men rise by night and walk about their chamber in their sleep—will so rise and hang himself; I can then see no other way but either bind him fast in his bed, or else essay whether that might hap to help him with which, the common tale goeth, a carver's wife helped her husband in such a frantic fancy. When, upon a Good Friday, he would needs have killed himself for Christ as Christ did for him, she said to him that it would then be fitting for him to die even after the same fashion. And that might not be by his own hands, but by the hand of another; for Christ, perdy, killed not himself. And because her husband would take no counsel (for that would he not, in no wise), she offered him that for God's sake she would secretly crucify him herself upon a great cross that he had made to nail a new-carved crucifix upon. And he was very glad thereof. Yet then she bethought her that Christ was bound to a pillar and beaten first, and afterward crowned with thorns. Thereupon, when she had by his own assent bound him fast to a post, she left not off beating, with holy exhortation to suffer, so much and so long that ere ever she left work and unbound him (praying nevertheless, that she might put on his head, and drive well down, a crown of thorns that she had wrought for him and brought him), he said he thought this was enough for that year. He would pray God to forbear him of the rest till Good Friday came again! But when it came again the next years, then was his desire past; he longed to follow Christ no further.

VINCENT: Indeed, uncle, if this help him not, then will nothing help him, I suppose.

ANTHONY: And yet, cousin, the devil may peradventure make him, toward such a purpose, first gladly suffer other pain; yea, and diminish his feeling in it, too, that he may thereby the less fear his death. And yet are peradventure sometimes such things and many more to be essayed. For as the devil may hap to make him suffer, so may he hap to miss, namely if his friends fall to prayer for him against his temptation. For that can he himself never do, while he taketh it for none.

But, for conclusion: If the man be surely proved so inflexibly set upon the purpose to destroy himself, as being commanded by God to do so, that no good counsel that men can give him nor any other thing that men may do to him can refrain him, but that he would surely shortly kill himself; then except only good prayer made by his friends for him, I can find no further shift but either to have him ever in sight or to bind him fast in his bed.

And so must he needs of reason be content to be ordered. For though he himself may take his fancy for a true revelation, yet since he cannot make us perceive it for such, likewise as he thinketh himself by his secret commandment bound to follow it, so must he needs agree that, since it is against the plain open prohibition of God, we are bound by the plain open precept to keep him from it.

VINCENT: In this point, uncle, I can go no further. But now, if he were, on the other hand, perceived to intend his destruction and go about it with heaviness of heart and thought and dullness—what way would there be to be used to him then?

ANTHONY: Then would his temptation, as I told you before, be properly pertaining to our matter, for then would he be in a sore tribulation and a very perilous. For then would it be a token that the devil had either, by bringing him into some great sin, brought him into despair, or peradventure, by his revelations being found false and reproved or by some secret sin of his being deprehended and divulged, had cast him both into despair of heaven through fear and into a weariness of this life for shame. For then he seeth his estimation lost among other folk of whose praise he was wont to be proud.

And therefore, cousin, in such a case as this, the man is to be fairly handled and sweetly, and with tender loving words to be put in good courage, and comforted in all that men goodly can. Here must they put him in mind that, if he despair not, but pull up his courage and trust in God's great mercy, he shall have in conclusion great cause to be glad of this fall. For before he stood in greater peril than he was aware of, while he took himself for better than he was. And God, for favour that he beareth him, hath suffered him to fall deep into the devil's danger, to make him thereby know what he was while he took himself for so sure. And therefore, as he suffered him then to fall for a remedy against over-bold pride, so will God now—if the man meek himself, not with fruitless despair but with fruitful penance—so set him up again upon his feet and so strengthen him with his grace, that for this one fall that the devil hath given him he shall give the devil a hundred.

And here must he be put in remembrance of Mary Magdalene, of the prophet David, and especially of St. Peter, whose high bold courage took a foul fall. And yet because he despaired not of God's mercy, but wept and called upon it, how highly God took him into his favour again is well testified in his holy scripture and well known through Christendom.

And now shall it be charitably done if some good virtuous folk, such as he himself somewhat esteemeth and hath afore longed to stand in estimation with, do resort sometimes to him, not only to give him counsel but also to ask advice and counsel of him in some cases of their own conscience. For so may they let him perceive that they esteem him now no less, but rather more than they did before, since they think him now by this fall better expert of the devil's craft and so not only better instructed himself but also better able to give good advice and counsel to others. This thing will, to my mind, well amend and lift up his courage from the peril of that desperate shame.

VINCENT: Methinketh, uncle, that this would be a perilous thing. For it may peradventure make him set the less by his fall, and thereby it may cast him into his first pride or into his other sin again, the falling in to which drove him into this despair.

ANTHONY: I do not mean, cousin, that every fool should at adventure fall in hand with him, for so might it happen to do harm indeed.

But, cousin, if a learned physician have a man in hand, he can well discern when and how long some certain medicine is necessary which, if administered at another time or at that time over-long continued, might put the patient in peril. If he have his patient in an ague, for the cure of which he needeth his medicines in their working cold, yet he may hap, ere that fever be full cured, to fall into some other disease such that, unless it were helped with hot medicine, would be likely to kill the body before the fever could be cured. The physician then would for the while have his most care to the cure of that thing in which would be the most present peril. And when that were once out of jeopardy, he would do then the more exact diligence afterward about the further cure of the fever.

And likewise, if a ship be in peril to fall into Scilla, the fear of falling into Charibdis on the other side shall never hinder any wise master thereof from drawing himself from Scilla toward Charibdis first, in all that ever he can. But when he hath himself once so far away from Scilla that he seeth himself safe out of that danger, then will he begin to take good heed to keep himself well from the other.

And likewise, while this man is falling down to despair and to the final destruction of himself, a good wise spiritual leech will first look unto that, and by good comfort lift up his courage. And when he seeth that peril well past, he will care for the cure of his other faults afterward. Howbeit, even in the giving of his comfort, he may find ways enough in such wise to temper his words that the men may take occasion of good courage and yet far from occasion of new relapse into his former sin. For the great part of his counsel shall be to encourage him to amendment, and that is, perdy, far from falling into sin again.

VINCENT: I think, uncle, that folk fall into this ungracious mind, through the devil's temptation, by many more means than one.

ANTHONY: That is, cousin, very true. For the devil taketh his occasions as he seeth them fall convenient for him. Some he stirreth to it for weariness of themselves after some great loss, some for fear of horrible bodily harm, and some (as I said) for fear of worldly shame.

One I knew myself who had been long reputed for a right honest man, who was fallen into such a fancy that he was well near worn away with it. But what he was tempted to do, that would he tell no man. But he told me that he was sore cumbered and that it always ran in his mind that folk's fancies were fallen from him, and that they esteemed not his wit as they were wont to do, but ever his mind gave him that the people began to take him for a fool. And folk of truth did not so at all, but reputed him both for wise and honest.

Two others I knew who were marvellous afraid that they would kill themselves, and could tell me no cause wherefore they so feared it except that their own mind so gave them. Neither had they any loss nor no such thing toward them, nor none occasion of any worldly shame (the one was in body very well liking and lusty), but wondrous weary were they both twain of that mind. And always they thought that they would not do it for anything, and nevertheless they feared they would. And wherefore they so feared neither of them both could tell. And the one, lest he should do it, desired his friends to bind him.

VINCENT: This is, uncle, a marvellous strange manner.

ANTHONY: Forsooth, cousin, I suppose many of them are in this case.

The devil, as I said before, seeketh his occasions. For as St. Peter saith, "Your adversary the devil as a roaring lion goeth about seeking whom he may devour." He marketh well, therefore, the state and condition that every man standeth in, not only concerning these outward things (lands, possessions, goods, authority, fame, favour, or hatred of the world), but also men's complexions within them—health or sickness, good humours or bad, by which they be light-hearted or lumpish, strong-hearted or faint and feeble of spirit, bold and hardy or timorous and fearful of courage. And according as these things minister him matter of temptation, so useth he himself in the manner of his temptation.

Now likewise as in such folk as are full of young warm lusty blood and other humours exciting the flesh to filthy voluptuous living, the devil useth to make those things his instruments in tempting them and provoking them to it; and as, where he findeth some folk full of hot blood and choler, he maketh those humours his instruments to set their hearts on fire in wrath and fierce furious anger; so where he findeth some folk who, through some dull melancholy humours, are naturally disposed to fear, he casteth sometimes such a fearful imagination into their mind that without help of God they can never cast it out of their heart.

Some, at the sudden falling of some horrible thought into their mind, have not only had a great abomination at it (which abomination they well and virtuously had), but the devil, using their melancholy humour and thereby their natural inclination to fear for his instruments, hath caused them to conceive therewith such a deep dread besides that they think themselves with that abominable thought to be fallen into such an outrageous sin that they are ready to fall into despair of grace, believing that God hath given them over for ever. Whereas that thought, were it never so horrible and never so abominable, is yet unto those who never like it, but ever still abhor it and strive still against it, matter of conflict and merit and not any sin at all.

Some have, with holding a knife in their hand, suddenly thought upon the killing of themselves, and forthwith, in devising what a horrible thing it would be if they should mishap to do so, have fallen into a fear that they would do so indeed. And they have, with long and often thinking thereon, imprinted that fear so sore in their imagination, that some of them have not afterwards cast it off without great difficulty. And some could never in their life be rid of it, but have afterward in conclusion miserably done it indeed. But like as, where the devil useth the blood of a man's own body toward his purpose in provoking him to lechery, the man must and doth with grace and wisdom resist it; so must the man do whose melancholy humours and devil abuseth, toward the casting of such a desperate dread into his heart.

VINCENT: I pray you, uncle, what advice would be to be given him in such a case?

ANTHONY: Surely, methinketh his help standeth in two things: counsel and prayer.

First, as concerning counsel: Like as it may be that he hath two things that hold him in his temptation; that is, some evil humours of his own body, and the cursed devil that abuseth them to his pernicious purpose, so must he needs against them twain the counsel of two manner of folk; that is, physicians for the body and physicians for the soul. The bodily physician shall consider what abundance of these evil humours the man hath, that the devil maketh his instruments, in moving the man toward that fearful affection. And he shall proceed by fitting diet and suitable medicines to resist them, as well as by purgations to disburden the body of them.

Let no man think it strange that I would advise a man to take counsel for the body, in such spiritual suffering. For since the body and the soul are so knit and joined together that they both make between them one person, the distemperance of either one engendereth sometimes the distemperance of both twain. And therefore I would advise every man in every sickness of the body to be shriven and to seek of a good spiritual physician the sure health of his soul. For this shall not only serve against peril that may peradventure grow further by that sickness than in the beginning men think were likely, but the comfort of it (and God's favour increasing with it) shall also do the body good. For this cause the blessed apostle St. James exhorteth men in their bodily sickness to call in the priests, and saith that it shall do them good both in body and soul. So likewise would I sometimes advise some men, in some sickness of the soul, besides their spiritual leech, to take also some counsel of the physician for the body. Some who are wretchedly disposed, and yet long to be more vicious than they are, go to physicians and apothecaries and enquire what things may serve them to make them more lusty to their foul fleshly delight. And would it then be any folly, on the other hand, if he who feeleth himself against his will much moved unto such uncleanness, should enquire of the physician what things, without diminishing his health, would be suitable for the diminishing of such foul fleshly motion?

Of spiritual counsel, the first is to be shriven, that the devil have not the more power upon him by reason of his other sins.

VINCENT: I have heard some say, uncle, that when such folk have been at shrift, their temptation hath been the more hot upon them than it was before.

ANTHONY: That think I very well, but that is a special token that shrift is wholesome for them, since the devil is most wroth with it. You find, in some places in the gospel, that the devil did most trouble the person whom he possessed when he saw that Christ would cast him out. Otherwise, we must let the devil do what he will, if we fear his anger, for with every good deed will he wax angry.

Then is it in his shrift to be told him that he not only feareth more than he needeth, but also feareth where he needeth not. And besides that, he is sorry for a thing for which, unless he will willingly turn his good into his harm, he hath more cause to be glad.

First, if he have cause to fear, yet feareth he more than he needeth. For there is no devil so diligent to destroy him as God is to preserve him; nor no devil so near him to do him harm as God is to do him good. Nor are all the devils in hell so strong to invade and assault him as God is to defend him if he distrust him not but faithfully put his trust in him.

He feareth also where he needeth not. For he dreadeth that he were out of God's favour, because such horrible thoughts fall into his mind, but he must understand that while they fall into his mind against his will they are not imputed unto him.

He is, finally, sad of that of which he may be glad. For since he taketh such thoughts displeasantly, and striveth and fighteth against them, he hath thereby a good token that he is in God's favour, and that God assisteth him and helpeth him. And he may make himself sure that so will God never cease to do, unless he himself fail and fall from him first. And beside that, this conflict that he hath against the temptation shall, if he will not fall where he need not, be an occasion of his merit and of a right great reward in heaven. And the pain that he taketh therein shall for so much, as Master Gerson well showeth, stand him in stead of his purgatory.

The manner of the fight against temptation must stand in three things: that is, in resisting, and in contemning, and in the invocation of help.

Resist must a man for his own part with reason, considering what a folly it would be to fall where he need not, since he is not driven to it in avoiding of any other pain or in hope of winning any manner of pleasure, but contrariwise he would by that fall lose everlasting bliss and fall into everlasting pain. And if it were in avoiding of other great pain, yet could he avoid none so great thereby as the one he should thereby fall into.

He must also consider that a great part of this temptation is in effect but the fear of his own fancy, the dread that he hath lest he shall once be driven to it. For he may be sure that (unless he himself will, of his own folly) all the devils in hell can never drive him to it, but his own foolish imagination may. For it fareth in his temptation like a man going over a high bridge who waxeth so afraid, through his own fancy, that he falleth down indeed, when he would otherwise be able enough to pass over without any danger. For a man upon such a bridge, if folk call upon him, "You fall, you fall!" may fall with the fancy that he taketh thereof; although, if folk looked merrily upon him and said, "There is no danger therein," he would pass over the bridge well enough—and he would not hesitate to run upon it, if it were but a foot from the ground. So, in this temptation, the devil findeth the man of his own foolish fancy afraid and then crieth in the ear of his heart, "Thou fallest, thou fallest!" and maketh the foolish man afraid that he should, at every foot, fall indeed. And the devil so wearieth him with that continual fear, if he give the ear of his heart to him, that at last he withdraweth his mind from due remembrance of God, and then driveth him to that deadly mischief indeed. Therefore, like as, against the vice of the flesh, the victory standeth not all in the fight, but sometimes also in the flight (saving that it is indeed a part of a wise warrior's fight to flee from his enemies' traps), so must a man in this temptation too, not only resist it always with reasoning against it, but sometimes set it clear at right naught and cast it off when it cometh and not once regard it so much as to vouchsafe to think thereon.

Some folk have been clearly rid of such pestilent fancies with very full contempt of them, making a cross upon their hearts and bidding the devil avaunt. And sometimes they laugh him to scorn too, and then turn their mind unto some other matter. And when the devil hath seen that they have set so little by him, after certain essays, made in such times as he thought most fitting, he hath given that temptation quite over. And this he doth not only because the proud spirit cannot endure to be mocked, but also lest, with much tempting the man to the sin to which he could not in conclusion bring him, he should much increase his merit.

The final fight is by invocation of help unto God, both praying for himself and desiring others also to pray for him—both poor folk for his alms and other good folk of their charity, especially good priests in that holy sacred service of the Mass. And not only them but also his own good angel and other holy saints such as his devotion specially doth stand unto. Or, if he be learned, let him use then the litany, with the holy suffrages that follow, which is a prayer in the church of marvellous old antiquity. For it was not made first, as some believe, by that holy man St. Gregory (which opinion arose from the fact that, in the time of a great pestilence in Rome, he caused the whole city to go in solemn procession with it), but it was in use in the church many years before St. Gregory's days, as well appeareth by the books of other holy doctors and saints, who were dead hundreds of years before St. Gregory was born.

And holy St. Bernard giveth counsel that every man should make suit unto angels and saints to pray for him to God in the things that he would have furthered by his holy hand. If any man will stick at that, and say it needs not, because God can hear us himself; and will also say that it is perilous to do so because (they say) we are not so counseled by scripture, I will not dispute the matter here. He who will not do it, I hinder him not to leave it undone. But yet for mine own part, I will as well trust to the counsel of St. Bernard, and reckon him for as good and as well learned in scripture, as any man whom I hear say the contrary. And better dare I jeopard my soul with the soul of St. Bernard than with that of him who findeth that fault in his doctrine.

Unto God himself every good man counseleth to have recourse above all. And, in this temptation, to have special remembrance of Christ's passion, and pray him for the honour of his death, the ground of man's salvation, to keep this person thus tempted form that damnable death.

Special verses may be drawn out of the psalter, against the devil's wicked temptations—as, for example, "Exsurgat Deus et dissipentur inimici eius, et fugiant qui oderunt eum a facie eius," and many others—which in such horrible temptation are pleasing to God and to the devil very terrible. But none is more terrible nor more odious to the devil than the words with which our Saviour drove him away himself: "Vade Sathana." And no prayer is more acceptable unto God, nor more effectual in its matter, than those words which our Saviour hath taught us himself, "Ne nos inducas in tentationem, sed libera nos a malo." And I doubt not, by God's grace, but that he who in such a temptation will use good counsel and prayer and keep himself in good virtuous business and good virtuous company and abide in the faithful hope of God's help, he shall have the truth of God (as the prophet saith in the verse afore rehearsed) so compass him about with a shield that he shall not need to dread this night's fear of this wicked temptation.

And thus will I finish this piece of the night's fear. And glad am I that we are past it, and come once unto the day, to those other words of the prophet, "A sagitta volante in die." For methinketh I have made it a long night!

VINCENT: Forsooth, uncle, so have you, but we have not slept in it, but been very well occupied. But now I fear that unless you make here a pause till you have dined, you shall keep yourself from your dinner overlong.

ANTHONY: Nay, nay, cousin, for I broke my fast even as you came in. And also you shall find this night and this day like a winter day and a winter night. For as the winter hath short days and long nights, so shall you find that I made you not this fearful night so long but what I shall make you this light courageous day as short.

And so shall the matter require well of itself indeed. For in these words of the prophet, "The truth of God shall compass thee round about with a shield from the arrow flying in the day," I understand the arrow of pride, with which the devil tempteth a man, not in the night (that is, in tribulation and adversity), for that time is too discomfortable and too fearful for pride, but in the day (that is, in prosperity), for that time is full of lightsome pleasure and courage. But surely this worldly prosperity in which a man so rejoiceth and of which the devil maketh him so proud, is but a very short winter day. For we begin, many full poor and cold, and up we fly like an arrow shot into the air. And yet when we be suddenly shot up into the highest, ere we be well warm there, down we come unto the cold ground again. And then even there stick we still. And yet for the short while that we be upward and aloft—Lord, how lusty and how proud we be, buzzing above busily, as a bumblebee flieth about in summer, never aware that she shall die in winter! And so fare many of us, God help us. For in the short winter day of worldly wealth and prosperity, this flying arrow of the devil, this high spirit of pride, shot out of the devil's bow and piercing through our heart, beareth us up in our affection aloft into the clouds, where we think we sit on the rainbow and overlook the world under us, accounting in the regard of our own glory such other poor souls as were peradventure wont to be our fellows for silly poor pismires and ants.

But though this arrow of pride fly never so high in the clouds, and though the man whom it carrieth up so high be never so joyful thereof, yet let him remember that, be this arrow never so light, it hath yet a heavy iron head. And therefore, fly it never so high, down must it needs come, and on the ground must it light. And sometimes it falleth not in a very cleanly place, but the pride turneth into rebuke and shame and there is then all the glory gone.

Of this arrow speaketh the wise man in the fifth chapter of the book of Wisdom, where he saith in the person of them that in pride and vanity passed the time of this present life, and after that so spent, passed hence into hell: "What hath pride profited us? Or what good hath the glory of our riches done unto us? Passed are all those things like a shadow ... or like an arrow shot out into the place appointed; the air that was divided is forthwith returned unto the place, and in such wise closed together again that the way is not perceived in which the arrow went. And in like wise we, as soon as we were born, are forthwith vanished away, and have left no token of any good virtue behind us, but are consumed and wasted and come to naught in our malignity. They, lo, that have lived here in sin, such words have they spoken when they lay in hell."

Here shall you, good cousin, consider, that whereas the scripture here speaketh of the arrow shot into its place appointed or intended, in the shooting of this arrow of pride there be divers purposings and appointings. For the proud man himself hath no certain purpose or appointment at any mark, butt, or prick upon earth, at which he determineth to shoot and there to stick and tarry. But ever he shooteth as children do, who love to shoot up cop-high, to see how high their arrow can fly up. But now doth the devil intend and appoint a certain mark, surely set in a place into which he purposeth—fly this arrow never so high and the proud heart on it—to have them both alight at last, and that place is in the very pit of hell. There is set the devil's well-acquainted prick and his very just mark. And with his pricking shaft of pride he hath by himself a plain proof and experience that down upon this prick (unless it be stopped by some grace of God on the way) the soul that flieth up with it can never fail to fall. For when he himself was in heaven and began to fly cop-high, with the lusty light flight of pride, saying, "I will fly up above the stars and set my throne on the sides of the north, and will be like unto the Highest," long ere he could fly up half so high as he said in his heart that he would, he was turned from a bright glorious angel into a dark deformed devil, and from flying any further upward, down was he thrown into the deep dungeon of hell.

Now may it, peradventure, cousin, seem that, since this kind of temptation of pride is no tribulation or pain, all this that we speak of this sorrow of pride flying forth in the day of prosperity, would be beside our matter.

VINCENT: Verily, mine uncle, and so seemed it unto me. And somewhat was I minded so to say to you, too, saving that, whether it were properly pertaining to the present matter or somewhat digressing from it, methought it was good matter and such as I had no wish to leave.

ANTHONY: But now must you consider, cousin, that though prosperity be contrary to tribulation, yet unto many a good man the devil's temptation to pride in prosperity is a greater tribulation, and more hath need of good comfort and good counsel both, than he who never felt it would believe. And that is the thing, cousin, that maketh me speak of it as of a thing proper to this matter. For, cousin, as it is a right hard thing to touch pitch and never defile the fingers, to put flax unto fire and yet keep them from burning, to keep a serpent in thy bosom and yet be safe from stinging, to put young men with young women without danger of foul fleshly desire—so it is hard for any person, either man or woman, in great worldly wealth and much prosperity, so to withstand the suggestions of the devil and occasions given by the world that they keep themselves from the deadly danger of ambitious glory. And if a man fall into it, there followeth upon it a whole flood of all unhappy mischief: arrogant manner, high solemn bearing, overlooking the poor in word and countenance, displeasant and disdainful behaviour, ravine, extortion, oppression, hatred and cruelty.

Now, many a good man, cousin, come into great authority, casteth in his mind the peril of such occasions of pride as the devil taketh of prosperity to make his instruments of, with which to move men to such high point of presumption as engendereth so many great evils. And, feeling the devil therewith offering him suggestions to it, he is sore troubled therewith. And some fall so afraid of it that even in the day of prosperity they fall into the night's fear of pusillanimity, and they leave the things undone in which they might use themselves well. And mistrusting the aid and help of God in holding them upright in their temptations, whereby for faint heart they leave off good business in which they would be well occupied. And, under pretext (as it seemeth to themselves) of humble heart and meekness, and of serving God in contemplation and silence, they seek their own ease and earthly rest unawares. And with this, if it be so, God is not well content.

Howbeit, if it be so that a man, by the experience that he hath of himself, perceiveth that in wealth and authority he doth his own soul harm, and cannot do the good that to his part appertaineth; but seeth the things that he should set his hands to sustain, decay through his default and fall to ruin under him, and seeth that to the amendment thereof he leaveth his own duty undone; then would I in any wise advise him to leave off that thing—be it spiritual benefice that he have, parsonage or bishopric, or temporal office and authority—and rather give it over quite and draw himself aside and serve God, than to take the worldly worship and commodity for himself, with incommodity of those whom his duty would be to profit.

But, on the other hand, he may not see the contrary but what he may do his duty conveniently well, and may fear nothing but that the temptations of ambition and pride may peradventure turn his good purpose and make him decline unto sin. I deny not that it is well done to stand always in moderate fear, for the scripture saith, "Blessed is the man that is always fearful," and St. Paul saith, "He that standeth, let him look that he fall not." Yet is over-much fear perilous and draweth toward the mistrust of God's gracious help. This immoderate fear and faint heart holy scripture forbiddeth, saying, "Be not feeble-hearted or timorous." Let such a man therefore temper his fear with good hope, and think that since God hath set him in that place (if he think that God have set him in it), God will assist him with his grace to use it well. Howbeit, if he came to it by simony or some such other evils means, then that would be one good reason wherefore he should rather leave it off. But otherwise let him continue in his good business. And, against the devil's provocation unto evil, let him bless himself and call unto God and pray, and look that the devil tempt him not to lean the more toward the contrary.

Let him pity and comfort those who are in distress and affliction. I mean not that he should let every malefactor pass forth unpunished, and freely run out and rob at random. But in his heart let him be sorry to see that of necessity, for fear of decaying the common weal, men are driven to put malefactors to pain. And yet where he findeth good tokens and likelihood of amendment, there let him help all that he can that mercy may be had. There shall never lack desperately disposed wretched enough besides, upon whom, as an example, justice can proceed. Let him think, in his own heart, that every poor beggar is his fellow.

VINCENT: That will be very hard, uncle, for an honourable man to do, when he beholdeth himself richly apparelled and the beggar rigged in his rags.

ANTHONY: If there were here, cousin, two men who were both beggars, and afterward a great rich man would take one unto him, and tell him that for a little time he would have him in his house, and thereupon arrayed him in silk and gave him a great bag by his side, filled even with gold, but giving him this catch therewith: that, within a little while, out he should go in his old rags again, and bear never a penny with him—if this beggar met his fellow now, while his gay gown was on, might he not, for all his gay gear, take him for his fellow still? And would he not be a very fool if, for a wealth of a few weeks, he would think himself far his better?

VINCENT: Yes, uncle, if the difference in their state were no other.

ANTHONY: Surely, cousin, methinketh that in this world, between the richest and the most poor, the difference is scant so much. For let the highest look on the most base, and consider how they both came into this world. And then let him consider further that, howsoever rich he be now, he shall yet, within a while— peradventure less than one week—walk out again as poor as that beggar shall. And then, by my troth, methinketh this rich man much more than mad if, for the wealth of a little while—haply less than one week—he reckon himself in earnest any better than the beggar's fellow.

And less than thus can no man think, who hath any natural wit and well useth it. But now a Christian man, cousin, who hath the light of faith, he cannot fail to think much further in this thing. For he will think not only upon his bare coming hither and his bare going hence again, but also the dreadful judgment of God, and upon the fearful pains of hell and the inestimable joys of heaven. And in the considering of these things, he will call to remembrance that peradventure when this beggar and he are both departed hence, the beggar may be suddenly set up in such royalty that well were he himself that ever was he born if he might be made his fellow. And he who well bethinketh him, cousin, upon these things, I verily think that the arrow of pride flying forth in the day of worldly wealth shall never so wound his heart that ever it shall bear him up one foot.

But now, to the intent that he may think on such things the better, let him use often to resort to confession. And there let him open his heart and, by the mouth of some virtuous ghostly father, have such things often renewed in his remembrance. Let him also choose himself some secret solitary place in his own house, as far from noise and company as he conveniently can, and thither let him sometimes secretly resort alone, imagining himself as one going out of the world even straight unto the giving up his reckoning unto God of his sinful living. There, before an altar or some pitiful image of Christ's bitter passion, the beholding of which may put him in remembrance of the thing and move him to devout compassion, let him then kneel down or fall prostrate as at the feet of almighty God, verily believing him to be there invisibly present, as without any doubt he is. There let him open his heart to God and confess his faults, such as he can call to mind, and pray God for forgiveness. Let him call to remembrance the benefits that God hath given him, either in general among other men or privately to himself, and give him humble hearty thanks for them. There let him declare unto God the temptations of the devil, the suggestions of the flesh, the occasions of the world—and of his worldly friends, much worse many times in drawing a man from God than are his most mortal enemies, as our Saviour witnesseth himself where he saith, "The enemies of a man are they that are his own familiars." There let him lament and bewail unto God his own frailty, negligence, and sloth in resisting and withstanding of temptation; his readiness and proneness to fall into it. There let him lamentably beseech God, of his gracious aid and help, to strengthen his infirmity—both to keep him from falling and, when he by his own fault misfortuneth to fall, then with the helping hand of his merciful grace to lift him up and set him on his feet in the state of his grace again. And let this man not doubt but that God heareth him and granteth him gladly his boon.

And so, dwelling in the faithful trust of God's help, he shall well use his prosperity, and persevere in his good profitable business, and shall have the truth of God so compass him about with a shield of his heavenly defence that he shall not need to dread of the devil's arrow flying in the day of worldly wealth.

VINCENT: Forsooth, uncle, I like this good counsel well. And I should think that those who are in prosperity and take such order therein, may do much good both to themselves and to other folk.

ANTHONY: I beseech our Lord, cousin, to put this and better in the mind of every man who needeth it.
And now will I touch one word or twain of the third temptation, of which the prophet speaketh in these words: "From the business walking in the darknesses." And then will we call for our dinner, leaving the last temptation—that is, "from the incursion and the devil of the midday"—till afternoon. And then shall we with that, God willing, make an end of all this matter.

VINCENT: Our Lord reward you, good uncle, for your good labour with me. But, for our Lord's sake, take good heed, uncle, that you forbear not your dinner over-long.

ANTHONY: Fear not that, cousin, I warrant you, for this piece will I make you but short.

## XVII

The prophet saith in the said psalm, "He that dwelleth in the faithful hope of God's help, he shall abide in the protection or safeguard of God in heaven. And thou who art such a one, the truth of him shall so compass thee about with a shield, that thou shalt not be afraid of the business walking about in the darknesses."

"Negotium, the business," is here, cousin, the name of the devil who is ever full of busy-ness in tempting folk to much evil business. His time of tempting is in the darknesses. For you know well that beside the full night, which is the deep dark, there are two times of darkness, the one ere the morning wax light, the other when the evening waxeth dark. Two times of like darkness are there also in the soul of man: the one ere the light of grace be well sprung up in the heart, the other when the light of grace beginneth out of the heart to walk fast away. In these two darknesses this devil who is called Business busily walketh about, and he carrieth about with him such foolish folk as will follow him and setteth them to work with many a manner of bumbling business.

He setteth some, I say, to seek the pleasures of the flesh in eating, drinking, and other filthy delight. And some he setteth about incessant seeking for these worldly goods. And of such busy folk whom this devil called Business, walking about in the darknesses, setteth to work with such business, our Saviour saith in the gospel, "He that walketh in darknesses knoweth not whither he goeth." And surely in such a state are they—they neither know which way they go, nor whither. For verily they walk round about as it were in a round maze; when they think themselves at an end of their business, they are but at the beginning again. For is not the going about the serving of the flesh a business that hath no end, but evermore from the end cometh to the beginning again? Go they never so full-fed to bed, yet evermore on the morrow, as new they are to be fed again as they were the day before. Thus fareth it by the belly; thus fareth it by those parts that are beneath the belly. And as for covetousness, it fareth like the fire—the more wood there cometh to it, the more fervent and the more greedy it is.

But now hath this maze a centre or middle place, into which these busy folk are sometimes conveyed suddenly when they think they are not yet far from the brink. The centre or middle place of this maze is hell. And into that place are these busy folk who with this devil of business walk about in this busy maze, in the darkness, sometimes suddenly conveyed, unaware whither they are going. And that may be even while they think that they have not walked far from the beginning, and that they have yet a great way to walk about before they should come to the end. But of these fleshly folk walking in this busy pleasant maze the scripture declareth the end: "They lead their life in pleasure, and at a pop down they descend into hell."

Of the covetous man saith St. Paul, "They that long to be rich do fall into temptation and into the snare of the devil, and into many unprofitable and harmful desires, which drown men into death and destruction." Lo, here in the middle place of this busy maze, the snare of the devil, the place of perdition and destruction, in which they fall and are caught and drowned ere they are aware!

The covetous rich man also that our Saviour speaketh of in the gospel, who had so great plenty of corn that his barns would not receive it, but intended to make his barns larger, and said unto himself that he would make merry many days—he thought, you know, that he had a great way yet to walk. But God said unto him, "Fool, this night shall they take thy soul from thee, and then all these goods that thou hast gathered, whose shall they be?" Here, you see, he fell suddenly into the deep centre of this busy maze, so that he was fallen full into it ere ever he had thought he should have come near to it.

Now this I know very well: Those who are walking about in this busy maze take not their business for any tribulation. And yet are there many of them as sore wearied in it, and sore panged and pained, their pleasures being so short, so little, and so few, and their displeasures and their griefs so great, so continual, and so many. It maketh me think on a good worshipful man who, when he divers times beheld what pain his wife took in tightly binding up her hair to make her a fair large forehead, and with tightly bracing in her body to make her middle small (both twain to her great pain) for the pride of a little foolish praise, he said unto her, "Forsooth, madam, if God give you not hell, he shall do you a great wrong. For it must needs be your own very right, for you buy it very dear and take very great pain therefore!"

Those who now lie in hell for their wretched living here do now perceive their folly in the more pain that they took here for the less pleasure. There confess they now their folly, and cry out, "We have been wearied in the way of wickedness." And yet, while they were walking in that way, they would not rest themselves, but ran on still in their weariness, and put themselves still unto more pain and more, for a little childish pleasure, short and soon gone. For that they took all that labour and pain, beside the everlasting pain that followed it for their further advantage afterward. So help me God, but I verily think many a man buyeth hell here with so much pain that he might have bought heaven with less than half!

But yet, as I say, while these fleshly and worldly busy folk are walking about in this round busy maze of the devil called Business who walketh about in these two times of darkness, their wits are so bewitched by the secret enchantment of the devil that they mark not the great long miserable weariness and pain that the devil maketh them take and endure about naught. And therefore they take it for no tribulation, so that they need no comfort. And therefore it is not for their sakes that I speak of all this, saving that it may serve them for counsel toward the perceiving of their own foolish misery, through the help of God's grace, beginning to shine upon them again. But there are very good folk and virtuous who are in the daylight of grace, and yet the devil tempteth them busily to such fleshly delight. And since they see plenty of worldly substance fall unto them, and feel the devil in like wise busily tempt them to set their hearts upon it, they are sore troubled therewith. And they begin to fear thereby that they are not with God in the light but with this devil that the prophet calleth Negotium—that is to say, Business—walking about in the two times of darknesses.

Howbeit, as I said before of those good folk and gracious who are in the worldly wealth of great power and authority and thereby fear the devil's arrow of pride, so say I now here again of these who stand in dread of fleshly foul sin and covetousness: they do well to stand ever in moderate fear, lest with waxing over-bold and setting the thing over-light, they might peradventure mishap to fall in thereto. Yet, since they are but tempted with it and follow it not, to vex and trouble themselves sorely with the fear of loss of God's favour is without necessity and not always without peril. For, as I said before, it withdraweth the mind of a man far from the spiritual consolation of the good hope that he should have in God's help. And as for those temptations, as long as he who is tempted followeth them not, the fight against them serveth him for matter of merit and reward in heaven, if he not only flee the deed, the consent, and the delectation, but also (so far as he conveniently can) flee from all occasions of them.

And this point is in those fleshly temptations a thing easy to perceive and plain enough. But in worldly business pertaining unto covetousness the thing is somewhat more dark and there is more difficulty in the perceiving. And very great troublous fear of it doth often arise in the hearts of very good folk, when the world falleth fast unto them, because of the sore words and terrible threats that God in holy scripture speaketh against those who are rich. As, where St. Paul saith, "They that will be rich fall into temptation, and into the snare of the devil." And where our Saviour saith himself, "It is more easy for a camel"—or, as some say, "for a great cable rope," for "camelus" so signifieth in the Greek tongue—"to go through a needle's eye than for a rich man to enter into the kingdom of God."

No marvel, now, if good folk who fear God take occasion of great dread at so dreadful words, when they see the worldly goods fall to them. And some stand in doubt whether it be lawful for them to keep any goods or not. But evermore, in all those places of scripture, the having of the worldly goods is not the thing that is rebuked and threatened, but the affection that the haver unlawfully beareth to them. For where St. Paul saith, "they that will be made rich," he speaketh not of the having but of the will and desire and affection to have, and the longing for it. For that cannot be lightly without sin. For the thing that folk sore long for, they will make many shifts to get and jeopard themselves for.

And to declare that the having of riches is not forbidden, but the inordinate affection of the mind sore set upon them, the prophet saith, "If riches flow unto you, set not your heart thereupon." And albeit that our Lord, by the said example of the camel or cable rope to come through the needle's eye, said that it is not only hard but also impossible for a rich man to enter into the kingdom of heaven, yet he declared that though the rich man cannot get into heaven of himself, yet God, he said, can get him in well enough. For unto men he said it was impossible, but not unto God, for "unto God," he said, "all things are possible." And yet, beside that, he told of which manner of rich man he meant, who could not get into the kingdom of heaven, saying, "My babes, how hard is it for them that put their trust and confidence in their money, to enter into the kingdom of God!"

VINCENT: This is, I suppose, uncle, very true—and otherwise God forbid! For otherwise the world would be in a full hard state, if every rich man were in such danger and peril.

ANTHONY: That would it be, cousin, indeed. And so I suppose it is yet. For I fear me that to the multitude there are very few who long not sorely to be rich. And of those who so long to be, there are also very few reserved who set not their heart very sorely thereon.

VINCENT: This is, uncle, I fear me, very true, but yet not the thing that I was about to speak of. But the thing that I would have said was this: I cannot well perceive (the world being such as it is, and so many poor people in it) how any man can be rich, and keep himself rich, without danger of damnation for it.

For all the while he seeth so many poor people who lack, while he himself hath wherewith to give them. And their necessity he is bound in such case of duty to relieve, while he hath wherewith to do so—so far forth that holy St. Ambrose saith that whosoever die for default, where we might help them, we kill them. I cannot see but that every rich man hath great cause to stand in great fear of damnation, nor can I perceive, as I say, how he can be delivered of that fear as long as he keepeth his riches. And therefore, though he might keep his riches if there lacked poor men and yet stand in God's favour therewith, as Abraham did and many another holy rich man since; yet with such an abundance of poor men as there is now in every country, any man who keepeth any riches must needs have an inordinate affection unto it, since he giveth it not out unto the poor needy persons, as the duty of charity bindeth and constraineth him to.

And thus, uncle, in this world at this day, meseemeth your comfort unto good men who are rich, and are troubled with fear of damnation for the keeping, can very scantly serve.

ANTHONY: Hard is it, cousin, in many manner of things, to bid or forbid, affirm or deny, reprove or approve, a matter nakedly proposed and put forth; or precisely to say "This thing is good," or "This thing is evil," without consideration of the circumstances.

Holy St. Austine telleth of a physician who gave a man in a certain disease a medicine that helped him. The selfsame man at another time in the selfsame disease took the selfsame medicine himself, and had of it more harm than good. This he told the physician, and asked him how the harm should have happened. "That medicine," quoth he, "did thee no good but harm because thou tookest it when I gave it thee not." This answer St. Austine very well approveth, because, though the medicine were the same, yet might there be peradventure in the sickness some such difference as the patient perceived not—yea, or in the man himself, or in the place, or in the time of the year. Many things might make the hindrance, for which the physician would not then have given him the selfsame medicine that he gave him before.

To peruse every circumstance that might, cousin, in this matter be touched, and were to be considered and weighed, would indeed make this part of this devil of Business a very busy piece of work and a long one! But I shall open a little the point that you speak of, and shall show you what I think therein, with as few words as I conveniently can. And then will we go to dinner.

First, cousin, he who is a rich man and keepeth all his goods, he hath, I think, very good cause to be very afraid indeed. And yet I fear me that such folk fear the least. For they are very far from the state of good men, since, if they keep all, they are then very far from charity, and do, as you know well, either little alms or none at all.

But now our question, cousin, is not in what case that rich man standeth who keepeth all, but whether we should suffer men to stand in a perilous dread and fear for the keeping of any great part. For if, by the keeping of so much as maketh a rich man still, they stand in the state of damnation, then are the curates bound to tell them so plainly, according to the commandment of God given unto them all in the person of Ezechiel: "If, when I say to the wicked man, 'Thou shalt die,' thou do not show it unto him, nor speak unto him that he may be turned from his wicked way and live, he shall soothly die in his wickedness and his blood shall I require of thine hand."

But, cousin, though God invited men unto the following of himself in wilful poverty, by the leaving of everything at once for his sake—as the thing by which, being out of solicitude of worldly business and far from the desire of earthly commodities, they may the more speedily get and attain the state of spiritual perfection, and the hungry desire and longing for celestial things—yet doth he not command every man to do so upon the peril of damnation. For where he saith, "He that forsaketh not all that ever he hath, cannot be my disciple," he declareth well, by other words of his own in the selfsame place a little before, what he meaneth. For there saith he more, "He that cometh to me, and hateth not his father, and his mother, and his wife, and his children, and his brethren, and his sisters, yea and his own life too, cannot be my disciple." Here meaneth our Saviour Christ that no one can be his disciple unless he love him so far above all his kin, and above his own life, too, that for the love of him, rather than forsake him, he shall forsake them all. And so meaneth he by those other words that whosoever do not so renounce and forsake all that ever he hath in his own heart and affection, so that he will lose it all and let it go every whit, rather than deadly to displease God with the reserving of any one part of it, he cannot be Christ's disciple. For Christ teacheth us to love God above all things, and he loveth not God above all things who, contrary to God's pleasure, keepeth anything that he hath. For he showeth himself to set more by that thing than by God, since he is better content to lose God than it. But, as I said, to give away all, or that no man should be rich or have substance, that find I no commandment of.

There are, as our Saviour saith, in the house of his father many mansions. And happy shall he be who shall have the grace to dwell even in the lowest. It seemeth verily by the gospel that those who for God's sake patiently suffer penury, shall not only dwell in heaven above those who live here in plenty in earth, but also that heaven in some manner of wise more properly belongeth unto them and is more especially prepared for them than it is for the rich. For God in the gospel counseleth the rich folk to buy (in a manner) heaven of them, where he saith unto the rich men, "Make yourselves friends of the wicked riches, that when you fail here they may receive you into everlasting tabernacles."

But now, although this be thus, in respect of the riches and the poverty compared together, yet if a rich man and a poor man be both good men, there may be some other virtue beside in which the rich man may peradventure so excel that he may in heaven be far above that poor man who was here on earth in other virtues far under him. And the proof appeareth clear in Lazarus and Abraham.

Nor I say not this to the intent to comfort rich men in heaping up riches, for a little comfort will bend them enough thereto. They are not so proud-hearted and obstinate but what they would, I daresay, with right little exhortation be very conformable to that counsel! But I say this for those good men to whom God giveth substance, and the mind to dispose it well, and yet not the mind to give it all away at once, but for good causes to keep some substance still. Let them not despair of God's favour for not doing the thing which God hath given them no commandment of, nor drawn them to by any special calling.

Zachaeus, lo, who climbed up into the tree, for desire that he had to behold our Saviour: at such a time as Christ called aloud unto him and said, "Zachaeus, make haste and come down, for this day must I dwell in thy house," he was glad and touched inwardly with special grace to the profit of his soul. All the people murmured much that Christ would call him and be so familiar with him as, of his own offer, to come unto his house. For they knew him for the chief of the publicans, who were custom-men or toll-gatherers of the Emperor's duties, all which whole company were among the people sore infamous for ravine, extortion, and bribery. And then Zachaeus not only was the chief of the fellowship but also was grown greatly rich, whereby the people accounted him in their own opinion for a man very sinful and wicked. Yet he forthwith, by the instinct of the spirit of God, in reproach of all such temerarious bold and blind judgment, given upon a man whose inward mind and sudden change they cannot see, shortly proved them all deceived. And he proved that our Lord had, at those few words outwardly spoken to him, so wrought in his heart within that whatsoever he was before, he was then, unawares to them all, suddenly waxed good. For he made haste and came down, and gladly received Christ, and said, "Lo, Lord, the one half of my goods here I give unto poor people. And yet, over that, if I have in anything deceived any man, here am I ready to recompense him fourfold as much."

VINCENT: This was, uncle, a gracious hearing. But yet I marvel me somewhat, wherefore Zachaeus used his words in that manner of order. For methinketh he should first have spoken of making restitution unto those whom he had beguiled, and then spoken of giving his alms afterward. For restitution is, you know, duty, and a thing of such necessity that in respect of restitution almsdeed is but voluntary. Therefore it might seem that to put men in mind of their duty in making restitution first, and doing their alms afterward, Zachaeus would have spoken more fittingly if he had said first that he would make every man restitution whom he had wronged, and then give half in alms of that which remained afterward. For only that might he call clearly his own.

ANTHONY: This is true, cousin, where a man hath not enough to suffice for both. But he who hath, is not bound to leave his alms ungiven to the poor man who is at hand and peradventure calleth upon him, till he go seek up all his creditors and all those whom he hath wronged—who are peradventure so far asunder that, leaving the one good deed undone the while, he may, before they come together, change that good intent again and do neither the one nor the other. It is good always to be doing some good out of hand, while we think on it; grace shall the better stand with us and increase also, to go the further in the other afterward.

And this I would answer, if the man had there done the one out of hand—the giving, I mean, of half in alms—and not so much as spoken of restitution till afterward. Whereas now, though he spoke the one in order before the other (and yet all at one time) it remained still in his liberty to put them both in execution, after such order as he should then think expedient. But now, cousin, did the spirit of God temper the tongue of Zachaeus in the utterance of these words in such wise that it may well appear that the saying of the wise man is verified in them, where he saith, "To God it belongeth to govern the tongue." For here, when he said that he would give half of his goods unto poor people and yet beside that not only recompense any man whom he had wronged but more than recompense him by three times as much again, he doubly reproved the false suspicion of the people. For they accounted him for so evil that they reckoned in their mind all his goods wrongly gotten, because he was grown to substance in that office that was commonly misused with extortion. But his words declared that he was deep enough in his reckoning so that, if half his goods were given away, he would yet be well able to yield every man his due with the other half—and yet leave himself no beggar either, for he said not he would give away all.

Would God, cousin, that every rich Christian man who is reputed right worshipful—yea, and (which yet, to my mind, is more) reckoned for right honest, too—would and could do the thing that little Zachaeus, that same great publican, were he Jew or were he paynim, said that he would do: that is, with less than half his goods, to recompense every man whom he had wronged four times as much. Yea, yea, cousin, as much for as much, hardly! And then they who receive it shall be content, I dare promise for them, to let the other thrice-as-much go, and forgive it. Because that was one of the hard points of the old law, whereas Christian men must be full of forgiving, and not require and exact their amends to the uttermost.

But now, for our purpose here: He promised neither to give away all nor to become a beggar—no, nor yet to leave off his office either. For, albeit that he had not used it before peradventure in every point so pure as St. John the Baptist had taught them the lesson: "Do no more than is appointed unto you," yet he might both lawfully use his substance that he intended to reserve, and lawfully might use his office, too, in receiving the prince's duty, according to Christ's express commandment, "Give the Emperor those things that are his," refusing all extortion and bribery besides. Yet our Lord, well approving his good purpose, and exacting no further of him concerning his worldly behaviour, answered and said, "This day is health come to this house, for he too is the son of Abraham."

But now I forget not, cousin, that in effect you conceded to me thus far: that a man may be rich and yet not out of the state of grace, nor out of God's favour. Howbeit, you think that, though it may be so in some time or in some other place, yet at this time and in this place, or any other such in which there be so many poor people, upon whom you think they are bound to bestow their goods, they can keep no riches with conscience.

Verily, cousin, if that reason would hold, I daresay the world was never such anywhere that any man might have kept any substance without the danger of damnation. For since Christ's days to the world's end, we have the witness of his own word that there hath never lacked poor men nor ever shall. For he said himself, "Poor men shall you always have with you, unto whom, when you will, you may do good." So that, as I tell you, if your rule should hold, then I suppose there would be no place, in no time, since Christ's days hitherto, nor I think in as long before that either, nor never shall there be hereafter, in which any man could abide rich without the danger of eternal damnation, even for his riches alone, though he demeaned himself never so well.

But, cousin, men of substance must there be. For otherwise shall you have more beggars, perdy, than there are, and no man left able to relieve another. For this I think in my mind a very sure conclusion: If all the money that is in this country were tomorrow brought together out of every man's hand and laid all upon one heap, and then divided out unto every man alike, it would be on the morrow after worse than it was the day before. For I suppose that when it were all equally thus divided among all, the best would be left little better then than almost a beggar is now. And yet he who was a beggar before, all that he shall be the richer for, that he should thereby receive, shall not make him much above a beggar still. But many a one of the rich men, if their riches stood but in movable substance, shall be safe enough from riches, haply for all their life after!

Men cannot, you know, live here in this world unless some one man provide a means of living for many others. Every man cannot have a ship of his own, nor every man be a merchant without a stock. And these things, you know, must needs be had. Nor can every man have a plough by himself. And who could live by the tailor's craft, if no man were able to have a gown made? Who could live by masonry, or who could live a carpenter, if no man were able to build either church or house? Who would be the makers of any manner of cloth, if there lacked men of substance to set sundry sorts to work? Some man who hath not two ducats in his house would do better to lose them both and leave himself not a farthing, but utterly lose all his own, rather than that some rich man by whom he is weekly set to work should lose one half of his money. For then would he himself be likely to lack work. For surely the rich man's substance is the wellspring of the poor man's living. And therefore here would it fare by the poor man as it fared by the woman in one of Æsop's fables. She had a hen that laid her every day a golden egg, till on a day she thought she would have a great many eggs at once. And therefore she killed her hen and found but one or twain in her belly, so that for a few she lost many.

But now, cousin, to come to your doubt how it can be that a man may with conscience keep riches with him, when he seeth so many poor men on whom he may bestow them. Verily, that might he not with conscience do, if he must bestow it upon as many as he can. And so much of truth every rich man do, if all the poor folk that he seeth are so specially by God's commandment committed unto his charge alone that, because our Saviour said, "Give to every man who asketh thee," therefore he is bound to give out still to every beggar who will ask him, as long as any penny lasteth in his purse. But verily, cousin, that saying hath (as St. Austine saith other places in scripture have) need of interpretation. For, as holy St. Austine saith, though Christ say, "Give to every man who asketh thee," he saith not yet, "Give them all that they will ask thee." But surely they would be the same, if he meant to bind me by commandment to give every man without exception something. For so should I leave myself nothing.

Our Saviour, in that place of the sixth chapter of St. Luke, speaketh both of the contempt that we should have in heart of these worldly things, and also of the manner that men should use toward their enemies. For there he biddeth us love our enemies, give good words for evil, and not only suffer injuries patiently (both the taking away of our goods and harm done unto our body), but also be ready to suffer the double, and over that to do good in return to those who do us the harm. And among these things he biddeth us give to every man who asketh, meaning that when we can conveniently do a man good, we should not refuse it, whatsoever manner of man he may be, though he were our mortal enemy, if we see that unless we help him ourselves, the person of that man should stand in peril of perishing. And therefore saith St. Paul, "If thine enemy be in hunger, give him meat."

But now, though I be bound to give every manner of man in some manner of his necessity, were he my friend or my foe, Christian man or heathen, yet am I not bound alike unto all men, nor unto any many in every case alike. But, as I began to tell you, the differences of the circumstances make great change in the matter. St. Paul saith, "He that provideth not for those that are his, is worse than an infidel." Those are ours who are belonging to our charge, either by nature or by law, or any commandment of God. By nature, as our children; by law, as our servants in our household. Albeit these two sorts be not ours all alike, yet would I think that the least ours of the twain—that is, the servants—if they need, and lack, we are bound to look to them and provide for their need, and see, so far as we can, that they lack not the things that should serve for their necessity while they dwell in our service. Meseemeth also that if they fall sick in our service, so that they cannot do the service that we retain them for, yet may we not in any wise turn them out of doors and cast them up comfortless, while they are not able to labour and help themselves. For this would be a thing against all humanity. And surely, if a man were but a wayfarer whom I received into my house as a guest, if he fell sick there and his money be gone, I reckon myself bound to keep him still, and rather to beg about for his relief than to cast him out in that condition to the peril of his life, whatsoever loss I should happen to sustain in the keeping of him. For when God hath by such chance sent him to me and there once matched me with him, I reckon myself surely charged with him until I may, without peril of his life, be well and conveniently discharged of him.

By God's commandment our parents are in our charge, for by nature we are in theirs. Since, as St. Paul saith, it is not the children's part to provide for the parents but the parents' to provide for the children. Provide, I mean, conveniently—good learning or good occupations to get their living by, with truth and the favour of God—but not to make provision for them of such manner of living as they should live the worse toward God for. But rather, if they see by their manner that too much would make them wicked, the father should then give them a great deal less. But although nature put not the parents in the children's charge, yet not only God commandeth but the order of nature compelleth, that the children should both in reverent behaviour honour their father and mother, and also in all their necessity maintain them. And yet, as much as God and nature both bind us to the sustenance of our father, his need may be so little (though it be somewhat) and another man's so great, that both nature and God also would that I should, in such unequal need, relieve that urgent necessity of a stranger—yea, my foe, and God's enemy too, the very Turk or Saracen—before a little need, and unlikely to do great harm, in my father and my mother too. For so ought they both twain themselves to be well content that I should.

But now, cousin, outside of such extreme need well perceived and known unto myself, I am not bound to give to every beggar who will ask; nor to believe every imposter that I meet in the street who will say himself that he is very sick; nor to reckon all the poor folk committed by God only so to my charge alone, that no other man should give them anything of his until I have first given out all mine. Nor am I bound either to have so evil opinion of all other folk save myself as to think that, unless I help, the poor folk shall all fail at once, for God hath left in all this quarter no more good folk now but me! I may think better of my neighbours and worse of myself than that, and yet come to heaven, by God's grace, well enough.

VINCENT: Marry, uncle, but some man will peradventure be right content, in such cases, to think his neighbours very charitable, to the intent that he may think himself at liberty to give nothing at all.

ANTHONY: That is, cousin, very true. Some will be content either to think so, or to make as though they thought so. But those are they who are content to give naught because they are naught! But our question is, cousin, not of them, but of good folk who, by the keeping of worldly goods, stand in great fear to offend God. For the quieting of their conscience speak we now, to the intent that they may perceive what manner of having of worldly goods, and keeping of them, may stand with the state of grace.

Now think I, cousin, that if a man keep riches about him for a glory and royalty of the world, taking a great delight in the consideration of it and liking himself for it, and taking him who is poorer for the lack of it as one far worse than himself, such a mind is very vain foolish pride and such a man is very wicked indeed. But on the other hand, there may be a man—such as would God there were many!—who hath no love unto riches, but having it fall abundantly unto him, taketh for his own part no great pleasure of it, but, as though he had it not, keepeth himself in like abstinence and penance privily as he would do in case he had it not. And, in such things as he doth openly, he may bestow somewhat more liberally upon himself in his house after some manner of the world, lest he should give other folk occasion to marvel and muse and talk of his manner and misreport him for a hypocrite. And therein, between God and him, he may truly protest and testify, as did the good queen Hester, that he doth it not for any desire thereof in the satisfying of his own pleasure, but would with as good will or better forbear the possession of riches, saving them—as perhaps in keeping a good household in good Christian order and fashion, and in setting other folk to work with such things as they gain their living the better by his means. If there be such a man, his having of riches methinketh I might in a manner match in merit with another man's forsaking of all. Or so would it be if there were no other circumstances more pleasing unto God added further unto the forsaking besides, as perhaps for the more fervent contemplation by reason of the solicitude of all worldly business being left off, which was the thing that made Mary Magdalene's part the better. For otherwise would Christ have given her much more thanks to go about and be busy in the helping her sister Martha to dress his dinner, than to take her stool and sit down at her ease and do naught.

Now, if he who hath these goods and riches by him, have not haply fully so perfect a mind, but somewhat loveth to keep himself from lack; and if he be not, so fully as a pure Christian fashion requireth, determined to abandon his pleasure—well, what will you more? The man is so much the less perfect than I would that he were, and haply than he himself would wish, if it were as easy to be it as to wish it. But yet is he not forthwith in the state of damnation, for all that. No more than every man is forthwith in a state of damnation who, forsaking all and entering into religion, is not yet always so clear purified from worldly affections as he himself would very fain that he were, and much bewaileth that he is not. Many a man, who hath in the world willingly forsaken the likelihood of right worshipful offices, hath afterward had much ado to keep himself from the desire of the office of cellarer or sexton, to bear yet at least some rule and authority, though it were but among the bellies. But God is more merciful to man's imperfection—if the man know it, and acknowledge it, and mislike it, and little by little labour to amend it—than to reject and cast off to the devil him who, according as his frailty can bear and suffer, hath a general intent and purpose to please him and to prefer or set by nothing in this world before him.

And therefore, cousin, to make an end of this piece withal—of this devil, I mean, whom the prophet calleth "Business walking in the darknesses": If a man have a mind to serve God and please him, and would rather lose all the goods he hath than wittingly to do deadly sin; and if he would, without murmur or grudge, give it every whit away in case God should so command him, and intend to take it patiently if God would take it from him; and if he would be glad to use it unto God's pleasure, and do his diligence to know and be taught what manner of using of it God would be pleased with; and if he be glad to follow therein, from time to time, the counsel of good virtuous men, though he neither give away all at once, nor give to every man who asketh him neither; and though every man should fear and think in this world that all the good that he doth or can do is a great deal too little—yet, for all that fear, let that man dwell in the faithful hope of God's help! And then shall the truth of God so compass him about, as the prophet saith, with a shield, that he shall not so need to dread the snares and the temptations of this devil whom the prophet calleth "Business walking about in the darknesses." But he shall, for all the having of riches and worldly substance, so avoid his snares and temptations, that he shall in conclusion, by the great grace and almighty mercy of God, get into heaven well enough.

And now was I, cousin, after this piece thus ended, about to bid them bring in our dinner. But now shall I not need to, lo, for here they come with it already.

VINCENT: Forsooth, good uncle, God disposeth and timeth your matter and your dinner both, I trust. For the end of your good tale—for which our Lord reward you!—and the beginning here of your good dinner too (from which it would be more than pity that you should any longer have tarried) meet even at the close together.

ANTHONY: Well, cousin, now will we say grace. And then for a while will we leave talking and essay how our dinner shall please us, and how fair we can fall to feeding. After that, you know my customary guise (for "manner" I cannot call it, because the guise is unmannerly) to bid you not farewell but steal away from you to sleep. But you know I am not wont to sleep long in the afternoon, but even a little to forget the world. And when I wake, I will again come to you. And then is, God willing, all this long day ours, in which we shall have time enough to talk much more than shall suffice for the finishing of this one part of our matter that now alone remaineth.

VINCENT: I pray you, good uncle, keep your customary manner, for "manner" may you call it well enough. For as it would be against good manners to look that a man should kneel down for courtesy when his knee is sore, so is it very good manners that a man of your age (aggrieved with such sundry sicknesses besides, that suffer you not always to sleep when you should) should not let his sleep slip away but should take it when he can. And I will, uncle, in the meanwhile steal from you, too, and speed a little errand and return to you again.

ANTHONY: Stay as long as you will, and when you have dined go at your pleasure. But I pray you, tarry not long.

VINCENT: You shall not need, uncle, to put me in mind of that, I would so fain have up the rest of our matter.

# BOOK THREE

VINCENT: I have tarried somewhat the longer, uncle, partly because I was loth to come over-soon, lest my soon-coming might have happed to have made you wake too soon. But I tarried especially for the reason that I was delayed by someone who showed me a letter, dated at Constantinople, by which it appeareth that the great Turk prepareth a marvellous mighty army. And yet whither he will go with it, that can there yet no man tell. But I fear in good faith, uncle, that his voyage shall be hither. Howbeit, he who wrote the letter saith that it is secretly said in Constantinople that a great part of his army shall be shipped and sent either into Naples or into Sicily.

ANTHONY: It may fortune, cousin, that the letter of a Venetian, dated at Constantinople, was devised at Venice. From thence come there some letters—and sometimes from Rome, too, and sometimes also from some other places—all stuffed full of such tidings that the Turk is ready to do some great exploit. These tidings they blow about for the furtherance of some such affairs as they have themselves then in hand.

The Turk hath also so many men of arms in his retinue at his continual charge that, lest they should lie still and do nothing, but peradventure fall in devising of some novelties among themselves, he is fain yearly to make some assembly and some changing of them from one place unto another, and part some asunder, that they wax not over-well acquainted by dwelling over-long together. By these ways also, he maketh those that he intendeth suddenly to invade indeed, to look the less for it, and thereby to make the less preparation before. For they see him so many times make a great visage of war when he intendeth it not, but then, at one time or another, they suddenly feel it when they fear it not.

Howbeit, cousin, it is of very truth full likely that into this realm of Hungary he will not fail to come. For neither is there any country throughout Christendom that lieth so convenient for him, nor never was there any time till now in which he might so well and surely win it. For now we call him in ourselves, God save us, as Æsop telleth that the sheep took in the wolf among them to keep them from the dogs.

VINCENT: Then are there, good uncle, all those tribulations very like to fall upon us here, that I spoke of in the beginning of our first communication here the other day.

ANTHONY: Very truth it is, cousin, that so there will of likelihood in a while, but not forthwith all at first. For since he cometh under the colour of aid for the one against the other, he will somewhat see the proof before he fully show himself. But in conclusion, if he be able to get it for that one, you shall see him so handle it that he shall not fail to get it from him, and that forthwith out of hand, ere ever he suffer him to settle himself oversure therein.

VINCENT: Yet say they, uncle, that he useth not to force any man to forsake his faith.

ANTHONY: Not any man, cousin? They say more than they can make good, those who tell you so. He maketh a solemn oath, among the ceremonies of that feast in which he first taketh upon him his authority, that he will diminish the faith of Christ, in all that he possibly can, and dilate the faith of Mahomet. But yet hath he not used to force every whole country at once to forsake their faith. For of some countries hath he been content only to take a tribute yearly and let them then live as they will. Out of some he taketh the whole people away, dispersing them for slaves among many sundry countries of his, very far from their own, without any sufferance of regress. In some countries, so great and populous that they cannot well be carried and conveyed thence, he destroyeth the gentlefolk and giveth the lands partly to such as he bringeth and partly to such as willingly will deny their faith, and keepeth the others in such misery that they might as well (in a manner) be dead at once. In rest he suffereth else no Christian man almost, but those that resort as merchants or those that offer themselves to serve him in his war.
But as for those Christian countries that he useth not only for tributaries, as he doth Chios, Cyprus, or Crete, but reckoneth for clear conquest and utterly taketh for his own, as Morea, Greece, and Macedonia, and such others—and as I verily think he will Hungary, if he get it—in all those he useth Christian people after sundry fashions. He letteth them dwell there, indeed, because they would be too many to carry all away, and too many to kill them all, too, unless he should either leave the land dispeopled and desolate or else, from some other countries of his own, should convey the people thither (which would not be well done) to people that land with. There, lo, those who will not be turned from their faith, of which God—lauded be his holy name!—keepeth very many, he suffereth to dwell still in peace. But yet is their peace for all that not very peaceable. For he suffereth them to have no lands of their own, honourable offices they bear none; with occasions of his wars, he plucketh them unto the bare bones with taxes and tallages. Their children he chooseth where he will in their youth, and taketh them from their parents, conveying them whither he will, where their friends never see them after, and abuseth them as he will. Some young maidens he maketh harlots, some young men he bringeth up in war, and some young children he causeth to be gelded—not their stones cut out as the custom was of old, but their whole members cut off by the body; how few escape and live he little careth, for he will have enough! And all whom he so taketh young, to any use of his own, are betaken unto such Turks or false renegades to keep, that they are turned from the faith of Christ every one. Or else they are so handled that, as for this world, they come to an evil end. For, besides many other contumelies and despites that

the Turks and the false renegade Christians many times do to good Christian people who still persevere and abide by the faith, they find the means sometimes to make some false knaves say that they heard such-and-such a Christian man speak opprobrious words against Mahomet. And upon that point, falsely testified, they will take occasion to compel him to forsake the faith of Christ and turn to the profession of their shameful superstitious sect, or else will they put him to death with cruel intolerable torments.

VINCENT: Our Lord, uncle, for his mighty mercy, keep those wretches hence! For, by my troth, if they hap to come hither, methinketh I see many more tokens than one that we shall have some of our own folk here ready to fall in with them.

For as before a great storm the sea beginneth sometimes to work and roar in itself, ere ever the winds wax boisterous, so methinketh I hear at mine ear some of our own here among us, who within these few years could no more have borne the name of Turk than the name of devil, begin now to find little fault in them—yea, and some to praise them little by little, as they can, more glad to find faults at every state of Christendom: priests, princes, rites, ceremonies, sacraments, laws, and customs spiritual, temporal, and all.

ANTHONY: In good faith, cousin, so begin we to fare here indeed, and that but even now of late. For since the title of the crown hath come in question, the good rule of this realm hath very sore decayed, as little a while as it is. And undoubtedly Hungary shall never do well as long as men's minds hearken after novelty and have their hearts hanging upon a change. And much the worse I like it, when their words walk so large toward the favour of the Turk's sect, which they were ever wont to have in so great abomination, as every true-minded Christian man—and Christian woman, too—must have.

I am of such age as you see, and verily from as far as I can remember, it hath been marked and often proved true, that when children in Buda have fallen in a fancy by themselves to draw together and in their playing make as it were corpses carried to church, and sing after their childish fashion the tune of the dirge, great death hath followed shortly thereafter. And twice or thrice I can remember in my day when children in divers parts of this realm have gathered themselves in sundry companies and made as it were troops and battles. And after their battles in sport, in which some children have yet taken great hurt, there hath fallen true battle and deadly war indeed. These tokens were somewhat like your example of the sea, since they are tokens going before, of things that afterward follow, through some secret motion or instinct of which the cause is unknown.

But, by St. Mary, cousin, these tokens like I much worse—these tokens, I say, not of children's play nor of children's songs, but old knaves' large open words, so boldly spoken in the favour of Mahomet's sect in this realm of Hungary, which hath been ever hitherto a very sure key of

Christendom. And without doubt if Hungary be lost and the Turk have it once fast in his possession, he shall, ere it be long afterward, have an open ready way into almost all the rest of Christendom. Though he win it not all in a week, the great part will be won, I fear me, within very few years after.

VINCENT: But yet evermore I trust in Christ, good uncle, that he shall not suffer that abominable sect of his mortal enemies in such wise to prevail against his Christian countries.

ANTHONY: That is very well said, cousin. Let us have our sure hope in him, and then shall we be very sure that we shall not be deceived. For we shall have either the thing that we hope for, or a better thing in its stead. For, as for the thing itself that we pray for and hope to have, God will not always send it to us. And therefore, as I said in our first communication, in all things save only for heaven, our prayer and our hope may never be too precise, although the thing may be lawful to ask.

Verily, if we people of the Christian nations were such as would God we were, I would little fear all the preparations that the great Turk could make. No, nor yet, being as bad as we are, I doubt not at all but that in conclusion, however base Christendom be brought, it shall spring up again, till the time be come very near to the day of judgment, some tokens of which methinketh are not come yet. But somewhat before that time shall Christendom be straitened sore, and brought into so narrow a compass that, according to Christ's words, "When the Son of Man shall come again"—that is, to the day of general judgment—"thinkest thou that he shall find faith in the earth?" as who should say, "but a little." For, as appeareth in the Apocalypse and other places of scripture, the faith shall be at that time so far faded that he shall, for the love of his elect, lest they should fall and perish too, abridge those days and accelerate his coming. But, as I say, methinketh I miss yet in my mind some of those tokens that shall, by the scripture, come a good while before that. And among others, the coming in of the Jews and the dilating of Christendom again before the world come to that strait. So I say for mine own mind I have little doubt that this ungracious sect of Mahomet shall have a foul fall, and Christendom spring and spread, flower and increase again. Howbeit, the pleasure and comfort shall they see who shall be born after we are buried, I fear me, both twain. For God giveth us great likelihood that for our sinful wretched living he goeth about to make these infidels, who are his open professed enemies, the sorrowful scourge of correction over evil Christian people who should be faithful and who are of truth his falsely professing friends.

And surely, cousin, albeit that methinketh I see divers evil tokens of this misery coming to us, yet can there not, to my mind, be a worse prognostication of it than this ungracious token that you note here yourself. For undoubtedly, cousin, this new manner of men's favourable fashion in their language toward these ungracious Turks declareth plainly not only that their minds give them that hither shall he come, but also that they can be content both to live under him and, beside that, to fall from the true faith of Christ into Mahomet's false abominable sect.

VINCENT: Verily, mine uncle, as I go about more than you, so must I needs hear more (which is a heavy hearing in mine ear) the manner of men in this matter, which increaseth about us here—I trust that in other places of this realm, by God's grace, it is otherwise. But in this quarter here about us, many of these fellows who are fit for the war were wont at first, as it were in sport, to talk as though they looked for a day when, with a turn to the Turk's faith, they should be made masters here of true Christian men's bodies and owners of all their goods. And, in a while after that, they began to talk so half between game and earnest—and now, by our Lady, not far from fair flat earnest indeed.

ANTHONY: Though I go out but little, cousin, yet hear I sometimes—when I say little!—almost as much as that. But since there is no man to whom we can complain for redress, what remedy is there but patience, and to sit still and hold our peace? For of these two who strive which of them both shall reign over us—and each of them calleth himself king, and both twain put the people to pain—one is, as you know well, too far from our quarter here to help us in this behalf. And the other, since he looketh for the Turk's aid, either will not, or (I suppose) dare not find any fault with them that favour the Turk and his sect. For of natural Turks this country lacketh none now; they are living here under divers pretexts, and of everything they advertise the great Turk full surely. And therefore, cousin, albeit that I would advise every man to pray still and call unto God to hold his gracious hand over us and keep away this wretchedness if his pleasure be, yet would I further advise every good Christian body to remember and consider that it is very likely to come. And therefore I would advise him to make his reckoning and count his pennyworths before, and I would advise every man (and every woman, too) to appoint with God's help in their own mind beforehand what they intend to do if the very worst should befall.

# I

VINCENT: Well fare your heart, good uncle, for this good counsel of yours! For surely methinketh that this is marvellous good.
But yet heard I once a right learned and very good man say that it would be great folly, and very perilous too, if a man should think upon any such thing or imagine any such question in his mind, for fear of double peril that may follow thereupon. For he shall be likely to answer himself that he will rather suffer any painful death than forsake his faith, and by that bold appointment should he fall into the fault of St. Peter, who of oversight made a proud promise and soon had a foul fall. Or else would he be likely to think that rather than abide the pain he would forsake God

indeed, and by that mind should he sin deadly through his own folly, whereas he needeth not do so, since he shall peradventure never come in the peril to be put thereto. And therefore it would be most wisdom never to think upon any such manner of question.

ANTHONY: I believe well, cousin, that you have heard some men who would so say. For I can show almost as much as that left in writing by a very good man and a great solemn doctor. But yet, cousin, although I should happen to find one or two more, as good men and as well learned too, who would both twain say and write the same, yet would I not fear for my part to counsel my friend to the contrary.

For, cousin, if his mind answer him as St. Peter answered Christ, that he will rather die than forsake him, though he say therein more unto himself than he should be peradventure able to make good if it came to the point, yet I perceive not that he doth in that thought any deadly displeasure unto God. For St. Peter, though he said more than he could perform, yet in his so saying offended not God greatly neither. But his offence was when he did not afterward so well as he said before. But now may this man be likely never to fall in the peril of breaking that appointment, since of some ten thousand that shall so examine themselves, never one shall fall in the peril. And yet for them to have that good purpose all their life seemeth me no more harm in the meanwhile than for a poor beggar who hath never a penny to think that, if he had great substance, he would give great alms for God's sake.

But now is all the peril if the man answer himself that he would in such case rather forsake the faith of Christ with his mouth and keep it still in his heart than for the confessing of it to endure a painful death. For by this mind he falleth in deadly sin, which he never would have fallen in if he had never put himself the question. But in good faith methinketh that he who, upon that question put unto himself by himself, will make himself that answer, hath the habit of faith so faint and so cold that, for the better knowledge of himself and of his necessity to pray for more strength of grace, he had need to have the question put to him either by himself or by some other man.

Besides this, to counsel a man never to think on that question is, to my mind, as reasonable as the medicine that I have heard taught someone for the toothache: to go thrice about a churchyard, and never think on a fox-tail! For if the counsel be not given them, it cannot serve them. And if it be given them, it must put the point of the matter in their mind. And forthwith to reject it, and think therein neither one thing nor the other, is a thing that may be sooner bidden than obeyed.

I think also that very few men can escape it. For though they would never think on it by themselves, yet in one place or another where they shall happen to come in company, they shall have the question by adventure so proposed and put forth that—like as, while a man heareth someone talking to him, he can close his eyes if he will, but he cannot make himself sleep—so shall they, whether they will or not, think one thing or the other therein.

Finally, when Christ spoke so often and so plain of the matter, that every man should, upon pain of damnation, openly confess his faith if men took him and by dread of death would drive him to the contrary, it seemeth me (in a manner) implied that we are bound conditionally to have evermore that mind—actually sometimes, and evermore habitually—that if the case should so befall, then with God's help so we would do. And thus much methinketh necessary, for every man and woman to be always of this mind and often to think thereon. And where they find, in the thinking thereon, that their hearts shudder and shrink in the remembrance of the pain that their imagination representeth to the mind, then must they call to mind and remember the great pain and torment that Christ suffered for them, and heartily pray for grace that, if the case should so befall, God should give them strength to stand. And thus, with exercise of such meditation, through men should never stand full out of fear of falling, yet must they persevere in good hope and in full purpose of standing.

And this seemeth to me, cousin, so far forth the mind that every Christian man and woman must needs have, that methinketh every curate should often counsel all his parishioners, beginning in their tender youth, to know this point and think on it, and little by little from their very childhood accustom them sweetly and pleasantly in the meditation thereof. Thereby the goodness of God shall not fail so to inspire the grace of his Holy Spirit into their hearts, in reward of that virtuous diligence, that through such actual meditation he shall confirm them in such a sure habit of spiritual faithful strength, that all the devils in hell, with all the wrestling that they can make, shall never be able to wrest it out of their heart.

VINCENT: By my troth, uncle, methinketh that you say very well.

ANTHONY: I say surely, cousin, as I think. And yet all this have I said concerning them that dwell in such places that they are never like in their lives to come in the danger to be put to the proof. Howbeit, many a man may think himself far from it, who yet may fortune to come to it by some chance or other, either for the truth of faith or for the truth of justice, which go almost all alike.

But now you and I, cousin, and all our friends here, are far in another point. For we are so likely to fall in the experience of it soon, that it would have been more timely for us, all other things set aside, to have devised upon this matter, and firmly to have settled ourselves upon a false point long ago, than to begin to commune and counsel upon it now.

VINCENT: In good faith, uncle, you say therein very truth, and would God it had come sooner in my mind. But yet is it better late than never. And I trust God shall yet give us respite and time. And that we lose no part thereof, uncle, I pray you proceed now with your good counsel therein.

ANTHONY: Very gladly, cousin, shall I now go forth in the fourth temptation, which alone remaineth to be treated of, and properly pertaineth wholly unto this present purpose.

## II

The fourth temptation, cousin, that the prophet speaketh of in the fore-remembered psalm is plain open persecution. And it is touched in these words: "Ab incursu et demonio meridiano."

And of all his temptations, this is the most perilous, the most bitter, the most sharp, and the most rigorous. For in other temptations he useth either pleasant allectives unto sin, or other secret sleights and snares; and cometh in the night and stealeth on in the dark unaware; or in some other part of the day flieth and passeth by like an arrow; so shaping himself sometimes in one fashion, sometimes in another, and dissimulating himself and his high mortal malice, that a man is thereby so blinded and beguiled that he cannot sometimes perceive well what he is. But in this temptation, this plain open persecution for the faith, he cometh even in the very midday—that is, even upon those who have a high light of faith shining in their hearts—and he openly suffereth himself to be perceived so plainly, by his fierce malicious persecution against the faithful Christians, for hatred of Christ's true Catholic faith, that no man having faith can doubt what he is. For in this temptation he showeth himself such as the prophet nameth him, "the midday devil," so lightsomely can he be seen with the eye of the faithful soul, by his fierce furious assault and incursion. For therefore saith the prophet that the truth of God shall compass that man round about who dwelleth in the faithful hope of his help with a shield "from the incursion and the devil of the midday," because this kind of persecution is not a wily temptation but a furious force and a terrible incursion. In other of his temptations, he stealeth on like a fox, but in this Turk's persecution for the faith, he runneth on roaring with assault like a ramping lion.

This temptation is, of all temptations, also the most perilous. For in temptations of prosperity he useth only delectable allectives to move a man to sin; and in other kinds of tribulation and adversity he useth only grief and pain to pull a man into murmuring, impatience, and blasphemy. But in this kind of persecution for the faith of Christ he useth both twain—that is, both his allectives of quiet and rest by deliverance from death and pain, with other pleasures also of this present life, and besides that the terror and infliction of intolerable pain and torment.

In other tribulation—as loss, or sickness, or death of our friends—though the pain be peradventure as great and sometimes greater too, yet is not the peril nowhere nigh half so much. For in other tribulations, as I said before, that necessity that the man must perforce abide and endure the pain, wax he never so wroth and impatient with it, is a great reason to move him to keep his patience in it and be content with it and thank God for it and of necessity make a virtue, that he may be rewarded for it. But in this temptation, this persecution for the faith—I mean not by fight in the field, by which the faithful man standeth at his defence and putteth the faithless in half the fear and half the harm too; but I mean where he is taken and held, and may for the forswearing or denying of his faith be delivered and suffered to live in rest and some in great worldly wealth also. In this case, I say, since he needeth not to suffer this trouble and pain unless he will, there is a marvellous great occasion for him to fall into the sin that the devil would drive him to—that is, the forsaking of the faith.

And therefore, I say, of all the devil's temptations, this temptation, this persecution for the faith, is the most perilous.

VINCENT: The more perilous, uncle, this temptation is—as indeed, of all the temptations, the most perilous it is—the more need have those who stand in peril of it to be well armed against it beforehand, with substantial advice and good counsel. For so may we the better bear that tribulation when it cometh, with the comfort and consolation thereof, and the better withstand the temptation.

ANTHONY: You say, Cousin Vincent, therein very truth. And I am content therefore to fall in hand with it.

But forasmuch, cousin, as methinketh that of this tribulation you are somewhat more afraid than I—and of truth somewhat more excusable it is in you than it would be in me, mine age considered and the sorrow that I have suffered already, with some other considerations upon my part besides—rehearse you therefore the griefs and pains that you think in this tribulation possible to fall unto you. And I shall against each of them give you counsel and rehearse you such occasion of comfort and consolation as my poor wit and learning can call unto my mind.

VINCENT: In good faith, uncle, I am not wholly afraid in this case only for myself, but well you know I have cause to care also for many others, and that folk of sundry sorts, men and women both, and that not all of one age.

ANTHONY: All that you have cause to fear for, cousin, for all of them, have I cause to fear with you, too, since almost all your kinsfolk are likewise kin to me. Howbeit, to say the truth, every man hath cause in this case to fear both for himself and for every other. For since, as the scripture saith, "God hath given every man care and charge of his neighbour," there is no man who hath any spark of Christian love and charity in his breast but what, in a matter of such peril as this is, in which the soul of man standeth in so great danger to be lost, he must needs care and take thought not only for his friends but also for his very foes. We shall therefore, cousin, not rehearse your harms or mine that may befall in this persecution, but all the great harms in general, as near as we can call to mind, that may happen unto any man.

## III

Since a man is made of the body and the soul, all the harm that any man can take, it must needs be in one of these two, either immediately or by the means of some such thing as serveth for the pleasure, welfare, or commodity of one of these two.

As for the soul first, we shall need no rehearsal of any harm that may attain to it by this kind of tribulation, unless by some inordinate love and affection that the soul bear to the body, she consent to slide from the faith and thereby do herself harm. Now there remains the body, and these outward things of fortune which serve for the maintenance of the body and minister matter of pleasure to the soul also, through the delight that she hath in the body for the while that she is matched with it.

Consider first the loss of those outward things, as being somewhat less in weight than the body itself. What may a man lose in them, and thereby what pain may he suffer?

VINCENT: He may lose, uncle, money, plate, and other movable substance (of which I should somewhat lose myself); then, offices and authority; and finally all the lands of his inheritance for ever that he himself and his heirs perpetually might otherwise enjoy. And of all these things, uncle, you know well that I myself have some—little, in respect of that which some others have here, but yet somewhat more than he who hath most here would be well content to lose.

Upon the loss of these things follow neediness and poverty; the pain of lacking, the shame of begging (of which twain I know not which is the most wretched necessity); besides, the grief and heaviness of heart, in beholding good men and faithful and his dear friends bewrapped in like misery, and ungracious wretches and infidels and his mortal enemies enjoying the commodities that he himself and his friends have lost.

Now, for the body very few words should serve us. For therein I see none other harm but loss of liberty, labour, imprisonment, and painful and shameful death.

ANTHONY: There needeth not much more, cousin, as the world is now. For I fear me that less than a fourth part of this will make many a man sore stagger in his faith, and some fall quite from it, who yet at this day, before he come to the proof, thinketh himself that he would stand very fast. And I beseech our Lord that all those who so think, and who would yet when they were brought to the point fall from the faith for fear or pain, may get of God the grace to think still as they do and not to be brought to the essay, where pain or fear would show them, as it showed St. Peter, how far they are deceived now.

But now, cousin, against these terrible things, what way shall we take in giving men counsel of comfort? If the faith were in our days as fervent as it hath been ere this in times past, little counsel and little comfort would suffice. We should not much need with words and reasoning to extenuate and diminish the vigour and asperity of the pains. For of old times, the greater and the more bitter the pain were, the more ready was the fervour of faith to suffer it. And surely, cousin, I doubt little in my mind but what, if a man had in his heart so deep a desire and love—longing to be with God in heaven, to have the fruition of his glorious face—as had those holy men who are martyrs in old time, he would no more now stick at the pain that he must pass between than those old holy martyrs did at that time. But alas, our faint and feeble faith, with our love to God less than lukewarm because of the fiery affection that we bear to our own filthy flesh, maketh us so dull in the desire of heaven that the sudden dread of every bodily pain woundeth us to the heart and striketh our devotion dead. And therefore hath every man, cousin, as I said before, much the more need to think upon this thing many a time and oft aforehand, ere any such peril befall, by much devising upon it before they see cause to fear it. Since the thing shall not appear so terrible unto them, reason shall better enter, and through grace working with their diligence, engender and set sure, not a sudden slight affection of suffering for God's sake, but, by a long continuance, a strong deep-rooted habit—not like a reed ready to wave with every wind, nor like a rootless tree scantly set up on end in a loose heap of light sand, that will with a blast or two be blown down.

## IV

Let us now consider, cousin, these causes of terror and dread that you have recited, which in his persecution for the faith this midday devil may, by these Turks, rear against us to make his incursion with. For so shall we well perceive, weighing them well with reason, that, albeit they be indeed somewhat, yet (every part of the matter pondered) they shall well appear in conclusion things not so much to be dreaded and fled from as they do suddenly seem to folk at the first sight.

## V

First let us begin at the outward goods, which are neither the proper goods of the soul nor those of the body, but are called the goods of fortune, and serve for the sustenance and commodity of man for the short season of this present life, as worldly substance, offices, honour, and authority.

What great good is there in these things of themselves, that they should be worthy so much as to bear the name by which the world, of a worldly favour, customarily calleth them? For if the having of strength make a man strong, and the having of heat make a man hot, and the having of virtue make a man virtuous, how can these things be verily and truly "goods," by the having of which he who hath them may as well be worse as better—and, as experience proveth, more often is worse than better? Why should a man greatly rejoice in that which he daily seeth most abound in the hands of many who are wicked? Do not now this great Turk and his pashas in all these advancements of fortune surmount very far above a Christian estate, and any lords living under him? And was there not, some twenty years ago, the great Sultan of Syria, who many a year together bore himself as high as the great Turk, and afterward in one summer unto the great Turk that whole empire was lost? And so may all his empire now—and shall hereafter, by God's grace—be lost into Christian men's hands likewise, when Christian people shall be amended and grow in God's favour again. But since whole kingdoms and mighty great empires are of so little surety to stand, but are so soon transferred from one man unto another, what great thing can you or I—yea, or any lord, the greatest in this land—reckon himself to have, by the possession of a heap of silver or gold? For they are but white and yellow metal, not so profitable of their own nature, save for a little glittering, as the rude rusty metal of iron.

## VI

Lands and possessions many men esteem much more yet than money, because the lands seem not so casual as money is, or plate. For though their other substance may be stolen and taken away, yet evermore they think that their land will lie still where it lay. But what are we the better that our land cannot be stirred, but will lie still where it lay, since we ourselves may be removed and not suffered to come near it? What great difference is there to us, whether our substance be movable or unmovable, since we be so movable ourselves that we may be removed from them both and lose them both twain? Yet sometimes in the money is the surety somewhat more. For when we be fain ourselves to flee, we may make shift to carry some of our money with us, whereas of our land we cannot carry one inch.

If our land be a thing of more surety than our money, how happeth it then that in this persecution we are more afraid to lose it? For if it be a thing of more surety, then can it not so soon be lost. In the transfer of these two great empires—Greece first, since I myself was born, and after Syria, since you were born too—the land was lost before the money was found!

Oh, Cousin Vincent, if the whole world were animated with a reasonable soul, as Plato thought it were, and if it had wit and understanding to mark and perceive everything, Lord God, how the ground on which a prince buildeth his palace would loud laugh its lord to scorn, when it saw him proud of his possession and heard him boast himself that he and his blood are for ever the very lords and owners of the land! For then would the ground think the while, to itself, "Ah, thou poor soul, who thinkest thou wert half a god, and art amid thy glory but a man in a gay gown! I who am the ground here, over whom thou are so proud, have had a hundred such owners of me as thou callest thyself, more than ever thou hast heard the names of. And some of them who went proudly over mine head now lie low in my belly, and my side lieth over them. And many a one shall, as thou does now, call himself mine owner after thee, who shall neither be kin to thy blood nor have heard any word of thy name."

Who owned your village, cousin, three thousand years ago?

VINCENT: Three thousand, uncle? Nay, nay, in any king, Christian or heathen, you may strike off a third part of that well enough—and, as far as I know, half of the rest, too. In far fewer years than three thousand it may well fortune that a poor ploughman's blood may come up to a kingdom, and a king's right royal kin on the other hand fall down to the plough and cart, and neither that king know that ever he came from the cart, nor that carter know that ever he came from the crown.

ANTHONY: We find, Cousin Vincent, in full ancient stories many strange changes as marvellous as that, come about in the compass of very few years, in effect. And are such things then in reason so greatly to be set by, that we should esteem the loss so great, when we see that in keeping them our surety is so little?

VINCENT: Marry, uncle, but the less surety we have to keep it, since it is a great commodity to have it, so much more the loth we are to forgo it.

ANTHONY: That reason shall I, cousin, turn against yourself. For if it be so as you say, that since the things be commodious, the less surety that you see you have of keeping them, the more cause you have to be afraid of losing them; then on the other hand the more a thing is of its nature such that its commodity bringeth a man little surety and much fear, that thing of reason the less we have cause to love. And then, the less cause we have to love a thing, the less cause have we to care for it or fear its loss, or be loth to go from it.

## VII

We shall yet, cousin, consider in these outward goods of fortune—as riches, good name, honest estimation, honourable fame, and authority—in all these things we shall, I say, consider that we love them and set by them either as things commodious unto us for the state and condition of this present life, or else as things that we purpose by the good use of them to make matter of our merit, with God's help, in the life to come.

Let us then first consider them as things set by and beloved for the pleasure and commodity of them for this present life.

## VIII

Now, as for riches, if we consider it well, the commodity that we take of it is not so great as our own foolish affection and fancy maketh us imagine it. I deny not that it maketh us go much more gay and glorious in sight, garnished in silk—but wool is almost as warm! It maketh us have great plenty of many kinds of delicate and delicious victuals, and thereby to make more excess—but less exquisite and less superfluous fare, with fewer surfeits and fewer fevers too, would be almost as wholesome! Then, the labour in getting riches, the fear in keeping them, and the pain in parting from them, do more than counterweight a great part of all the pleasure and commodity that they bring.

Besides this, riches are the thing that taketh many times from its master all his pleasure and his life, too. For many a man is slain for his riches. And some keep their riches as a thing pleasant and commodious for their life, take none other pleasure of it in all their life than as though they bore the key of another man's coffer. For they are content to live miserably in neediness all their days, rather than to find it in their heart to diminish their hoard, they have such a fancy to look thereon. Yea, and some men, for fear lest thieves should steal it from them, are their own thieves and steal it from themselves. For they dare not so much as let it lie where they themselves may look on it, but put it in a pot and hide it in the ground, and there let it lie safe till they die—and sometimes seven years thereafter. And if the pot had been stolen away from that place five years before the man's death, then all the same five years he lived thereafter, thinking always that his pot lay safe still, since he never occupied it afterward, what had he been the poorer?

VINCENT: By my troth, uncle, not one penny, for aught that I perceive.

## IX

ANTHONY: Let us now consider good name, honest estimation, and honourable fame. For these three things are of their own nature one, and take their differences in effect only of the manner of the common speech in diversity of degree. For a good name may a man have, be he never so poor. Honest estimation, in the common understanding of the people, belongeth not unto any man but him that is taken for one of some countenance and possessions, and among his neighbours had in some reputation. In the word of "honourable fame," folk conceive the renown of great estates, much and far spoken of, by reason of their laudable acts.

Now, all this gear, used as a thing pleasant and commodious for this present life, may seem pleasant to him who fasteneth his fancy thereon. But of the nature of the thing itself I perceive no great commodity that it hath—I say of the nature of the thing itself, because it may by chance be some occasion of some commodity. For it may hap that for the good name the poor man hath, or for the honest estimation that a man of some possessions and substance standeth in among his neighbours, or for the honourable fame with which a great estate is renowned—it may hap, I say, that some man, bearing them the better, will therefore do them some good. And yet, as for that, like as it may sometimes so hap (and sometimes doth so hap indeed), so may it hap sometimes on the other hand (and on the other hand so it sometimes happeth indeed) that such folk are envied and hated by others, and as readily take harm by them who envy and hate them as they take good by them that love them.

But now, to speak of the thing itself in its own proper nature, what is it but a blast of another man's mouth, as soon past as spoken? He who setteth his delight on it, feedeth himself but with wind; be he never so full, he hath little substance therein. And many times shall he much deceive himself. For he shall think that many praise him who never speak word of him. And they that do, say yet much less than he thinketh and far more seldom too. For they spend not all the day, he may be sure, in talking of him alone. And those who so commend him the most will yet, I daresay, in every four-and-twenty hours, shut their eyes and forget him once! Besides this, while one speaketh well of him in one place, another sitteth and saith as ill of him in another. And finally, some who most praise him in his presence, behind his back mock him as fast and loud laugh him to scorn, and sometimes slily to his own face, too. And yet are there some fools so fed with this foolish fancy of fame that they rejoice and glory to think how they are continually praised all about, as though all the world did nothing else, day nor night, but ever sit and sing "Sanctus sanctus, sanctus" upon them!

## X

And into this pleasant frenzy of much foolish vainglory are there some men brought sometimes by those whom they themselves do (in a manner) hire to flatter them. And they would not be content if a man should do otherwise, but would be right angry—not only if a man told them truth when they do evil indeed, but also if they praise it but slenderly.

VINCENT: Forsooth, uncle, this is very truth. I have been ere this, and not very long ago, where I saw so proper experience of this point that I must stop your tale long enough to tell you mine.

ANTHONY: I pray you, cousin, tell on.

VINCENT: When I was first in Germany, uncle, it happed me to be somewhat favoured by a great man of the church and a great estate, one of the greatest in all that country there. And indeed, whosoever could spend as much as he could for one thing and another, would be a right great estate in any country of Christendom. But vainglorious was he, very far above all measure. And that was great pity, for it did harm and made him abuse many great gifts that God had given him. Never was he satiated with hearing his own praise.

So happed it one day, that he had in a great audience made an oration in a certain manner, in which he liked himself so well that at his dinner he thought he sat on thorns till he might hear how those who sat with him at his board would commend it. He sat musing a while, devising, as I thought afterward, upon some pretty proper way to bring it in withal. And at last, for lack of a better, lest he should have forborne the matter too long, he brought it even bluntly forth and asked us all who sat at his board's end—for at his own place in the midst there sat but himself alone—how well we liked his oration that he had made that day. But in faith, uncle, when that problem was once proposed, till it was full answered, no man, I believe, ate one morsel of meat more—every man was fallen in so deep a study for the finding of some exquisite praise. For he who should have brought out but a vulgar and common commendation, would have thought himself shamed for ever. Ten said we our sentences, by row as we sat, from the lowest unto the highest in good order, as though it had been a great matter of the common weal in a right solemn council. When it came to my part—I say it not, uncle, for a boast—methought that, by our Lady, for my part, I quit myself well enough! And I liked myself the better because methought that, being but a foreigner, my words went yet with some grace in the German tongue, in which, letting my Latin alone, it pleased me to show my skill. And I hoped to be liked the better because I saw that he who sat next to me, and should say his sentence after me, was an unlearned priest, for he could speak no Latin at all. But when he came forth for his part with my lord's commendation, the wily fox had been so well accustomed in court to the craft of flattery that he went beyond me by far. And then might I see by him what excellence a right mean wit may come to in one craft, if in all his life he studieth and busieth his wit about no more but that one. But I made afterward a solemn vow unto myself that if ever he and I were matched together at that board again, when we should fall to our flattery I would flatter in Latin, that he might contend with me no more. For though I could be content to be outrun by a horse, yet would I no more abide it to be outrun by an ass.

But, uncle, here began now the game: he that sat highest and was to speak last, was a great beneficed man, and not only a doctor but also somewhat learned indeed in the laws of the church. A world was it to see how he marked every man's word who spoke before him! And it seemed that the more proper every word was, the worse he liked it, for the cumbrance that he had to study out a better one to surpass it. The man even sweated with the labour, so that he was fain now and then to wipe his face. Howbeit, in conclusion, when it came to his course, we who had spoken before him had so taken up all among us before that we had not left him one wise word to speak afterward.

ANTHONY: Alas, good man—among so many of you, some good fellow should have lent him one!

VINCENT: It needed not, as it happened, uncle. For he found out such a shift that in his flattering he surpassed us all.

ANTHONY: Why, what said he, cousin?

VINCENT: By our Lady, uncle, not one word. But he did as I believe Pliny telleth of Apelles the painter, in the picture that he painted of the sacrifice and death of Iphigenia, in the making of the sorrowful countenances of the noble men of Greece who beheld it. He reserved the countenance of King Agamemnon her father for the last, lest, if he made his visage before, he must in some of the others afterward either have made the visage less dolorous than he could, and thereby have forborne some part of his praise, or, doing the uttermost of his craft, might have happed to make some other look more heavily for the pity of her pain than her own father, which would have been yet a far greater fault in his painting. When he came, therefore, to the making of her father's face last of all, he had spent out so much of his craft and skill that he could devise no manner of new heavy cheer and countenance for him but what he had made there aleady in some of the others a much more heavy one before. And therefore, to the intent that no man should see what manner of countenance it was that her father had, the painter was fain to paint him holding his face in his handkerchief!

The like pageant (in a manner) played us there this good ancient honourable flatterer. For when he saw that he could find no words of praise that would surpass all that had been spoken before already, the wily fox would speak never a word. But as one who were ravished heavenward with the wonder of the wisdom and eloquence that my lord's grace had uttered in that oration, he set up a long sigh with an "Oh!" from the bottom of his breast, and held up both his hands, and lifted up his head, and cast up his eyes into the welkin, and wept.

ANTHONY: Forsooth, cousin, he played his part very properly. But was that great prelate's oration, cousin, at all praiseworthy? For you can tell, I see well. For you would not, I suppose, play as Juvenal merrily describeth the blind senator, one of the flatterers of Tiberius the emperor, who among the rest so magnified the great fish that the emperor had sent for them to show them. This blind senator—Montanus, I believe they called him—marvelled at the fish as much as any that marvelled most. And many things he spoke of it, with some of his words directed unto it, looking himself toward his left side, while the fish lay on his right side! You would not, I am sure, cousin, have taken upon you to praise it so, unless you had heard it.

VINCENT: I heard it, uncle, indeed, and, to say the truth, it was not to dispraise. Howbeit, surely, somewhat less praise might have served it— less by a great deal more than half. But this I am sure: had it been the worst that ever was made, the praise would not have been the less by one hair. For those who used to praise him to his face never considered how much the thing deserved, but how great a laud and praise they themselves could give his good Grace.

ANTHONY: Surely, cousin, as Terence saith, such folk make men of fools even stark mad. And much cause have their lords to be right angry with them.

VINCENT: God hath indeed, and is, I daresay. But as for their lords, uncle, if they would afterward wax angry with them for it, they would, to my mind, do them very great wrong. For it is one of the things that they specially keep them for. For those who are of such vainglorious mind, be they lords or be they meaner men, can be much better contented to have their devices commended than amended. And though they require their servant and their friend never so specially to tell them the very truth, yet shall he better please them if he speak them fair than if he telleth them the truth.

For they be in the condition that Marciall speaketh of in an epigram, unto a friend of his who required his judgment how he liked his verses, but prayed him in any wise to tell him even the very truth. To him, Marciall made answer in this wise:

"The very truth of me thou dost require.
The very truth is this, my friend dear:
The very truth thou wouldst not gladly hear."

And in good faith, uncle, the selfsame prelate that I told you my tale of—I dare be bold to swear it, I know it so surely—had one time drawn up a certain treaty that was to serve for a league between that country and a great prince. In this treaty he himself thought that he had devised his articles so wisely and composed them so well, that all the world would approve them. Thereupon, longing sore to be praised, he called unto him a friend of his, a man well learned and of good worship, and very well expert in those matters, as one who had been divers times ambassador for that country and had made many such treaties himself. When he gave him the treaty and he had read it, he asked him how he liked it, and said, "But I pray you heartily, tell me the very truth." And that he spake so heartily that the other thought he would fain have heard the truth, and in that trust he told him a fault in the treaty. And at the hearing of it he swore in great anger, "By the mass, thou art a very fool!" The other afterward told me that he would never tell him the truth again.

ANTHONY: Without question, cousin, I cannot greatly blame him. And thus they themselves make every man mock them, flatter them, and deceive them—those, I say, who are of such a vainglorious mind. For if they be content to hear the truth, let them then make much of those who tell them the truth, and withdraw their ears from them who falsely flatter them, and they shall be more truly served than with twenty requests praying men to tell them true.

King Ladislaus—our Lord absolve his soul!—used much this manner among his servants. When one of them praised any deed of his or any quality in him, if he perceived that they said but the truth he would let it pass by uncontrolled. But when he saw that they set a gloss on it for his praise of their own making besides, then would he shortly say unto them, "I pray thee, good fellow, when thou sayest grace at my board, never bring in a Gloria Patri without a sicut erat. Any act that ever I did, if thou report it again to mine honour with a Gloria Patri, never report it but with a sicut erat—that is, even as it was and none otherwise. And lift me not up with lies, for I love it not." If men would use this way with them that this noble king used, it would diminish much of their false flattery.

I can well approve that men should commend such things as they see praiseworthy in other men—keeping them within the bounds of truth—to give them the greater courage to the increase of them. For men keep still in that point one quality of children, that praise must prick them forth. But better it were to do well and look for none. Howbeit, those who cannot find it in their hearts to commend another man's good deed show themselves either envious or else of nature very cold and dull. But without question, he who putteth his pleasure in the praise of the people hath but a foolish fancy. For if his finger do but ache of a hot blain, a great many men's mouths blowing out his praise will scantly do him, among them all, so much ease as to have one boy blow on his finger!

## XI

Let us now consider likewise what great worldly wealth ariseth unto men by great offices and authority—to those worldly-disposed people, I say, who desire them for no better purpose. For of those who desire them for better, we shall speak after anon.

The great thing that they all chiefly like therein is that they may bear a rule, command and control other men, and live uncommanded and uncontrolled themselves. And yet this commodity took I so little heed of, that I never was aware it was so great, until a good friend of ours merrily told me once that his wife once in a great anger taught it to him. For when her husband had no desire to grow greatly upward in the world, nor would labour for office of authority, and beside that forsook a right worshipful office when it was offered him, she fell in hand with him, he told me. And she all berated him, and asked him, "What will you do, that you will not put yourself forth as other folk do? Will you sit by the fire and make goslings in the ashes with a stick, as children do? Would God I were a man—look what I would do!" "Why, wife," quoth her husband, "what would you do?" "What? By God, go forward with the best! For, as my mother was wont to say—God have mercy on her soul—it is evermore better to rule than to be ruled. And therefore, by God, I would not, I warrant you, be so foolish as to be ruled where I might rule." "By my troth, wife," quoth her husband, "in this I daresay you say truth, for I never found you willing to be ruled yet."

VINCENT: Well, uncle, I follow you now, well enough! She is indeed a stout master-woman. And in good faith, for aught that I can see, even that same womanish mind of hers is the greatest commodity that men reckon upon in offices of authority.

ANTHONY: By my troth, and methinketh there are very few who attain any great commodity therein. For first there is, in every kingdom, but one who can have an office of such authority that no man may command him or control him. No officer can stand in that position but the king himself; he only, uncontrolled or uncommanded, may control and command all. Now, of all the rest, each is under him. And yet almost every one is under more commanders and controllers, too, than one. And many a man who is in a great office commandeth fewer things and less labour to many men who are under him than someone that is over him commandeth him alone.

VINCENT: Yet it doth them good, uncle, that men must make courtesy to them and salute them with reverence and stand bareheaded before them, or unto some of them peradventure kneel, too.

ANTHONY: Well, cousin, in some part they do but play at gleek—they receive reverence, and to their cost they pay honour again therefor. For except, as I said, a king alone, the greatest in authority under him receiveth not so much reverence from any man as according to reason he himself doth honour to the king. Nor twenty men's courtesies do him not so much pleasure as his own once kneeling doth him pain if his knee hap to be sore. And I once knew a great officer of the king's to say—and in good faith I believe he said but as he thought—that twenty men standing bareheaded before him kept not his head half so warm as to keep on his own cap. And he never took so much ease with their being bareheaded before him, as he once caught grief with a cough that came upon him by standing long bareheaded before the king.

But let it be that these commodities be somewhat, such as they be. Yet then consider whether any incommodities be so joined with them that a man might almost as well lack both as have both. Goeth everything evermore as every one of them would have it? That would be as hard as to please all the people at once with one weather, since in one house the husband would have fair weather for his corn and his wife would have rain for her leeks! So those who are in authority are not all evermore of one mind, but sometimes there is variance among them, either for the respect of profit or the contention of rule, or for maintenance of causes, sundry parts for their sundry friends, and it cannot be that both the parties can have their own way. Nor often are they content who see their conclusions fail, but they take the missing of their intent ten times more displeasantly than poor men do. And this goeth not only for men of mean authority, but unto the very greatest. The princes themselves cannot have, you know, all their will. For how would it be possible, since almost every one of them would, if he could, be lord over all the rest? Then many men, under their princes in authority, are in such a position that many bear them privy malice and envy in heart. And many falsely speak them full fair and praise them with their mouth, who when there happeth any great fall unto them, bark and bite upon them like dogs.

Finally, there is the cost and charge, the danger and peril of war, in which their part is more than a poor man's is, since that matter dependeth more upon them. And many a poor ploughman may sit still by the fire while they must arise and walk.

And sometimes their authority falleth by change of their master's mind. And of that we see daily, in one place or another, such examples and so many that the parable of that philosopher can lack no testimony, who likened the servants of great princes unto the counters with which men do reckon accounts. For like as that counter that standeth sometimes for a farthing is suddenly set up and standeth for a thousand pound, and afterward as soon is set down beneath to stand for a farthing again; so fareth it sometimes with those who seek the way to rise and grow up in authority by the favour of great princes—as they rise up high, so fall they down again as low.

Howbeit, though a man escape all such adventures, and abide in great authority till he die, yet then at least every man must leave at last. And that which we call "at last" hath no very long time to it. Let a man reckon his years that are past of his age ere ever he can get up aloft; and let him, when he hath it first in his fist, reckon how long he shall be likely to live thereafter; and I daresay that then the most part shall have little cause to rejoice. They shall see the time likely to be so short that their honour and authority by nature shall endure, beside the manifold chances by which they may lose it sooner. And then, when they see that they must needs leave it—the thing which they did much more set their hearts upon than ever they had reasonable cause—what sorrow they take for it, that shall I not need to tell you.

And thus it seemeth unto me, cousin, in good faith, that since in the having of authority the profit is not great, and the displeasures neither small nor few; and since of the losing there are so many sundry chances and by no means a man can keep it long; and since to part from it is such a painful grief: I can see no very great cause for which, as a high worldly commodity, men should greatly desire it.

## XII

And thus far have we considered hitherto, in these outward goods that are called the gifts of fortune, only the slender commodity that worldly-minded men have by them. But now, if we consider further what harm to the soul they take by them who desire them only for the wretched wealth of this world, then shall we well perceive how far more happy is he who well loseth them than he who ill findeth them.

These things are such as are of their own nature indifferent—that is, of themselves neither good nor bad—but are matter that may serve to the one or the other according as men will use them. Yet need we little doubt but that for those who desire them only for their worldly pleasure and for no further godly purpose the devil shall soon turn them from things indifferent and make them things very evil. For though they be indifferent of their nature, yet cannot the use of them lightly stand indifferent, but must be determinately either good or bad. And therefore he who desireth them only for worldly pleasure, desireth them not for any good. And for better purpose than he desireth them, to better use is he not likely to put them. And therefore will he use them not unto good but consequently to evil.

And for example, first consider it in riches, and in him who longeth for them as for things of temporal commodity and not for any godly purpose. What good they shall do him, St. Paul declareth, when he writeth unto Timothy, "They that long to be rich fall into temptation and into the snare of the devil, and into many desires unprofitable and noxious, which drown men into death and into perdition." And the holy scripture saith also in the twenty-fourth chapter of the Proverbs, "He that gathereth treasures shall be shoved into the snares of death." So that whereas God saith by the mouth of St. Paul that they shall fall into the devil's snare, he saith in the other place that they shall be pushed and shoved in by violence. And of truth, while a man desireth riches not for any good godly purpose but only for worldly wealth, it must needs be that he shall have little conscience in the getting. But, by all evil ways that he can invent, shall he labour to get them. And then shall he either niggardly heap them up together, which is, as you well know, damnable; or else shall he wastefully misspend them upon worldly pomp, pride, and gluttony, with occasion of many sins more, and that is yet much more damnable.

As for fame and glory desired only for worldly pleasure, they do unto the soul inestimable harm. For they set men's hearts upon high devices and desires of such things as are immoderate and outrageous. And by help of false flatterers, they puff up a man in pride and make a brittle man—lately made of earth, that shall again shortly be laid full low in earth and there lie and rot and turn again into earth—take himself in the meantime for a god here upon earth and think to win himself to be lord of all the earth. This maketh battles between these great princes, with much trouble to much people, and great effusion of blood, and one king looking to reign in five realms, who cannot well rule one. For how many hath now this great Turk? And yet he aspireth to more. And those that he hath, he ordereth evilly—and yet he ordereth himself worst.

Then, offices of authority: If men desire them only for their worldly fancies, who can look that ever they shall occupy them well, and not rather abuse their authority and do thereby great hurt? For then shall they fall from indifference and maintain false suits for their friends. And they shall bear up their servants, and such as depend upon them, with bearing down of other innocent folk, who are not so able to do hurt as easy to take harm. Then the laws that are made against malefactors shall they make, as an old philosopher said, to be much like unto cobwebs, in which the little gnats and flies stick still and hang fast, but the great humble-bees break them and fly quite through. And then the laws that are made as a buckler in the defence of innocents, those shall they make serve for a sword to cut and sore wound them with—and therewith wound they their own souls sorer.

And thus you see, cousin, that of all these outward goods which men call the goods of fortune, there is never one that, unto those who long for it not for any godly purpose but only for their worldly welath, hath any great commodity to the body. And yet are they all, beside that, very deadly destruction unto the soul.

## XIII

VINCENT: Verily, good uncle, this thing is so plainly true that no man can with any good reason deny it. But I think also, uncle, that no man will do so. For I see no man who will confess, for very shame, that he desireth riches, honour, renown, and offices of authority only for his worldly pleasure. For every man would fain seem as holy as a horse. And therefore will every man say—and would it were so believed, too—that he desireth these things, though for his worldly wealth a little so, yet principally to merit thereby through doing some good with them.

ANTHONY: This is, cousin, very surely so, that so doth every man say. But first he who in the desire of these things hath his respect unto his worldly wealth, as you say, "but a little so," so much as he himself thinketh but a little, may soon prove a great deal too much. And many men will say so, too, who have principal respect unto their worldly commodity, and toward God little or none at all. And yet they pretend the contrary, and that unto their own harm. For "God cannot be mocked."

And some peradventure know not well their own affection themselves. But there lieth more imperfection secretly in their affection than they themselves are well aware of, which only God beholdeth. And therefore saith the prophet unto God, "Mine imperfection have thine eyes beheld." And therefore the prophet prayeth, "From mine hidden sins cleanse thou me, good Lord."

But now, cousin, this tribulation of the Turk: If he so persecute us for the faith that those who will forsake their faith shall keep their goods, and those shall lose their goods who will not leave their faith—lo, this manner of persecution shall try them like a touchstone. For it shall show the feigned from the true-minded, and it shall also teach them who think they mean better than they do indeed, better to discern themselves. For there are some who think they mean well, while they frame themselves a conscience, and ever keep still a great heap of superfluous substance by them, thinking ever still that they will bethink themselves upon some good deed on which they will well bestow it once—or else that their executors shall! But now, if they lie not unto themselves, but keep their goods for any good purpose to the pleasure of God indeed, then shall they, in this persecution, for the pleasure of God in keeping his faith, be glad to depart from them.

And therefore, as for all these things—the loss, I mean, of all these outward things that men call the gifts of fortune—this is, methinketh, in this Turk's persecution for the faith, consolation great and sufficient: Every man who hath them either setteth by them for the world or for God. He who setteth by them for the world hath, as I have showed you, little profit by them to the body and great harm unto the soul. And therefore, he might well, if he were wise, reckon that he won by the loss, although he lost them but by some common cause. And much more happy can he then be, since he loseth them by such a meritorious means. And on the other hand, he who keepeth them for some good purpose, intending to bestow them for the pleasure of God, the loss of them in this Turk's persecution for keeping of the faith can be no manner of grief to him. For by so parting from them he bestoweth them in such wise unto God's pleasure that at the time when he loseth them by no way could he bestow them unto his high pleasure better. For though it would have been peradventure better to have bestowed them well before, yet since he kept them for some good purpose he would not have left them unbestowed if he had foreknown the chance. But being now prevented so by persecution that he cannot bestow them in that other good way that he would have, yet since he parteth from them because he will not part from the faith, though the devil's escheator violently take them from him, yet willingly giveth he them to God.

## XIV

VINCENT: In good faith, good uncle, I can deny none of this. And indeed, unto those who were despoiled and robbed by the Turk's overrunning of the country, and all their substance movable and unmovable bereft and lost already, their persons only fled and safe, I think that these considerations—considering also that, as you lately said, their sorrow could not amend their chance—might unto them be good occasion of comfort, and cause them, as you said, to make a virtue of necessity.

But in the case, uncle, that we now speak of, they have yet their substance untouched in their own hands, and the keeping or the losing shall both hang in their own hands, by the Turk's offer, upon the retaining or the renouncing of the Christian faith. Here, uncle, I find it, as you said, that this temptation is most sore and most perilous. For I fear me that we shall find few of such as have much to lose who shall find it in their hearts so suddenly to forsake their goods, with all those other things before rehearsed on which their worldly wealth dependeth.

ANTHONY: That fear I much, cousin, too. But thereby shall it well appear, as I said, that, seemed they never so good and virtuous before, and flattered they themselves with never so gay a gloss of good and gracious purpose that they kept their goods for, yet were their hearts inwardly in the deep sight of God not sound and sure such as they should be (and as peradventure some had themselves thought they were) but like a puff-ring of Paris—hollow, light, and counterfeit indeed.

And yet, they being even such, this would I fain ask one of them. And I pray you, cousin, take you his person upon you, and in this case answer for him. "What hindereth you," would I ask, "your Lordship," (for we will take no small man for an example in this part, nor him who would have little to lose, for methinketh such a one who would cast away God for a little, would be so far from all profit, that he would not be worth talking with). "What hindereth you," I say, therefore, "that you be not gladly content, without any deliberation at all, in this kind of persecution, rather than to leave your faith, to let go all that ever you have at once?"

VINCENT: Since you put it unto me, uncle, to make the matter more plain, that I should play that great man's part who is so wealthy and hath so much to lose, albeit that I cannot be very sure of another man's mind, nor of what another man would say, yet as far as mine own mind can conjecture, I shall answer in his person what I think would be his hindrance. And therefore to your question I answer that there hindereth me the thing that you yourself may lightly guess: the losing of the many commodities which I now have—riches and substance, lands and great possessions of inheritance, with great rule and authority here in my country. All of which things the great Turk granteth me to keep still in peace and have them enhanced, too, if I will forsake the faith of Christ. Yea, I may say to you, I have a motion secretly made me further, to keep all this yet better cheap; that is, not to be compelled utterly to forsake Christ nor all the whole Christian faith, but only some such parts of it as may not stand with Mahomet's law. And only granting Mahomet for a true prophet and serving the Turk truly in his wars against all Christian kings, I shall not be hindered to praise Christ also, and to call him a good man, and worship and serve him too.

ANTHONY: Nay, nay, my lord—Christ hath not so great need of your Lordship as, rather than to lose your service, he would fall at such covenants with you as to take your service at halves, to serve him and his enemy both! He hath given you plain warning already by St. Paul that he will have in your service no parting-fellow: "What fellowship is there between light and darkness? Between Christ and Belial?" And he hath also plainly told you himself by his own mouth, "No man can serve two lords at once." He will have you believe all that he telleth you, and do all that he biddeth you, and forbear all that he forbiddeth you, without any manner of exception. Break one of his commandments, and you break all. Forsake one point of his faith, and you forsake all, as for any thanks that you get of him for the rest. And therefore, if you devise, as it were, indentures between God and you—what you will do for him and what you will not do, as though he should hold himself content with such service of yours as you yourself care to appoint him—if you make, I say, such indentures, you shall seal both the parts yourself, and you get no agreement thereto from him.

And this I say: Though the Turk would make such an appointment with you as you speak of, and would, when he had made it, keep it—whereas he would not, I warrant you, leave you so when he had once brought you so far forth. But he would, little by little, ere he left you, make you deny Christ altogether and take Mahomet in his stead. And so doth he in the beginning, when he will not have you believe him to be God. For surely, if he were not God, he would be no good man either, since he plainly said he was God. But through he would go never so far forth with you, yet Christ will, as I said, not take your service by halves, but will that you shall love him with all your whole heart. And because, while he was living here fifteen hundred years ago, he foresaw this mind of yours that you have now, with which you would fain serve him in some such fashion that you might keep your worldly substance still, but rather forsake his service than put all your substance from you, he telleth you plainly fifteen hundred years ago with his own mouth that he will have no such service of you, saying, "You cannot serve both God and your riches together."

And therefore, this thing being established for a plain conclusion, which you must needs grant if you have faith—and if you be gone from that ground of faith already, then is all our disputation, you know, at an end. For how should you then rather lose your goods than forsake your faith, if you have lost your faith and let it go already? This point, I say, therefore, being put first for a ground, between us both twain agreed, that you have yet the faith still and intend to keep it always still in your heart, and are only in doubt whether you will lose all your worldly substance rather than forsake your faith in your word alone; now shall I reply to the point of your answer, wherein you tell me the lothness of the loss and the comfort of the keeping hinder you from forgoing your goods and move you rather to forsake your faith.

I let pass all that I have spoken of the small commodity of them unto your body and of the great harm that the having of them doth to your soul. And since the promise of the Turk, made unto you for the keeping of them, is the thing that moveth you and maketh you thus to doubt, I ask you first whereby you know that, when you have done all that he will have you do against Christ, to the harm of your soul—whereby know you, I say, that he will keep you his promise in these things that he promiseth you concerning the retaining of your well-beloved worldly wealth, for the pleasure of your body?

VINCENT: What surety can a man have of such a great prince

except his promise, which for his own honour it cannot become him to break?

ANTHONY: I have known him, and his father before him too, to break more promises than five, as great as this is that he should here make with you. Who shall come and cast it in his teeth, and tell him it is a shame for him to be so fickle and so false of his promise? And then what careth he for those words that he knoweth well he shall never hear? Not very much, though they were told him too!

If you might come afterward and complain your grief unto his own person yourself, you should find him as shamefast as a friend of mine, a merchant, once found the Sultan of Syria. Being certain years about his merchandise in that country, he gave to the Sultan a great sum of money for a certain office for him there for the while. But he had scantly granted him this and put it in his hand when, ere ever it was worth aught to him, the Sultan suddenly sold it to another of his own sect, and put our Hungarian out. Then came he to him and humbly put him in remembrance of his grant, spoken with his own mouth and signed with his own hand. Thereunto the Sultan answered him, with a grim countenance, "I will have thee know, good-for-nothing, that neither my mouth nor mine hand shall be master over me, to bind all my body at their pleasure. But I will be lord and master over them both, that whatsoever the one say and the other write, I will be at mine own liberty to do what I like myself, and ask them both no leave. And therefore, go get thee hence out of my countries, knave!" Think you now, my lord, that Sultan and this Turk, being both of one false sect, you may not find them both alike false of their promise?

VINCENT: That must I needs jeopard, for other surety can there none be had.

ANTHONY: An unwise jeoparding, to put your soul in peril of damnation for the keeping of your bodily pleasures, and yet without surety to jeopard them too!

But yet go a little further, lo. Suppose me that you might be very sure that the Turk would break no promise with you. Are you then sure enough to retain all your substance still?

VINCENT: Yea, then.

ANTHONY: What if a man should ask you how long?

VINCENT: How long? As long as I live.

ANTHONY: Well, let it be so, then. But yet, as far as I can see, though the great Turk favour you never so much and let you keep your goods as long as ever you live, yet if it hap that you be this day fifty years old, all the favour he can show you cannot make you one day younger tomorrow. But every day shall you wax older than the day before, and then within a while must you, for all his favour, lose all.

VINCENT: Well, a man would be glad, for all that, to be sure not to lack while he liveth.

ANTHONY: Well, then, if the great Turk give you your goods, can there then in all your life none other take them from you again?
VINCENT: Verily, I suppose not.

ANTHONY: May he not lose this country again unto Christian men, and you, with the taking of this way, fall in the same peril then that you would now eschew?

VINCENT: Forsooth, I think that if he get it once, he will never lose it after again in our days.

ANTHONY: Yes, by God's grace. But yet if he lose it after our day, there goeth your children's inheritance away again! But be it now that he could never lose it; could none take your substance from you then?

VINCENT: No, in good faith, none.

ANTHONY: No, none at all? Not God?

VINCENT: God? Why, yes, perdy. Who doubteth of that?

ANTHONY: Who? Marry, he who doubteth whether there be any God or no. And that there lacketh not some such, the prophet testifieth where he said, "The fool hath said in his heart, there is no God." With the mouth the most foolish will forbear to say it unto other folk, but in the heart they forbear not to say it softly to themselves. And I fear me there be many more such fools than every man would think. And they would not hesitate to say it openly, too, if they forbore it not more for dread or for shame of men than for any fear of God. But now those who are so frantic foolish as to think there were no God, and yet in their words confess him, though (as St. Paul saith) in their deeds they deny him—we shall let them pass till it please God to show himself unto them, either inwardly, in time, by his merciful grace, or else outwardly, but over-late for them, by his terrible judgment.

But unto you, my Lord, since you believe and confess, as a wise man should, that though the Turk keep you his promise in letting you keep your substance, because you do him pleasure in the forsaking of your faith, yet God, whose faith you forsake, and thereby do him displeasure, may so take them from you that the great Turk, with all the power he hath, is not able to keep you them—why will you be so unwise with the loss of your soul to please the great Turk for your goods, since you know well that God whom you displease therewith may take them from you too?

Besides this, since you believe there is a God, you cannot but believe also that the great Turk cannot take your goods from you without his will or sufferance, no more than the devil could from Job. And think you then that, if he will suffer the Turk to take away your goods albeit that by the keeping and confessing of his faith you please him, he will, when you displease him by forsaking his faith, suffer you to rejoice or enjoy any benefit of those goods that you get or keep thereby?

VINCENT: God is gracious, and though men offend him, yet he suffereth them many times to live in prosperity long after.

ANTHONY: Long after? Nay, by my troth, that doth he no man! For how can that be, that he should suffer you to live in prosperity long after, when your whole life is but short in all-together, and either almost half of it or more than half, you think yourself, I daresay, spent out already before? Can you burn out half a short candle, and then have a long one left of the rest?

There cannot in this world be a worse mind than for a man to delight and take comfort in any commodity that he taketh by sinful means. For it is the very straight way toward the taking of boldness and courage in sin, and finally to falling into infidelity and thinking that God careth not or regardeth not what things men do here nor of what mind we be. But unto such-minded folk speaketh holy scripture in this wise: "Say not, I have sinned and yet there hath happed me none harm, for God suffereth before he strike." But, as St. Austine saith, the longer he tarrieth ere he strike, the sorer is the stroke when he striketh.

And therefore, if you will do well, reckon yourself very sure that when you deadly displease God for the getting or the keeping of your goods, God shall not suffer those goods to do you good. But either he shall shortly take them from you, or else suffer you to keep them for a little while to your more harm and afterward, when you least look for it, take you away from them.

And then, what a heap of heaviness will there enter into your heart, when you shall see that you shall so suddenly go from your goods and leave them here in the earth in one place, and that your body shall be put in the earth in another place, and—which then shall be the most heaviness of all—when you shall fear (and not without great cause) that your soul first forthwith, and after that at the final judgment your body, shall be driven down deep toward the centre of the earth into the fiery pit and dungeon of the devil of hell, there to tarry in torment, world without end! What goods of this world can any man imagine, the pleasure and commodity of which could be such in a thousand years as to be able to recompense that intolerable pain that there is to be suffered in one year? Yea, or in one day or one hour, either? And then what a madness is it, for the poor pleasure of your worldly goods of so few years, to cast yourself both body and soul into the everlasting fire of hell, which is not diminished by the amount of a moment by lying there the space of a hundred thousand years?

And therefore our Saviour, in few words, concluded and confuted all these follies of those who, for the short use of this worldly substance, forsake him and his faith and sell their souls unto the devil for ever. For he saith, "What availeth it a man if he won all the whole world, and lost his soul?" This would be, methinketh, cause and occasion enough, to him who had never so much part of this world in his hand, to be content rather to lose it all than for the retaining or increasing of his worldly goods to lose and destroy his soul.

VINCENT: This is, good uncle, in good faith very true. And what other thing any of them who would not for this be content, have to allege in reason for the defence of their folly, that can I not imagine. I care not in this matter to play the part any longer, but I pray God give me the grace to play the contrary part in deed. And I pray that I may never, for any goods or substance of this wretched world, forsake my faith toward God either in heart or tongue. And I trust in his great goodness that so I never shall.

## XV

ANTHONY: Methinketh, cousin, that this persecution shall not only, as I said before, try men's hearts when it cometh and make them know their own affections—whether they have a corrupt greedy covetous mind or not—but also the very fame and expectation of it may teach them this lesson, ere ever the thing fall upon them itself. And this may be to their no little fruit, if they have the wit and the grace to take it in time while they can. For now may they find sure places to lay their treasure in, so that all the Turk's army shall never find it out.

VINCENT: Marry, uncle, that way they will not forget, I warrant you, as near as their wits will serve them. But yet have I known some who have ere this thought that they had hid their money safe and sure enough, digging it full deep in the ground, and yet have missed it when they came again and found it digged out and carried away to their hands.

ANTHONY: Nay, from their hands, I think you would say. And it was no marvel. For some such have I known, too, but they have hid their goods foolishly in such place as they were well warned before that they should not. And that were they warned by him whom they well knew for such a one as knew well enough what would come of it.

VINCENT: Then were they more than mad. But did he tell them too where they should have hid it, to make it sure?

ANTHONY: Yea, by St. Mary, did he! For else he would have told them but half a tale. But he told them a whole tale, bidding them that they should in no wise hide their treasure in the ground. And he showed them a good cause, for there thieves dig it out and steal it away.

VINCENT: Why, where should they hide it, then, said he? For thieves may hap to find it out in any place.

ANTHONY: Forsooth, he counselled them to hide their treasure in heaven and there lay it up, for there it shall lie safe. For thither, he said, there can no thief come, till he have left his theft and become a true man first. And he who gave this counsel knew well enough what he said, for it was our Saviour himself, who in the sixth chapter of St. Matthew saith, "Hoard not up your treasures in earth, where the rust and the moth fret it out and where thieves dig it out and steal it away. But hoard up your treasures in heaven, where neither the rust nor the moth fret them out, and where thieves dig them not out nor steal them away. For where thy treasure is, there is thine heart too."

If we would well consider these words of our Saviour Christ, methinketh we should need no more counsel at all, nor no more comfort either, concerning the loss of our temporal substance in this Turk's persecution for the faith. For here our Lord in these words teacheth us where we may lay up our substance safe, before the persecution come. If we put it into the poor men's bosoms, there shall it lie safe, for who would go search a beggar's bag for money? If we deliver it to the poor for Christ's sake, we deliver it unto Christ himself. And then what persecutor can there be, so strong as to take it out of his hand?

VINCENT: These things, uncle, are undoubtedly so true that no man can with words wrestle therewith. But yet ever there hangeth in a man's heart a lothness to lack a living!

ANTHONY: There doth indeed, in theirs who either never or but seldom hear any good counsel against it, or who, when they hear it, hearken to it but as they would to an idle tale, rather for a pastime or for the sake of manners than for any substantial intent and purpose to follow good advice and take any fruit by it. But verily, if we would lay not only our ear but also our heart to it, and consider that the saying of our Saviour Christ is not a poet's fable or a harper's song but the very holy word of almighty God himself, we would be full sore ashamed of ourselves—and well we might! And we would be full sorry too, when we felt in our affection those words to have in our hearts no more strength and weight but what we remain still of the same dull mind as we did before we heard them.

This manner of ours, in whose breasts the great good counsel of God no better settleth nor taketh no better root, may well declare to us that the thorns and briars and brambles of our worldly substance grow so thick and spring up so high in the ground of our hearts that they strangle, as the

Gospel saith, the word of God that was sown therein. And therefore is God a very good lord unto us, when he causeth, like a good husbandman, his folk to come on the field—for the persecutors are his folk, to this purpose—and with their hooks and their stocking-irons to grub up these wicked weeds and bushes of our earthly substance and carry them quite away from us, that the word of God sown in our hearts may have room there, and a glade round about for the warm sun of grace to come to it and make it grow. For surely those words of our Saviour shall we find full true, "Where thy treasure is, there is also thine heart." If we lay up our treasure in earth, in earth shall be our hearts. If we send our treasure into heaven, in heaven shall we have our hearts. And surely, the greatest comfort any man can have in his tribulation is to have his heart in heaven.

If thine heart were indeed out of this world and in heaven, all the kinds of torments that all this world could devise could put thee to no pain here. Let us then send our hearts hence thither in such a manner as we may, by sending hither our worldly substance hence. And let us never doubt but we shall, that once done, find our hearts so conversant in heaven, with the glad consideration of our following the gracious counsel of Christ, that the comfort of his Holy Spirit, inspired in us for that, shall mitigate, diminish, assuage, and (in a manner) quench the great furious fervour of the pain that we shall happen to have by his loving sufferance of our further merit in our tribulation.

If we saw that we should be within a while driven out of this land, and fain to fly into another, we would think that a man were mad who would not be content to forbear his goods here for the while and send them before him into that land where he saw he should live all the rest of his life. So may we verily think yet ourselves much more mad—seeing that we are sure it cannot be long ere we shall be sent, spite of our teeth, out of this world—if the fear of a little lack or the love to see our goods here about us and the lothness to part from them for this little while that we may keep them here, shall be able to keep us from the sure sending them before us into the other world. For we may be sure to live there wealthily with them if we send them thither, or else shortly leave them here behind us and then stand in great jeopardy there to live wretches for ever.

VINCENT: In good faith, good uncle, methinketh that concerning the loss of these outward things, these considerations are so sufficient comforts, that for mine own part I would methinketh desire no more, save only grace well to remember them.

## XVI

ANTHONY: Much less than this may serve, cousin, with calling and trusting upon God's help, without which much more than this cannot serve. But the fervour of the Christian faith so sore fainteth nowadays and decayeth, coming from hot unto luke-warm and from luke-warm almost to key-cold, that men must now be fain to lay many dry sticks to it, as to a fire that is almost out, and use much blowing at it.

But else I think, by my troth, that unto a warm faithful man one thing alone, of which we have spoken yet no word, would be comfort enough in this kind of persecution, against the loss of all his goods.

VINCENT: What thing may that be, uncle?

ANTHONY: In good faith, cousin, even the bare remembrance of the poverty that our Saviour willingly suffered for us. For I verily suppose that if there were a great king who had so tender love for a servant of his that he had, to help him out of danger, forsaken and lost all his worldly wealth and royalty and become poor and needy for his sake, that servant could scantly be found who would be of such a base unnatural heart that if he himself came afterward to some substance he would not with better will lose it all again than shamefully to forsake such a master.

And therefore, as I say, I surely suppose that if we would well remember and inwardly consider the great goodness of our Saviour toward us, when we were not yet his poor sinful servants but rather his adversaries and his enemies, and what wealth of this world he willingly forsook for our sakes—for he was indeed universal king of this world, and so having the power in his own hand to have used it if he had wished, instead of which, to make us rich in heaven, he lived here in neediness and poverty all his life and neither would have authority nor keep either lands or goods. If we would remember this, the deep consideration and earnest advisement of this one point alone would be able to make any true Christian man or woman well content rather for his sake in return to give up all that ever God hath lent them (and lent them he hath, all that they have) than unkindly and unfaithfully to forsake him. And him they forsake if, for fear, they forsake the confessing of his Christian faith.

And therefore, to finish this piece withal, concerning the dread of losing our outward worldly goods, let us consider the slender commodity that they bring; with what labour they are bought; what a little while they abide with whomsoever they abide with longest; what pain their pleasure is mingled with; what harm the love of them doth unto the soul; what loss is in the keeping if Christ's faith is refused for them; what winning is in the loss, if we lose them for God's sake; how much more profitable they are when well given than when ill kept; and finally what ingratitude it would be if we would not forsake them for Christ's sake rather than for them to forsake Christ unfaithfully, who while he lived for our sake forsook all the world, beside the suffering of shameful and painful death, of which we shall speak afterward.

If we will consider well these things, I say, and will pray God with his holy hand to print them in our hearts, and will abide and dwell still in the hope of his help, his truth shall, as the prophet saith, so compass us about with a shield that we shall not need to be afraid of this incursion of this midday devil—this plain open persecution of the Turk—for any loss that we can take by the bereaving from us of our wretched worldly goods. For their short and small pleasure in this life forborne, we shall be with heavenly substance everlastingly recompensed by God, in joyful bliss and glory.

## XVII

VINCENT: Forsooth, uncle, as for these outward goods, you have said enough. No man can be sure what strength he shall have or how faint and feeble he may find himself when he shall come to the point, and therefore I can make no warranty of myself, seeing that St. Peter so suddenly fainted at a woman's word and so cowardly forsook his master, for whom he had so boldly fought within so few hours before, and by that fall in forsaking well perceived that he had been too rash in his promise and was well worthy to take a fall for putting so full trust in himself. Yet in good faith methinketh now (and God will, I trust, help me to keep this thought still) that if the Turk should take all that I have, unto my very shirt, unless I would forsake my faith, and should offer it all to me again with five times as much if I would fall into his sect, I would not once stick at it—rather to forsake it every whit, than to forsake any point of Christ's holy faith.

But surely, good uncle, when I bethink me further on the grief and the pain that may turn unto my flesh, here find I the fear that forceth my heart to tremble.

ANTHONY: Neither have I cause to marvel at that, nor have you, cousin, cause to be dismayed for it. The great horror and fear that our Saviour had in his own flesh, against his painful passion, maketh me little to marvel. And I may well make you take this comfort, too, that for no such manner of grudging felt in your sensual parts, the flesh shrinking in the meditation of pain and death, your reason shall give over, but resist it and manly master it. And though you would fain fly from the painful death and be loth to come to it, yet may the meditation of our Saviour's great grievous agony move you. And he himself shall, if you so desire him, not fail to work with you therein, and to get and give you the grace to submit and conform your will unto his, as he did his unto his Father. And thereupon shall you be so comforted with the secret inward inspiration of his Holy Spirit, as he was with the personal presence of that angel who after his agony came and comforted him. And so shall you as his true disciple follow him, and with good will, without grudge, do as he did, and take your cross of pain and suffering upon your back and die for the truth with him, and thereby reign with him crowned in eternal glory.

And this I say to give you warning of the truth, to the intent that when a man feeleth such a horror of death in his heart, he should not thereby stand in outrageous fear that he were falling. For many such a man standeth, for all that fear, full fast, and finally better abideth the brunt, when God is so good unto him as to bring him to it and encourage him therein, than doth some other man who in the beginning feeleth no fear at all. And yet may he never be brought to the brunt, and most often so it is. For God, having many mansions, and all wonderful wealthful, in his Father's house, exalteth not every good man up to the glory of a martyr. But foreseeing their infirmity, that though they be of good will before and peradventure of right good courage too, they would yet play St. Peter if they were brought to the point, and thereby bring their souls into the peril of eternal damnation, he provideth otherwise for them before they come there. And he findeth a way that men shall not have the mind to lay any hands upon them, as he found for his disciples when he himself was willingly taken. Or else, if they set hands on them, he findeth a way that they shall have no power to hold them, as he found for St. John the Evangelist, who let his sheet fall from him, upon which they caught hold, and so fled himself naked away and escaped from them. Or, though they hold them and bring them to prison too, yet God sometimes delivereth them hence, as he did St. Peter. And sometimes he taketh them to him out of the prison into heaven, and suffereth them not to come to their torment at all, as he hath done by many a good holy man. And some he suffereth to be brought into the torments and yet suffereth them not to die in them, but to live many years afterward and die their natural death, as he did by St. John the Evangelist and by many another more, as we may well see both by sundry stories and in the epistles of St. Ciprian also. And therefore, which way God will take with us, we cannot tell.

But surely, if we be true Christian men, this can we well tell: that without any bold warranty of ourselves or foolish trust in our own strength, we are bound upon pain of damnation not to be of the contrary mind but what we will with his help, however loth we feel in our flesh thereto, rather than forsake him or his faith before the world—which if we do, he hath promised to forsake us before his Father and all his holy company of heaven—rather, I say, than we would do so, we would with his help endure and sustain for his sake all the tormentry that the devil with all his faithless tormentors in this world would devise. And then, if we be of this mind, and submit our will unto his, and call and pray for his grace, we can tell well enough that he will never suffer them to put more upon us than his grace will make us able to bear, but will also with their temptation provide for us a sure way. For "God is faithful," saith St. Paul, "who suffereth you not to be tempted above what you can bear, but giveth also with the temptation a way out." For either, as I said, he will keep us out of their hands, though he before suffered us to be afraid of them to prove our faith (that we may have, by the examination of our mind, some comfort in hope of his grace and some fear of our own frailty to drive us to call for grace), or else, if we call into their hands, provided that we fall not from the trust of him nor cease to call for his help, his truth shall, as the prophet saith, so compass us about with a shield that we shall not need to fear this incursion of this midday devil. For these Turks his tormentors, who shall enter this land and persecute us, shall either not have the power to touch our bodies at all, or else the short pain that they shall put into our bodies shall turn us to eternal profit both in our souls and in our bodies too. And therefore, cousin, to begin with, let us be of good comfort. For we are by our faith very sure that holy scripture is the very word of God, and that the word of God cannot but be true. And we see by the mouth of his holy prophet and by the mouth of his blessed apostle also that God hath made us faithful promise that he will not suffer us to be tempted above our power, but will both provide a way out for us and also compass us round about with his shield and defend us that we shall have no cause to fear this midday devil with all his persecution. We cannot therefore but be very sure (unless we are very shamefully cowardous of heart and out of measure faint in faith toward God, and in love less than luke-warm or waxed even key-cold) we may be very sure, I say, either that God will not suffer the Turks to invade this land; or that, if they do, God shall provide such resistance that they shall not prevail; or that, if they prevail, yet if we take the way that I have told you we shall by their persecution take little harm or rather none harm at all, but that which shall seem harm indeed be to us no harm at all but good. For if God make us and keep us good men, as he hath promised to do if we pray well therefore, then saith holy scripture, "Unto good folk all things turn them to good."

And therefore, cousin, since God knoweth what shall happen and not we, let us in the meanwhile with a good hope in the help of God's grace have a good purpose of standing sure by his holy faith against all persecutions. And if we should hereafter, either for fear or pain or for lack of his grace lost in our own default, mishap to decline from his good purpose—which our Lord forbid—yet we would have won the well-spent time beforehand, to the diminishment of our pain, and God would also be much the more likely to lift us up after our fall and give us his grace again. Howbeit, if this persecution come, we are, by this meditation and well-continued intent and purpose beforehand, the better strengthened and confirmed, and much more likely to stand indeed. And if it so fortune, as with God's grace at men's good prayers and amendment of our evil lives it may well fortune, that the Turks shall either be well withstood and vanquished or peradventure not invade us at all, then shall we, perdy, by this good purpose get ourselves of God a very good cheap thank!

And on the other hand, while we now think on it—and not to think on it, in so great likelihood of it, I suppose no wise man can—if we should for the fear of worldly loss or bodily pain, framed in our own minds, think that we would give over and to save our goods and lives forsake our Saviour by denial of his faith, then whether the Turks come or come not, we are meanwhile gone from God. And then if they come not indeed, or come and are driven to flight, what a shame should that be to us, before the face of God, in so shameful cowardly wise to forsake him for fear of that pain that we never felt or that never was befalling us!

VINCENT: By my troth, uncle, I thank you. Methinketh that though you never said more in the matter, yet have you, even with this that you have spoken here already of the fear of bodily pain in this persecution, marvellously comforted mine heart.

ANTHONY: I am glad, cousin, if your heart have taken comfort thereby. But if you so have, give God the thanks and not me, for that work is his and not mine. For neither am I able to say any good thing except by him, nor can all the good words in the world—no, not the holy words of God himself, and spoken also with his own holy mouth—profit a man with the sound entering at his ear, unless the Spirit of God also inwardly work in his soul. But that is his goodness ever ready to do, unless there be hindrance through the untowardness of our own froward will.

## XVIII

And now, being somewhat in comfort and courage before, we may the more quietly consider everything, which is somewhat more hard and difficult to do when the heart is before taken up and oppressed with the troublous affection of heavy sorrowful fear. Let us therefore examine now the weight and the substance of those bodily pains which you rehearsed before as the sorest part of this persecution. They were, if I remember you right, thraldom, imprisonment, and painful and shameful death. And first let us, as reason is, begin with the thraldom, for that was, as I remember it, the first.

VINCENT: I pray you, good uncle, say then somewhat of that. For methinketh, uncle, that captivity is a marvellous heavy thing, namely when they shall (as they most commonly do) carry us far from home into a strange unknown land.

ANTHONY: I cannot deny that some grief it is, cousin, indeed. But yet, as for me, it is not half so much as it would be if they could carry me out into any such unknown country that God could not know where nor find the means to come at me!
But now in good faith, cousin, if my migration into a strange country were any great grief unto me, the fault should be much in myself. For since I am very sure that whithersoever man convey me, God is no more verily here than he shall be there, if I get (as I can, if I will) the grace to set mine whole heart upon him and long for nothing but him, it can then make no matter to my mind, whether they carry me hence or leave me here. And then, if I find my mind much offended therewith, that I am not still here in mine own country, I must consider that the cause of my grief is mine own wrong imagination, whereby I beguile myself with an untrue persuasion, thinking that this were mine own country. Whereas in truth it is not so, for, as St. Paul saith, "We have here no city nor dwelling-country at all, but we seek for one that we shall come to." And in whatsoever country we walk in this world, we are but as pilgrims and wayfaring men. And if I should take

any country for mine own, it must be the country to which I come and not the country from which I came. That country, which shall be to me then for a while so strange, shall yet perdy be no more strange to me—nor longer strange to me, neither—than was mine own native country when first I came into it. And therefore if my being far from hence be very grievous to me, and I find it a great pain that I am not where I wish to be, that grief shall in great part grow for lack of sure setting and settling my mind in God, where it should be. And when I mend that fault of mine, I shall soon ease my grief.

Now, as for all the other griefs and pains that are in captivity, thraldom, and bondage, I cannot deny that many there are and great. Howbeit, they seem yet somewhat the more—what say I, "somewhat"? I may say a great deal the more—because we took our former liberty for a great deal more than indeed it was.

Let us therefore consider the matter thus: Captivity, bondage, or thraldom, what is it but the violent restraint of a man, being so subdued under the dominion, rule, and power of another that he must do whatever the other please to command him, and may not do at his liberty such things as he please himself? Now, when we shall be carried away by a Turk and be fain to be occupied about such things as he please to set us, we shall lament the loss of our liberty and think we bear a heavy burden of our servile condition. And we shall have, I grant well, many times great occasion to do so. But yet we should, I suppose, set somewhat the less by it, if we would remember well what liberty that was that we lost, and take it for no larger than it was indeed. For we reckon as though we might before do what we would, but in that we deceive ourselves. For what free man is there so free that he can be suffered to do what he please? In many things God hath restrained us by his high commandment—so many, that of those things which we would otherwise do, I daresay it be more than half. Howbeit, because (God forgive us) we forbear so little for all that, but do what we please as though we heard him not, we reckon our liberty never the less. But then is our liberty much restrained by the laws made by man, for the quiet and politic governance of the people. And these too would, I suppose, hinder our liberty but little, were it not for the fear of the penalties that fall thereupon. Look then, whether other men who have authority over us never command us some business which we dare not but do, and therefore often do it full sore against our wills. Some such service is sometimes so painful and so perilous too, that no lord can command his bondsmen worse, and seldom doth command him half so sore. Let every free man who reckoneth his liberty to stand in doing what he please, consider well these points, and I daresay he shall then find his liberty much less than he took it for before.

And yet have I left untouched the bondage that almost every man is in who boasteth himself for free—the bondage, I mean, of sin. And that it be a true bondage, I shall have our Saviour himself to bear me good record. For he saith, "Every man who committeth sin is the thrall, or the bondsman, of sin." And then if this be thus (as it must needs be, since God saith it is so), who is there then who can make so much boast of his liberty that he should take it for so sore a thing and so strange to become through chance of war, bondsman unto a man, since he is already through sin become willingly thrall and bondsman unto the devil?

Let us look well how many things, and of what vile wretched sort, the devil driveth us to do daily, through the rash turns of our blind affections, which we are fain to follow, for our faultful lack of grace, and are too feeble to refrain. And then shall we find in our natural freedom our bondservice such that never was there any man lord of any so vile a bondsman that he ever would command him to so shameful service. And let us, in the doing of our service to the man that we be slave unto, remember what we were wont to do about the same time of day while we were at our free liberty before, and would be well likely, if we were at liberty, to do again. And we shall peradventure perceive that it were better for us to do this business than that. Now we shall have great occasion of comfort, if we consider that our servitude, though in the account of the world it seem to come by chance of war, cometh unto us yet in very deed by the provident hand of God, and that for our great good if we will take it well, both in remission of sins and also as matter of our merit.

The greatest grief that is in bondage or captivity, I believe, is this: that we are forced to do such labour as with our good will we would not. But then against that grief, Seneca teacheth us a good remedy: "Endeavour thyself evermore that thou do nothing against thy will, but the things that we see we shall needs do, let us always put our good will thereto."

VINCENT: That is soon said, uncle, but it is hard to do.

ANTHONY: Our froward mind maketh every good thing hard, and that to our own more hurt and harm. But in this case, if we will be good Christian men, we shall have great cause gladly to be content, for the great comfort that we may take thereby. For we remember that in the patient and glad doing of our service unto that man for God's sake, according to his high commandment by the mouth of St. Paul, "Servi obedite dominis carnalibus," we shall have our thanks and our whole reward of God.

Finally, if we remember the great humble meekness of our Saviour Christ himself—that he, being very almighty God, "humbled himself and took the form of a bondsman or slave," rather than that his Father should forsake us—we may think ourselves very ungrateful caitiffs (and very frantic fools, too) if, rather than to endure this worldly bondage for awhile, we would forsake him who hath by his own death delivered us out of everlasting bondage to the devil, and who will for our short bondage give us everlasting liberty.

VINCENT: Well fare you, good uncle, this is very well said! Albeit that bondage is a condition that every man of any spirit would be very glad to eschew and very loth to fall in, yet have you well made it so open that it is a thing neither so strange nor so sore as it before seemed to me. And specially is it far from such as any man who hath any wit should, for fear of it, shrink from the confession of his faith. And now, therefore, I pray you, speak somewhat of imprisonment.

## XIX

ANTHONY: That shall I, cousin, with good will. And first, if we could consider what thing imprisonment is of its own nature methinketh we should not have so great horror of it. For of itself it is, perdy, but a restraint of liberty, which hindereth a man from going whither he would.

VINCENT: Yes, by St. Mary, uncle, but methinketh it is much more sorry than that. For beside the hindrance and restraint of liberty, it hath many more displeasures and very sore griefs knit and adjoined to it.

ANTHONY: That is, cousin, very true indeed. And those pains, among many sorer than those, thought I not afterward to forget. Howbeit, I purpose now to consider first imprisonment as imprisonment alone, without any other incommodity besides. For a man may be imprisoned, perdy, and yet not set in the stocks or collared fast by the neck. And a man may be let walk at large where he will, and yet have a pair of fetters fast riveted on his legs. For in this country, you know, and Seville and Portugal too, so go all the slaves. Howbeit, because for such things men's hearts have such horror of it, albeit that I am not so mad as to go about to prove that bodily pain were no pain, yet since it is because of this manner of pains that we so especially abhor the state and condition of prisoners, methinketh we should well perceive that a great part of our horror groweth of our own fancy. Let us call to mind and consider the state and condition of many other folk in whose state and condition we would wish ourselves to stand, taking them for no prisoners at all, who stand yet for all that in many of the selfsame points that we abhor imprisonment for. Let us therefore consider these things in order. First, those other kinds of grief that come with imprisonment are but accidents unto it. And yet they are neither such accidents as be proper unto it, since they may almost all befall man without it; nor are they such accidents as be inseparable from it, since imprisonment may fall to a man and none of them therein. We will, I say, therefore begin by considering what manner of pain or incommodity we should reckon imprisonment to be of itself and of its own nature alone. And then in the course of our communication, you shall as you please increase and aggravate the cause of your horror with the terror of those painful accidents.

VINCENT: I am sorry that I did interrupt your tale, for you were about, I see well, to take an orderly way therein. And as you yourself have devised, so I beseech you proceed. For though I reckon imprisonment much the sorer thing by sore and hard handling therein, yet reckon I not the imprisonment of itself any less than a thing very tedious, although it were used in the most favourable manner that it possibly could be.

For, uncle, if a great prince were taken prisoner upon the field, and in the hand of a Christian king, such as are accustomed, in such cases, for the consideration of their former estate and mutable chance of war, to show much humanity to them, and treat them in very favourable wise—for these infidel emperors handle oftentimes the princes that they take more villainously than they do the poorest men, as the great Tamberlane kept the great Turk, when he had taken him, to tread on his back always when he leapt on horseback. But, as I began to say, by the example of a prince taken prisoner, were the imprisonment never so favourable, yet it would be, to my mind, no little grief in itself for a man to be penned up, though not in a narrow chamber. But although his walk were right large and right fair gardens in it too, it could not but grieve his heart to be restrained by another man within certain limits and bounds, and lose the liberty to be where he please.

ANTHONY: This is, cousin, well considered of you. For in this you perceive well that imprisonment is, of itself and of its own very nature alone, nothing else but the retaining of a man's person within the circuit of a certain space, narrower or larger as shall be limited to him, restraining his liberty from going further into any other place.

VINCENT: Very well said, methinketh.

ANTHONY: Yet I forgot, cousin, to ask you one question.

VINCENT: What is that, uncle?

ANTHONY: This, lo: If there be two men kept in two several chambers of one great castle, of which two chambers the one is much larger than the other, are they prisoners both, or only the one who has the less room to walk in?

VINCENT: What question is it, uncle, but that they are both prisoners, as I said myself before, although the one lay fast locked in the stocks and the other had all the whole castle to walk in?

ANTHONY: Methinketh verily, cousin, that you say the truth. And then, if imprisonment be such a thing as you yourself here agree it is—that is, but a lack of liberty to go whither we please—now would I fain know of you what one man you know who is at this day out of prison?

VINCENT: What one man, uncle? Marry, I know almost none other! For surely I am acquainted with no prisoner, that I remember.

ANTHONY: Then I see well that you visit poor prisoners seldom.

VINCENT: No, by my troth, uncle, I cry God mercy. I send them sometimes mine alms, but by my troth I love not to come myself where I should see such misery.

ANTHONY: In good faith, Cousin Vincent (though I say it before you) you have many good qualities, but surely (though I say that before you, too) that is not one of them. If you would amend it, then should you have yet the more good qualities by one—and peradventure the more by three or four. For I assure you it is hard to tell how much good it doth to a man's soul, the personal visiting of poor prisoners.

But now, since you can name me none of them that are in prison, I pray you name me some one of all those whom you are, you say, better acquainted with—men, I mean, who are out of prison. For I know, methinketh, as few of them as you know of the others.

VINCENT: That would, uncle, be a strange case. For every man is out of prison who may go where he will, though he be the poorest beggar in the town. And, in good faith, uncle (because you reckon imprisonment so small a matter of itself) meseemeth the poor beggar who is at his liberty and may walk where he will is in better case than is a king kept in prison, who cannot go but where men give him leave.

ANTHONY: Well, cousin, whether every way-walking beggar be, by this reason, out of prison or no, we shall consider further when you will. But in the meanwhile I can by this reason see no prince who seemeth to be out of prison. For if the lack of liberty to go where a man will, be imprisonment, as you yourself say it is, then is the great Turk, by whom we fear to be put in prison, in prison already himself, for he may not go where he will. For if he could he would go into Portugal, Italy, Spain, France, Germany, and England, and as far in the other direction too—both into Prester John's land and into the Grand Cham's too.

Now, the beggar that you speak of, if he be (as you say he is) by reason of his liberty to go where he will, in much better case than a king kept in prison, because he cannot go but where men give him leave; then is that beggar in better case, not only than a prince in prison but also than many a prince out of prison too. For I am sure there is many a beggar who may without hindrance walk further upon other men's ground than many a prince at his best liberty may walk upon his own. And as for walking out abroad upon other men's, that prince might be withstood and held fast, where that beggar, with his bag and staff, might be suffered to go forth and keep on his way.

But forasmuch, cousin, as neither the beggar nor the prince is at free liberty to walk where they will, but neither of them would be suffered to walk in some places without men withstanding them and saying them nay; therefore if imprisonment be, as you grant it is, a lack of liberty to go where we please, I cannot see but the beggar and the prince, whom you reckon both at liberty, are by your own reason restrained in prison both.

VINCENT: Yea, but uncle, both the one and the other have way enough to walk—the one in his own ground and the other in other men's, or in the common highway, where they may both walk till they be weary of walking ere any man say them nay.

ANTHONY: So may, cousin, that king who had, as you yourself put the case, all the whole castle to walk in. And yet you deny not that he is prisoner for all that—though not so straitly kept, yet as verily prisoner as he that lieth in the stocks.

VINCENT: But they may go at least to every place that they need, or that is commodious for them, and therefore they do not wish to go anywhere but where they may. And therefore they are at liberty to go where they will.

ANTHONY: I need not, cousin, to spend the time about impugning every part of this answer. Let pass by that, though a prisoner were brought with his keeper into every place where need required, yet since he might not when he wished go where he wished for his pleasure alone, he would be, as you know well, a prisoner still. And let pass over also that it would be needful for this beggar, and commodious for this king, to go into divers places where neither of them may come. And let pass also that neither of them is lightly so temperately determined by what they both fain would so do indeed, if this reason of yours put them out of prison and set them at liberty and made them free, as I will well grant it doth if they so do indeed—that is, if they have no will to go anywhere but where they may go indeed.

Then let us look on our other prisoners enclosed within a castle, and we shall find that the straitest kept of them both, if he get the wisdom and grace to quiet his mind and hold himself content with that place, and not long (as a woman with child longeth for her desires) to be gadding out anywhere else, is by the same reason of yours, while his will is not longing to be anywhere else, he is, I say, at his free liberty to be where he will. And so he is out of prison too.

And, on the other hand, if, though his will be not longing to be anywhere else, yet because if his will so were he should not be so suffered, he is therefore not at his free liberty but a prisoner still, since your free beggar that you speak of and the prince that you call out of prison too, though they be (which I daresay few be) by some special wisdom so temperately disposed that they will have not the will to be anywhere but where they see that they may be suffered to be, yet, since if they did have that will they could not then be where they would, they lack the effect of free liberty and are both twain in prison too.

VINCENT: Well, uncle, if every man universally is by this reason in prison already, after the proper nature of imprisonment, yet to be imprisoned in this special manner which alone is commonly called imprisonment is a thing of great horror and fear, both for the straitness of the keeping and for the hard handling that many men have therein. Of all the griefs that you speak of, we feel nothing at all. And therefore every man abhorreth the one, and would be loth to come into it. And no man abhorreth the other, for they feel no harm and find no fault therein.

Therefore, uncle, in good faith, though I cannot find fitting answers with which to avoid your arguments, yet (to be plain with you and tell you the very truth) my mind findeth not itself satisfied on this point. But ever methinketh that these things, with which you rather convince and conclude me than induce a credence and persuade me that every man is in prison already, are but sophistical fancies, and that except those that are commonly called prisoners, other men are not in any prison at all.

ANTHONY: Well fare thine heart, good Cousin Vincent! There was, in good faith, no word that you spoke since we first talked of these matters that I liked half so well as these that you speak now. For if you had assented in words and your mind departed unpersuaded, then, if the thing be true that I say, yet had you lost the fruit. And if it be peradventure false, and I myself deceived therein, then, since I should have supposed that you liked it too, you would have confirmed me in my folly. For, in good faith, cousin, such an old fool am I that this thing (in the persuading of which unto you I had thought I had quit me well, and yet which, when I have all done, appeareth to your mind but a trifle and sophistical fancy) I myself have so many years taken it for so very substantial truth that as yet my mind cannot give me to think it any other. But I would not play the part of that French priest who had so long used to say Dominus with the second syllable long that at least he thought it must needs be so, and was ashamed to say it short. So to the intent that you may the better perceive me and I may the better perceive myself, we shall here between us a little more consider the thing. So spit well on your hands boldly, and take good hold, and give it not over against your own mind, for then we would be never the nearer.

VINCENT: Nay, by my troth, uncle, that intend I not to do. Nor have I done it yet since we began. And that may you well perceive by some things which, without any great cause, save for the further satisfaction of my own mind, I repeated and debated again.

ANTHONY: That guise, cousin, you must hold on boldly still. For I purpose to give up my part in this matter, unless I make you yourself perceive both that every man universally is a very prisoner in very prison—plainly, without any sophistry at all—and also that there is no prince living upon earth who is not in a worse case prisoner by this general imprisonment that I speak of, than is many a simple ignorant wretch by that special imprisonment that you speak of. And beside this, that in this general imprisonment that I speak of, men are for the time that they are in it, so sore handled and so hardly and in such painful wise, that men's hearts have with reason great cause to abhor this hard handling that is in this imprisonment as sorely as they do the other that is in that.

VINCENT: By my troth, uncle, these things would I fain see well proved.

ANTHONY: Tell me, then, cousin, first by your troth: If a man were attainted of treason or felony; and if, after judgment had been given of his death and it were determined that he should die, the time of his execution were only delayed till the king's further pleasure should be known; if he were thereupon delivered to certain keepers and put up in a sure place out of which he could not escape—would this man be a prisoner, or not?

VINCENT: This man, quoth he? Yea, marry, that would he be in very deed, if ever man were!

ANTHONY: But now what if, for the time that were between his attainder and his execution, he were so favourably handled that he were suffered to do what he would, as he did while he was free—to have the use of his lands and his goods, and his wife and his children to have license to be with him, and his friends leave at liberty to resort unto him, and his servants not forbidden to abide about him. And add yet thereunto that the place were a great castle royal with parks and other pleasures in it, a very great circuit about. Yes, and add yet, if you like, that he were suffered to go and ride also, both when he wished and whither he wished; only this one point always provided and foreseen, that he should ever be surely seen to, and safely kept from escaping. So though he had never so much of his own will in the meanwhile (in all matters save escaping), yet he should well know that escape he could not, and that when he were called for, to execution and to death he should go.

Now, Cousin Vincent, what would you call this man? A prisoner, because he is kept for execution? Or no prisoner, because he is in the meanwhile so favourably handled and suffered to do all that he would, save escape? And I bid you not here be hasty in your answer, but advise it well that you grant no such thing in haste as you would afterward at leisure mislike, and think yourself deceived.

VINCENT: Nay, by my troth, uncle, this thing needeth no study at all, to my mind. But, for all this favour showed him and all this liberty lent him, yet being condemned to death, and being kept for it, and kept with sure watch laid upon him that he cannot escape, he is all that while a very plain prisoner still.

ANTHONY: In good faith, cousin, methinketh you say very true. But then one thing must I yet desire you, cousin, to tell me a little further. If there were another laid in prison for a brawl, and through the jailors' displeasure were bolted and fettered and laid in a low dungeon in the stocks, where he might lie peradventure for a while and abide in the meantime some pain but no danger of death at all, but that out again he should come well enough—which of these two prisoners would stand in the worse case? He that hath all this favour, or he that is thus hardly handled?

VINCENT: By our Lady, uncle, I believe that most men, if they should needs choose, had liefer be such prisoners in every point as he who so sorely lieth in the stocks, than in every point such as he who walketh at such liberty about the park.

ANTHONY: Consider, then, cousin, whether this thing seem any sophistry to you that I shall show you now. For it shall be such as seemeth in good faith substantially true to me. And if it so happen that you think otherwise, I will be very glad to perceive which of us both is beguiled.

For it seemeth to me, cousin, first, that every man coming into this world here upon earth as he is created by God, so cometh he hither by the providence of God. Is this any sophistry first, or not?

VINCENT: Nay, verily, this is very substantial truth.

ANTHONY: Now take I this, also, for very truth in my mind: that there cometh no man nor woman hither into the earth but what, ere ever they come alive into the world out of the mother's womb, God condemneth them unto death by his own sentence and judgment, for the original sin that they bring with them, contracted in the corrupted stock of our forefather Adam. Is this, think you, cousin, verily thus or not?

VINCENT. This is, uncle, very true indeed.

ANTHONY: Then seemeth this true further unto me: that God hath put every man here upon the earth under so sure and so safe keeping that of all the whole people living in this wide world, there is neither man, woman, nor child—would they never so far wander about and seek it—who can possibly find any way by which they can escape from death. Is this, cousin, a fond imagined fancy, or is it very truth indeed?

VINCENT: Nay, this is no imagination, uncle, but a thing so clearly proved true that no man is so mad as to deny it.

ANTHONY: Then need I say no more, cousin. For then is all the matter plain and open evident truth, which I said I took for truth. And it is yet a little more now than I told you before, when you took my proof yet but for a sophistical fancy, and said that, for all my reasoning that every man is a prisoner, yet you thought that, except those whom the common people call prisoners, there is else no man a very prisoner indeed. And now you grant yourself again for very substantial truth, that every man, though he be the greatest king upon earth, is set here by the ordinance of God in a place, be it never so large, yet a place, I say (and you say the same) out of which no man can escape. And you grant that every man is there put under sure and safe keeping to be readily set forth when God calleth for him, and that then he shall surely die. And is not then, cousin, by your own granting before, every man a very prisoner, when he is put in a place to be kept to be brought forth when he would not, and himself knows not whither?

VINCENT: Yes, in good faith, uncle, I cannot but well perceive this to be so.

ANTHONY: This would be true, you know, even though a man were but taken by the arm and in a fair manner led out of this world unto his judgment. But now, we well know that there is no king so great but what, all the while he walketh here, walk he never so loose, ride he with never so strong an army for his defence, yet he himself is very sure—though he seek in the meantime some other pastime to put it out of his mind—yet is he very sure, I say, that escape he cannot. And very well he knoweth that he hath already sentence given upon him to die, and that verily die he shall. And though he hope for long respite of his execution, yet can he not tell how soon it will be. And therefore, unless he be a fool, he can never be without fear that, either on the morrow or on the selfsame day, the grisly cruel hangman Death, who from his first coming in hath ever hoved aloof and looked toward him, and ever lain in wait for him, shall amid all his royalty and all his main strength neither kneel before him nor make him any reverence, nor with any good manner desire him to come forth. But he shall rigorously and fiercely grip him by the very breast, and make all his bones rattle, and so by long and divers sore torments strike him stark dead in his prison. And then shall he cause his body to be cast into the ground in a foul pit in some corner of the same, there to rot and be eaten by the wretched worms of the earth, sending yet his soul out further into a more fearful judgment. Of that judgment at his temporal death his success is uncertain and therefore, though by God's grace not out of good hope, for all that in the meanwhile in very sore dread and fear and peradventure in peril inevitable of eternal fire, too.

Methinketh therefore, cousin, that, as I told you, this keeping of every man in this wretched world for execution of death is a very plain imprisonment indeed. And it is, as I say, such that the greatest king is in this prison in much worse case, for all his wealth, than is many a man who, in the other imprisonment, is sore and hardly handled. For while some of those lie not there attainted nor condemned to death, the greatest man of this world and the most wealthy in this universal prison is laid in to be kept undoubtedly for death.

VINCENT: But yet, uncle, in that case is the other prisoner too, for he is as sure that he shall die, perdy.

ANTHONY: This is very true, cousin, indeed, and well objected too.

But then you must consider that he is not in danger of death by reason of the prison into which he is put peradventure but for a little brawl, but his danger of death is by the other imprisonment, by which he is prisoner in the great prison of this whole earth, in which prison all the princes of the world be prisoners as well as he.

If a man condemned to death were put up in a large prison, and while his execution were respited he were, for fighting with his fellows, put up in a strait place, part of that prison, then would he be in danger of death in that strait prison, but not by the being in that, for there is he but for the brawl. But his deadly imprisonment was the other—the larger, I say, into which he was put for death. So the prisoner that you speak of is, beside the narrow prison, a prisoner of the broad world, and all the princes of the world are prisoners there with him. And by that imprisonment both they and he are in like danger of death, not by that strait imprisonment that is commonly called imprisonment, but by that imprisonment which, because of the large walk, men call liberty—and which you therefore thought but a sophistical fancy to prove it a prison at all!

But now may you, methinketh, very plainly perceive that this whole earth is not only for all the whole of mankind a very plain prison indeed, but also that all men without exception (even those that are most at their liberty in it, and reckon themselves great lords and possessors of very great pieces of it, and thereby wax with wantonness so forgetful of their state that they think they stand in great wealth) do stand for all that indeed, by reason of their imprisonment in this large prison of the whole earth, in the selfsame condition that the others do stand who, in the narrow prisons which alone are called prisons, and which alone are reputed prisons in the opinion of the common people, stand in the most fearful and in the most odious case—that is, condemned already to death.

And now, cousin, if this thing that I tell you seem but a sophistical fancy of your mind, I would be glad to know what moveth you so to think. For, in good faith, as I have told you twice, I am no wiser but what I verily think that it is very plain truth indeed.

## XX

VINCENT: In good faith, uncle, thus far I not only cannot make resistance against it with any reason, but also I see very clearly proved that it cannot be otherwise. For every man must be in this world a very prisoner, since we are all put here into a sure hold to be kept till we be put unto execution, as folk all already condemned to death.

But yet, uncle, the strait-keeping, collaring, bolting, and stocking, with lying on straw or on the cold ground (which manner of hard handling is used in these special imprisonments that alone are commonly called by that name) must needs make that imprisonment much more odious and dreadful than the general imprisonment with which we are every man universally imprisoned at large, walking where we will round about the wide world. For in this broad prison, outside of those narrow prisons, there is no such hard handling used with the prisoners.

ANTHONY: I said, I think, cousin, that I purposed to prove to you further that in this general prison—the large prison, I mean, of this whole world—folk are, for the time that they are in it, as sore handled and as hardly, and wrenched and wrung and broken in such painful wise, that our hearts (save that we consider it not) have with reason good and great cause to grudge against the hard handling that there is in this prison—and, as far as pertaineth only to the respect of pain, as much horror to conceive against it—as against the other that there is in that one.

VINCENT: Indeed, uncle, it is true that you said you would prove this.

ANTHONY: Nay, so much said I not, cousin! But I said that I would if I could, and if I could not, then would I therein give over my part. But I trust, cousin, that I shall not need to do that—the thing seemeth to me so plain.
For, cousin, not only the prince and king but also the chief jailor over this whole broad prison the world (though he have both angels and devils who are jailors under him) is, I take it, God. And that I suppose you will grant me, too.

VINCENT: That will I not deny, uncle.

ANTHONY: If a man, cousin, be committed unto prison for no cause but to be kept, though there be never so great a charge against him, yet his keeper, if he be good and honest, is neither so cruel as to pain the man out of malice, nor so covetous as to put him to pain to make him seek his friends and pay for a pennyworth of ease. If the place be such that he is sure to keep him safe otherwise, or if he can get surety for the recompense of more harm than he seeth he should have if he escaped, he will never handle him in any such hard fashion as we most abhor imprisonment for. But marry, if the place be such that the keeper cannot otherwise be sure, then is he compelled to keep him to that extent the straiter. And also if the prisoner be unruly and fall to fighting with his fellows or do some other manner of ill turns, then useth the keeper to punish him in some such fashions as you yourself have spoken of.
Now, cousin, God—the chief jailor, as I say, of this broad prison the world—is neither cruel nor covetous. And this prison is also so sure and so subtly built that, albeit that it lieth open on every side without any wall in the world, yet, wander we never so far about in it, we shall never find the way to get out. So God neither needeth to collar us nor to stock us for any fear of our escaping away. And therefore, unless he see some other cause than only our keeping for death, he letteth us in the meanwhile, for as long as he pleases to respite us, walk about in the prison and do there what we

will, using ourselves in such wise as he hath, by reason and revelation, from time to time told us his pleasure.

And hence it cometh, lo, that by reason of this favour for a time we wax, as I said, so wanton, that we forget where we are. And we think that we are lords at large, whereas we are indeed, if we would consider, even poor wretches in prison. For, of very truth, our very prison this earth is. And yet we apportion us out divers parts of it diversely to ourselves, part by covenants that we make among ourselves, and part by fraud and violence too. And we change its name from the odious name of prison, and call it our own land and our livelihood. Upon our prison we build; our prison we garnish with gold and make it glorious. In this prison they buy and sell; in this prison they brawl and chide. In this they run together and fight; in this they dice; in this they play at cards. In this they pipe and revel; in this they sing and dance. And in this prison many a man who is reputed right honest forbeareth not, for his pleasure in the dark, privily to play the knave.

And thus, while God our king and our chief jailor too, suffereth us and letteth us alone, we think ourselves at liberty. And we abhor the state of those whom we call prisoners, taking ourselves for no prisoners at all. In this false persuasion of wealth and forgetfulness of our own wretched state, which is but a wandering about for a while in this prison of this world, till we be brought unto the execution of death, we forget in our folly both ourselves and our jail, and our under-jailors the angels and devils both, and our chief jailor God too—God, who forgetteth not us, but seeth us all the while well enough. And being sore discontent to see so ill rule kept in the jail, he sendeth the hangman Death to put some to execution here and there, sometimes by the thousands at once. And he handleth many of the rest, whose execution he forbeareth yet unto a farther time, even as hardly and punisheth them as sorely, in this common prison of the world, as there are any handled in those special prisons which, for the hard handling used in them, you say your heart hath in such horror and so sore abhorreth.

VINCENT: The rest will I not gainsay, for methinketh I see it so indeed. But that God, our chief jailor in this world, useth any such prisonly fashion of punishment, that point must I needs deny. For I see him neither lay any man in the stocks, nor strike fetters on his legs, nor so much as shut him up in a chamber, neither.

ANTHONY: Is he no minstrel, cousin, who playeth not on a harp? Maketh no man melody but he who playeth on a lute? He may be a minstrel and make melody, you know, with some other instrument—a strange-fashioned one, peradventure, that never was seen before.

God, our chief jailor, as he himself is invisible, so useth he in his punishments invisible instruments. And therefore are they not of like fashion as those the other jailors use, but yet of like effect, and as painful in feeling as those. For he layeth one of his prisoners with a hot fever as ill at ease in a warm bed as the other jailor layeth his on the cold ground. He wringeth them by the brows with a migraine; he collareth them by the neck with a quinsy; he bolteth them by the arms with a palsy, so that they cannot lift their hands to their head; he manacleth their hands with the gout in their fingers; he wringeth them by the legs with the cramp in their shins; he bindeth them to the bed with the crick in the back; and he layeth one there at full length, as unable to rise as though he lay fast by the feet in the stocks.

A prisoner of another jail may sing and dance in his two fetters, and fear not his feet for stumbling at a stone, while God's prisoner, who hath his one foot fettered with the gout, lieth groaning on a couch, and quaketh and crieth out if he fear that there would fall on his foot no more than a cushion.

And therefore, cousin, as I said, if we consider it well, we shall find this general prison of this whole earth a place in which the prisoners are as sore handled as they are in the other. And even in the other some make as merry too as there do some in this one, who are very merry at large out of that. And surely as we think ourselves out of prison now, so if there were some folk born and brought up in a prison, who never came on the wall or looked out at the door or heard of another world outside, but saw some, for ill turns done among themselves, locked up in a straiter room; and if they heard them alone called prisoners who were so served and themselves ever called free folk at large; the like opinion would they have there of themselves then as we have here of ourselves now. And when we take ourselves for other than prisoners now, verily are we now as deceived as those prisoners would be then.

VINCENT: I cannot, uncle, in good faith deny that you have performed all that you promised. But yet, since, for all this, there appeareth no more but that as they are prisoners so are we too, and that as some of them are sore handled so are some of us too; we know well, for all this, that when we come to those prisons we shall not fail to be in a straiter prison than we are now, and to have a door shut upon us where we have none shut upon us now. This shall we be sure of at least if there come no worse—and then there may come worse, you know well, since it cometh there so commonly. And therefore is it yet little marvel that men's hearts grudge much against it.

ANTHONY: Surely, cousin, in this you say very well. Howbeit, your words would have touched me somewhat the nearer if I had said that imprisonment were no displeasure at all. But the thing that I say, cousin, for our comfort in the matter, is that our fancy frameth us a false opinion by which we deceive ourselves and take it for sorer than it is. And that we do because we take ourselves for more free before than we were, and imprisonment for a stranger thing to us than it is indeed. And thus far, as I say, I have proved truth in very deed.

But now the incommodities that you repeat again—those, I say, that are proper to the imprisonment of its own nature; that is, to have less room to walk and to have the door shut upon us—these are, methinketh, so very slender and slight that in so great a cause as to suffer for God's sake we might be sore ashamed so much as once to think upon them.

Many a good man there is, you know, who, without any force at all, or any necessity wherefor he should do so, suffereth these two things willingly of his own choice, with much other hardness more. Holy monks, I mean, of the Charterhouse order, such as never pass their cells save only to the church, which is set fast by their cells, and thence to their cells again. And St. Brigit's order, and St. Clare's much alike, and in a manner all enclosed religious houses. And yet anchorites and anchoresses most especially, all whose whole room is less than a good large chamber. And yet are they there as well content many long years together as are other men—and better, too—who walk about the world. And therefore you may see that the lothness of less room and the door shut upon us, since so many folk are so well content with them and will for God's love choose to live so, is but a horror enhanced of our own fancy.

And indeed I knew a woman once who came into a prison, to visit of her charity a poor prisoner there. She found him in a chamber that was fair enough, to say the truth—at least, it was strong enough! But with mats of straw the prisoner had made it so warm, both under foot and round about the walls, that in these things, for the keeping of his health, she was on his behalf very glad and very well comforted. But among many other displeasures that for his sake she was sorry for, one she lamented much in her mind. And that was that he should have the chamber door made fast upon him by night, by the jailor who was to shut him in. "For, by my troth," quoth she, "if the door should be shut upon me, I think it would stop up my breath!" At that word of hers the prisoner laughed in his mind—but he dared not laugh aloud or say anything to her, for indeed he stood somewhat in awe of her, and he had his food there in great part of her charity for alms. But he could not but laugh inwardly, for he knew well enough that she used to shut her own chamber door full surely on the inside every night, both door and windows too, and used not to open them all the long night. And what difference, then, as to the stopping of the breath, whether they were shut up within or without?

And so surely, cousin, these two things that you speak of are neither one of so great weight that in Christ's cause they ought to move a Christian man. And one of the twain is so very childish a fancy, that in a matter almost of three chips (unless it were a chance of fire) it should never move any man.

As for those other accidents of hard handling, I am not so mad as to say that they are no grief, but I say that our fear may imagine them much greater grief than they are. And I say that such as they be, many a man endureth them—yea, and many a woman too—who afterward fareth full well.

And then would I know what determination we take—whether for our Saviour's sake to suffer some pain in our bodies, since he suffered in his blessed body so great pain for us, or else to give him warning and be at a point utterly to forsake him rather than to suffer any pain at all? He who cometh in his mind unto this latter point—from which kind of unkindness God keep every man!—he needeth no comfort, for he will flee the need. And counsel, I fear, availeth him little, if grace be so far gone from him. But, on the other hand, if, rather than to forsake our Saviour, we determine ourselves to suffer any pain at all, I cannot then see that the fear of hard handling should anything stick with us and make us to shrink so that we would rather forsake his faith than suffer for his sake so much as imprisonment. For the handling is neither such in prison but what many men, and many women too, live with it many years and sustain it, and afterward yet fare full well. And yet it may well fortune that, beside the bare imprisonment, there shall happen to us no hard handling at all. Or else it may happen to us for only a short while—and yet, beside all this, peradventure not at all. And which of all these ways shall be taken with us, lieth all in his will for whom we are content to take it, and who for that intent of ours favoureth us and will suffer no man to put more pain to us than he well knoweth we shall be able to bear. For he himself will give us the strength for it, as you have heard his promise already by the mouth of St. Paul: "God is faithful, who suffereth you not to be tempted above what you may bear, but giveth also with the temptation a way out."

But now, if we have not lost our faith already before we come to forsake it for fear, we know very well by our faith that, by the forsaking of our faith, we fall into that state to be cast into the prison of hell. And that can we not tell how soon; but, as it may be that God will suffer us to live a while here upon earth, so may it be that he will throw us into that dungeon beneath before the time that the Turk shall once ask us the question. And therefore, if we fear imprisonment so sore, we are much more than mad if we fear not most the imprisonment that is far more sore. For out of that prison shall no man ever get, and in this other shall no man abide but a while.

In prison was Joseph while his brethren were at large; and yet afterward were his brethren fain to seek upon him for bread. In prison was Daniel, and the wild lions about him; and yet even there God kept him harmless and brought him safe out again. If we think that he will not do the like for us, let us not doubt that he will do for us either the like or better, for better may he do for us if he suffer us there to die. St. John the Baptist was, you know, in prison, while Herod and Herodias sat full merry at the feast, and the daughter of Herodias delighted them with her dancing, till with her dancing she danced off St. John's head. And now sitteth he with great feast in heaven at God's board, while Herod and Herodias full heavily sit in hell burning both twain, and to make them sport withal the devil with the damsel dance in the fire before them.

Finally, cousin, to finish this piece, our Saviour was himself taken prisoner for our sake. And prisoner was he carried, and prisoner was he kept, and prisoner was he brought forth before Annas, and prisoner from Annas carried unto Caiphas. Then prisoner was he carried from Caiphas unto Pilate, and prisoner was he sent from Pilate to King Herod, and prisoner from Herod unto Pilate again. And so was he kept as prisoner to the end of his passion. The time of his imprisonment, I grant you, was not long. But as for hard handling, which our hearts most abhor, he had as much in that short while as many men among them all in a much longer time. And surely, then, if we consider of what estate he was and also that he was prisoner in that wise for our sake, we shall, I think, unless we be worse than wretched beasts, never so shamefully play the ungrateful coward as sinfully to forsake him for fear of imprisonment.

Nor shall we be so foolish either as, by forsaking him, to give him the occasion to forsake us in turn. For so should we, with the avoiding of an easier prison, fall into a worse. And instead of the prison that cannot keep us long, we should fall into that prison out of which we can never come, though the short imprisonment should have won us everlasting liberty.

## XXI

VINCENT: Forsooth, uncle, if we feared not further, beside imprisonment, the terrible dart of shameful and painful death, I would verily trust that, as for imprisonment, remembering these things which I have here heard from you (our Lord reward you for them!) rather than that I should forsake the faith of our Saviour, I would with help of grace never shrink at it.

But now are we come, uncle, with much work at last unto the last and uttermost point of the dread that maketh this incursion of this midday devil—this open invasion of the Turk and his persecution against the faith—seem so terrible unto men's minds. Although the respect of God vanquish all the rest of the trouble that we have hitherto perused (as loss of goods, lands, and liberty), yet, when we remember the terror of shameful and painful death, that point suddenly putteth us in oblivion of all that should be our comfort. And we feel (all men, I fear me, for the most part) the fervour of our faith wax so cold and our hearts so faint that we find ourselves at the point of falling even for fear.

ANTHONY: I deny not, cousin, that indeed in this point is the sore pinch. And yet you see, for all this, that even this point too taketh increase or diminishment of dread according to the difference of the affections that are beforehand fixed and rooted in the mind—so much so, that you may see a man set so much by his worldly substance that he feareth less the loss of his life than the loss of lands. Yea, you may see a man abide deadly torment, such as some other man had rather die than endure, rather than to bring out the money that he hath hid. And I doubt not but that you have heard by right authentic stories of many men who (some for one cause, some for another) have not hesitated willingly to suffer death, divers in divers kinds, and some both with despiteful rebuke and painful torment too. And therefore, as I say, we may see that the affection of the mind toward the increase or decrease of dread maketh much of the matter.

Now the affections of men's minds are imprinted by divers means. One way is by means of the bodily senses, moved by such things, pleasant or unpleasant, as are outwardly offered unto them through sensible worldly things. And this manner of receiving the impression of affections is common unto men and beasts. Another manner of receiving affections is by means of reason, which both ordinately tempereth those affections that the five bodily senses imprint, and also disposeth a man many times to some spiritual virtues very contrary to those affections that are fleshly and sensual. And those reasonable dispositions are spiritual affections, and proper to the nature of man, and above the nature of beasts. Now, as our ghostly enemy the devil enforceth himself to make us lean to the sensual affections and beastly, so doth almighty God of his goodness by his Holy Spirit inspire us good motions, with the aid and help of his grace, toward the other spiritual affections. And by sundry means he instructeth our reason to lean to them, and not only to receive them as engendered and planted in our soul, but also in such wise to water them with the wise advertisement of godly counsel and continual prayer, that they may become habitually radicated and surely take deep root therein. And according as the one kind of affection or the other beareth the strength in our heart, so are we stronger or feebler against the terror of death in this cause.

And therefore, cousin, will we essay to consider what things there are for which we have cause in reason to master the fearful affection and sensual. And though we cannot clean avoid it and put it away, yet will we essay in such wise to bridle it at least that it run not out so far like a headstrong horse that, in spite of our teeth, it carry us out unto the devil.

Let us therefore now consider and well weigh this thing that we dread so sore—that is, shameful and painful death.

## XXII

And first I perceive well by these two things that you join unto "death"—that is, "shameful" and "painful"—that you would esteem death so much the less if it should come along without either shame or pain.

VINCENT: Without doubt, uncle, a great deal the less. But yet, though it should come without them both, by itself, I know well many a man would be for all that very loth to die.

ANTHONY: That I believe well, cousin, and the more pity it is. For that affection happeth in very few without the cause being either lack of faith, lack of hope, or finally lack of wit.

Those who believe not the life to come after this, and think themselves here in wealth, are loth to leave this life, for then they think they lose all. And thence come the manifold foolish unfaithful words which are so rife in our many mouths: "This world we know, and the other we know not." And some say in sport (and think in earnest), "The devil is not so black as he is painted," and "Let him be as black as he will, he is no blacker than a crow!" with many such other foolish fancies of the same sort.

There are some who believe well enough but who, through lewdness of living, fall out of good hope of salvation. And then I very little marvel that they are loth to die. Howbeit, some who purpose to mend and would fain have some time left them longer to bestow somewhat better, may peradventure be loth to die also forthwith. And albeit that a very good will gladly to die and to be with God would be, to my mind, so thankful that it would be well able to purchase as full remission both of sin and pain as peradventure he would be like to purchase, if he lived, in many years' penance, yet will I not say but what such a kind of lothness to die may be approvable before God.

There are some also who are loth to die, who are yet very glad to die and long for to be dead.

VINCENT: That would be, uncle, a very strange case!

ANTHONY: The case, I fear me, cousin, falleth not very often. But yet sometimes it doth, as where there is any man of that good mind that St. Paul was. For the longing that he had to be with God, he would fain have been dead, but for the profit of other folk he was content to live here in pain, and defer and forbear for the while his inestimable bliss in heaven: "Desiderium habens dissolvi et esse cum Christo, multo magis melius, permanere autem in carne, necessarium propter vos."

But of all these kinds of folk, cousin, who are loth to die (except for the first kind only, who lack faith), there is I suppose none who would hesitate, for the bare respect of death alone, unless the fear of shame or sharp pain joined unto death should be the hindrance, to depart hence with good will in this case of the faith. For he would well know by his faith that his death, taken for the faith, should cleanse him clean of all his sins and send him straight to heaven. And some of these (namely the last kind) are such that shame and pain both joined unto death would be unlikely to make them loathe death or fear death so sore but what they would suffer death in this case with good will, since they know well that the refusing of the faith, for any cause in this world (seemed the cause never so good), should yet sever them from God, with whom, save for other folk's profit, they so fain would be. And charity it cannot be, for the profit of the whole world, deadly to displease him who made it.

Some are these, I say also, who are loth to die for lack of wit. Albeit that they believe in the world that is to come and hope also to come thither, yet they love so much the wealth of this world and such things as delight them therein, that they would fain keep them as long as ever they can, even with tooth and nail. And when they can be suffered in no wise to keep it longer, but death taketh them from it, then, if it can be no better, they will agree to be, as soon as they be hence, hauled up into heaven and be with God forthwith! These folk as as very idiot fools as he who had kept from his childhood a bag full of cherry stones, and cast such a fancy to it that he would not go from it for a bigger bag filled with gold.

These folk fare, cousin, as Æsop telleth in a fable that the snail did. For when Jupiter (whom the poets feign for the great god) invited all the poor worms of the earth unto a great solemn feast that it pleased him upon a time—I have forgotten upon what occasion—to prepare for them, the snail kept her at home and would not come. And when Jupiter asked her afterward wherefore she came not to his feast, where he said she would have been welcome and have fared well, and would have seen a goodly palace and been delighted with many goodly pleasures, she answered him that she loved no place so well as her own house. With this answer Jupiter waxed so angry that he said, since she loved her house so well, she should never after go from home, but should always afterward bear her house upon her back wheresoever she went. And so hath she ever done since, as they say. And at least I know well she doth so now and hath done so as long as I can remember.

VINCENT: Forsooth, uncle, I should think the tale were not all feigned, for I think verily that so much of your tale is true!

ANTHONY: Æsop meant by that feigned fable to touch the folly of such folk as so set their fancy upon some small simple pleasure that they cannot find it in their heart to forbear it, either for the pleasure of a better man or for the gaining of a better thing. For by this foolish froward fashion they sometimes fall in great disgrace and take by it no little harm.

And surely such Christian folk as, by their foolish affection, which they have set like the snail upon their own house here on earth, cannot, for the lothness of leaving that house, find it in their hearts to go with good will to the great feast that God prepareth in heaven and of his goodness so graciously calleth them to—they are, I fear me, unless they mend that mind in time, like to be served as the snail was, and yet much worse too. For they are like to have their house here, the earth, bound fast on their backs for ever, and not to walk with it where they will, as the snail creepeth about with hers, but to lie fast bound in the midst of it with the foul fire of hell about them. For into this folly they bring themselves by their own fault, as the drunken man bringeth himself into drunkenness, whereby the evil that he doth in his drunkenness is not forgiven him for his folly, but to his pain is imputed to his fault.

VINCENT: Surely, uncle, this seemeth not unlikely, and by their fault they fall in such folly indeed. And yet, if this be folly indeed, then are some folk fools who think themselves right wise.

ANTHONY: Who think themselves wise? Marry, I never saw a fool yet who thought himself other than wise! For as it is one spark of soberness left in a drunken head when he perceiveth himself to be drunk and getteth himself fair to bed, so if a fool perceive himself a fool that point is no folly but a little spark of wit.

But now, cousin, as for these kind of fools, who are loth to die for the love that they bear to their worldly fancies which they would, by their death, leave behind them and forsake: Those who would for that cause rather forsake the faith than die, would rather forsake it than lose their worldly goods, though there were no peril of death offered them at all. And then, as touching those who are of that mind, we have, you know, said as much as you yourself thought sufficient this afternoon here before.

VINCENT: Verily, uncle, that is very true. And now have you rehearsed, as far as I can remember, all the other kinds of them that would be loth to die for any other respect than the grievous qualities of shame and pain joined unto death. And of all these kinds, except the kind of infidelity—when no comfort can help, but only counsel to the attaining of faith, for faith must be presupposed to the receiving of comfort and had ready before, as you showed in the beginning of our communication the first day that we talked of the matter. But else, I say, except that one kind, there is none of the rest of those that were before untouched who would be likely to forsake their faith in this persecution for the fear and dread of death, save for those grievous qualities—pain, I mean, and shame—that they see well would come with it.

And therefore, uncle, I pray you, give us some comfort against those twain. For in good faith, if death should come without them, in such a case at this is, in which by the losing of this life we should find a far better, mine own reason giveth me that, save for the other griefs going before the change, no man who hath wit would anything stick at all.

ANTHONY: Yes, peradventure suddenly they would, before they gather their wits unto them and well weigh the matter. But, cousin, those who will consider the matter well, reason, grounded upon the foundation of faith, shall show they very great substantial causes for which the dread of those grievous qualities that they see shall come with death—shame, I mean, and pain also—shall not so sore abash them as sinfully to drive them to that point. And for the proof thereof, let us first begin at the consideration of the shame.

## XXIII

How can any faithful wise man dread death so sore, for any respect of shame, when his reason and his faith together can shortly make him perceive that there is no true shame in it at all? For how can that death be shameful that is glorious? Or how can it be anything but glorious to die for the faith of Christ, if we die both for the faith and in the faith, joined with hope and charity? For the scripture plainly saith, "Precious in the sight of God is the death of his saints." Now if the death of his saints be glorious in the sight of God, it can never be shameful in very deed, however shameful it seem here in the sight of men. For here we may see and be sure that not only at the death of St. Stephen, to whom it pleased him to show himself with the heaven open over his head, but at the death also of every may who so dieth for the faith, God with his heavenly company beholdeth his whole passion and verily looketh on.

Now if it were so, cousin, that you should be brought through the broad high-street of a great long city; and if, all along the way that you were going, there were on one side of the way a rabble of ragged beggars and madmen, who would despise and dispraise you with all the shameful names that they could call you and all the villainous words that they could say to you; and if there were then, all along the other side of the same street where you should come by, a goodly company standing in a fair range, a row of wise and worshipful folk, lauding and commending you, more than fifteen times as many as that rabble of ragged beggars and railing madmen—would you willingly turn back, thinking that you went unto your shame, for the shameful jesting and railing of those mad foolish wretches? Or would you hold on your way with a good cheer and a glad heart, thinking yourself much honoured by the laud and approbation of that other honourable company?

VINCENT: Nay, by my troth, uncle, there is no doubt but that I would much regard the commendation of those commendable folk, and regard not a rush the railing of all those ribalds.

ANTHONY: Then, cousin, no man who hath faith can account himself shamed here, by any manner of death that he suffereth for the faith of Christ. For however vile and shameful it seem in the sight here of a few worldly wretches, it is lauded and approved for very precious and honourable in the sight of God and all the glorious company of heaven, who as perfectly stand and behold it as those foolish people do. And they are in number more than a hundred to one; and of that hundred, every one a hundred times more to be regarded and esteemed than a hundred such whole rabbles of the other.

And now, if a man would be so mad as to be ashamed, for fear of the rebuke that he should have of such rebukeful beasts, to confess the faith of Christ, then, with fleeing from a shadow of shame, he would fall into a true shame—and a deadly painful shame indeed! For then hath our Saviour made a sure promise that he will show himself ashamed of that man before the Father of heaven and all his holy angels, saying in the ninth chapter of Luke, "He who is ashamed of me and my words, of him shall the Son of Man be ashamed when he shall come in the majesty of himself and of his Father and of his holy angels." And what manner of shameful shame shall that be, then? If a man's cheeks glow sometimes for shame in this world, they will fall on fire for shame when Christ shall show himself ashamed of them there!

The blessed apostles reckoned it for great glory to suffer for Christ's faith the thing that we worldly wretched fools think to be villainy and shame. For they, when they were scourged, with despite and shame, and thereupon commanded to speak no more of the name of Christ, "went their way from the council joyful and glad that God had vouchsafed to do them the worship to suffer shameful despite for the name of Jesus." And so proud were they of the shame and villainous pain put unto them, that for all the forbidding of that great council assembled, they ceased not every day to preach out the name of Jesus still—not only in the temple, out of which they were set and whipped for the same before, but also, to double it with, they went preaching the name about from house to house, too.

Since we regard so greatly the estimation of worldly folk, I wish that we would, among the many wicked things that they do, regard also some such as are good. For it is a manner among them, in many places, that some by handicraft, some by merchandise, some by other kinds of living, arise and come forward in the world. And commonly folk are in their youth set forth to suitable masters, under whom they are brought up and grow. But now, whensoever they find a servant such that he disdaineth to do such things as his master did while he was himself a servant, that servant every man accounteth for a proud unthrift, never like to come to good proof. Let us, lo, mark and consider this, and weigh it well withal: Our master Christ (who is not only the master, but the maker too, of all this whole world) was not so proud as to disdain for our sakes the most villainous and most shameful death, after the worldly count, that then was used in the world. And he endured the most despiteful mocking therewith, joined to the most grievous pain, as crowning him with sharp thorn, so that the blood ran down about his face. Then they gave him a reed in his hand for a sceptre, and kneeled down to him and saluted him like a king in scorn, and beat then the reed upon the sharp thorns about his holy head. Now our Saviour saith that the disciple or servant is not above his master. And therefore, since our master endured so many kinds of painful shame, very proud beasts may we well think ourselves if we disdain to do as our master did. And whereas he through shame ascended into glory, we would be so mad that we would rather fall into everlasting shame, both before heaven and hell, than for fear of a short worldly shame to follow him to everlasting glory.

## XXIV

VINCENT: In good faith, uncle, as for the shame, you shall need to take no more pains. For I suppose surely that any man who hath reason in his head shall hold himself satisfied with this.

But, of truth, uncle, all the pinch is in the pain. For as for shame, I perceive well now that a man may with wisdom so master it that it shall nothing move him at all—so much so that it is become a common proverb in almost every country that "shame is as it is taken." But, by God, uncle, all the wisdom in this world can never so master pain but that pain will be painful, in spite of all the wit in this world!

ANTHONY: Truth it is, cousin, that no man can, with all the reason he hath, in such wise change the nature of pain that in the having of pain he feel it not. For unless it be felt, perdy, it is no pain. And that is the natural cause, cousin, for which a man may have his leg stricken off at the knee and it grieve him not—if his head be off but half an hour before!

But reason may make a reasonable man not to shrink from it and refuse it to his more hurt and harm. Though he would not be so foolish as to fall into it without cause, yet upon good causes—either of gaining some kind of great profit or avoiding some kind of great loss, or eschewing thereby the suffering of far greater pain—he would be content and glad to sustain it for his far greater advantage and commodity.

And this doth reason alone in many cases, where it hath much less help to take hold of than it hath in this matter of faith. For you know well that to take a sour and bitter potion is great grief and displeasure, and to be lanced and have the flesh cut is no little pain. Now, when such things are to be ministered either to a child or to some childish man, they will by their own wills let their sickness and their sore grow, unto their more grief, till it become incurable, rather than abide the pain of the curing in time. And that for faint heart, joined with lack of discretion. But a man who hath more wisdom, though without cause he would no more abide the pain willingly than would the other, yet, since reason showeth him what good he shall have by the suffering, and what harm by refusing it, this maketh him well content and glad also to take it.

Now then, if reason alone be sufficient to move a man to take pain for the gaining of worldly rest or pleasure and for the avoiding of another pain (though the pain he take be peradventure more, yet to be endured but for a short season), why should not reason, grounded upon the sure foundation of faith, and helped toward also with the aid of God's grace—as it ever is, undoubtedly, when folk for a good mind in God's name come together, our Saviour saying himself, "Where there are two or three are gathered together in my name, there am I also even in the very midst of them." Why should not then reason, I say, thus furthered with faith and grace, be much more able first to engender in us such an affection, and afterward, by long and deep meditation thereof, so to continue that affection that it shall turn into a habitual purpose, fast-rooted and deep, of patiently suffering the painful death of this body here in earth for the gaining of everlasting wealthy life in heaven and avoiding of everlasting painful death in hell?

VINCENT: By my troth, uncle, I can find no words that should have any reason with them—faith being always presupposed, as you protested in the beginning, for a ground—words, I say, I can find none with which I might reasonably counter-plead this that you have said here already.

But yet I remember the fable that Æsop telleth of a great old hart that had fled from a little bitch, which had made pursuit after him and chased him so long that she had lost him, and (he hoped) more than half given him over. Having then some time to talk, and meeting with another of his fellows, he fell into deliberation with him as to what it were best for him to do—whether to run on still and fly farther from her, or to turn again and fight with her. The other hart advised him to fly no farther, lest the bitch might happen to find him again when he would be out of breath by the labour of farther fleeing, and thereby all out of strength too, and so would he be killed lying where he could not stir himself. Whereas, if he would turn and fight, he would be in no peril at all. "For the man with whom she hunteth," he said, "is more than a mile behind her. And she is but a little body, scant half so much as thou, and thy horns can thrust her through before she can touch thy flesh, by more than ten times her tooth-length." "By my troth," quoth the other hart, "I like your counsel well, and methinketh that the thing is even soothly as you say. But I fear me that when I hear once that cursed bitch bark, I shall fall to my feet and forget all together. But yet, if you will go back with me, then methinketh we shall be strong enough against that one bitch between us both." The other hart agreed, and they both appointed them thereon. But even as they were about to busk them forward to it, the bitch had found the scent again, and on she came yalping toward the place. And as soon as the harts heard her, off they went both twain apace!

And in good faith, uncle, even so I fear it would fare by myself and many others too. Though we think it reason, what you say, and in our minds agree that we should do as you say—yea, and peradventure think also that we would indeed do as you say—yet as soon as we should once hear those hell-hounds the Turks come yalping and howling upon us, our hearts should soon fall as clean from us as those other harts fled from the hounds.

ANTHONY: Cousin, in those days that Æsop speaketh of, though those harts and other brute beasts had (if he say sooth) the power to speak and talk, and in their talking power to talk reason too, yet they never had given them the power to follow reason and rule themselves thereby. And in good faith, cousin, as for such things as pertain to the conducting of reasonable men to salvation, I think that without the help of grace men's reasoning shall do little more. But then are we sure, as I said before, that if we desire grace, God is at such reasoning always present and very ready to give it. And unless men will afterward willingly cast it away, he is ever ready still to keep it and glad from time to time to increase it. And therefore our Lord biddeth us, by the mouth of the prophet, that we should not be like such brutish and unreasonable beasts as were those harts, and as are horses and mules: "Be not you like a horse and a mule, that hath no understanding." And therefore, cousin, let us never dread but what, if we will apply our minds to the gathering of comfort and courage against our persecutions, and hear reason and let it sink into our heart and cast it not out again (nor vomit it up, nor even there choke it up and stifle it with pampering in and stuffing up our stomachs with a surfeit of worldly vanities), God shall so well work with it that we shall feel strength therein. And so we shall not in such wise have all such shameful cowardous hearts as to forsake our Saviour and thereby lose our own salvation and run into eternal fire for fear of death joined therein—though bitter and sharp, yet short for all that, and (in a manner) a momentary pain.

VINCENT: Every man, uncle, naturally grudgeth at pain, and is very loth to come to it.

ANTHONY: That is very true, and no one biddeth any man to go run into it, unless he be taken and cannot flee. Then, we say that reason plainly telleth us that we should rather suffer and endure the less and the shorter pain here, than in hell the sorer and so far the longer too.

VINCENT: I heard of late, uncle, where such a reason was made as you make me now, which reason seemed undoubted and inevitable to me. Yet heard I lately, as I say, a man answer it thus: He said that if a man in this persecution should stand still in the confession of his faith and thereby fall into painful tormentry, he might peradventure happen, for the sharpness and bitterness of the pain, to forsake our Saviour even in the midst of it, and die there with his sin, and so be damned forever. Whereas, by the forsaking of the faith in the beginning, and for the time—and yet only in word, keeping it still nevertheless in his heart—a man might save himself from that painful death and afterward ask mercy and have it, and live long and do many good deeds, and be saved as St. Peter was.

ANTHONY: That man's reason, cousin, is like a three-footed stool—so tottering on every side that whosoever sits on it may soon take a foul fall. For these are the three feet of this tottering stool: fantastical fear, false faith, and false flattering hope.

First, it is a fantastical fear that the man conceiveth, that it should be perilous to stand in the confession of the faith at the beginning, lest he might afterward, through the bitterness of the pain, fall to the forsaking and so die there in the pain, out of hand, and thereby be utterly damned. As though, if a man were overcome by pain and so forsook his faith, God could not or would not as well give him grace to repent again, and thereupon give him forgiveness, as he would give it to him who forsook his faith in the beginning and set so little by God that he would rather forsake him than suffer for his sake any manner of pain at all! As though the more pain that a man taketh for God's sake, the worse would God be to him! If this reason were not unreasonable, then should our Saviour not have said, as he did, "Fear not them that may kill the body, and after that have nothing that they can do further." For he should, by this reason, have said,

"Dread and fear them that may slay the body, for they may, by the torment of painful death (unless thou forsake me betimes in the beginning and so save thy life, and get of me thy pardon and forgiveness afterward) make thee peradventure forsake me too late, and so be damned forever."

The second foot of this tottering stool is a false faith. For it is but a feigned faith for a man to say to God secretly that he believeth him, trusteth him, and loveth him, and then openly, where he should to God's honour tell the same tale and thereby prove that he doth so, there to God's dishonour flatter God's enemies as much as in him is, and do them pleasure and worship, with the forsaking of God's faith before the world. And such a one either is faithless in his heart too, or else knoweth well that he doth God this despite even before his own face. For unless he lack faith, he cannot but know that our Lord is everywhere present, and that, while he so shamefully forsaketh him, he full angrily looketh on.

The third foot of this tottering stool is false flattering hope. For since the thing that he doth, when he forsaketh his faith for fear, is forbidden by the mouth of God upon the pain of eternal death, though the goodness of God forgiveth many folk for the fault, yet to be bolder in offending for the hope of forgiving is a very false pestilent hope, with which a man flattereth himself toward his own destruction.

He who, in a sudden turn for fear or other affection, unadvisedly falleth, and after, in labouring to rise again, comforteth himself with hope of God's gracious forgiveness, walketh in the ready way toward his salvation. But he who with the hope of God's mercy to follow, doth encourage himself to sin, and thereby offendeth God first—I have no power to keep the hand of God from giving out his pardon where he will (nor would I if I could, but rather help to pray for it), but yet I very sorely fear that such a man may miss the grace to ask it in such effectual wise as to have it granted. Nor can I now instantly remember any example or promise expressed in holy scripture that the offender in such a case shall have the grace offered afterward, in such wise to seek for pardon that God, by his other promises of remission promised to penitents, would be bound himself to grant it. But this kind of presumption, under pretext of hope, seemeth rather to draw near on the one side (as despair doth, on the other) toward the abominable sin of blasphemy against the Holy Ghost. And against that sin, concerning either the impossibility or at least the great difficulty of forgiveness, our Saviour himself hath spoken in the twelfth chapter of St. Matthew and in the third chapter of St. Mark, where he saith that blasphemy against the Holy Ghost shall never be forgiven, neither in this world nor in the world to come.

And where the man that you speak of took in his reason an example of St. Peter, who forsook our Saviour and got forgiveness afterward, let him consider again on the other hand that he forsook him not upon the boldness of such a sinful trust, but was overcome and vanquished by a sudden fear. And yet, by that forsaking, St. Peter won but little, for he did but delay his trouble for a little while, as you know well. For beside that, he repented forthwith very sorely that he had so done, and wept for it forthwith full bitterly. He came forth at the Whitsuntide ensuing, and confessed his Master again, and soon after that, he was imprisoned for it. And not ceasing so, he was thereupon sore scourged for the confession of his faith, and yet after that imprisoned again afresh. And, being from thence delivered, he stinted not to preach on still until, after manifold labours, travails, and troubles, he was in Rome crucified and with cruel torment slain.

And in like wise I think I might (in a manner) well warrant that no man who denieth our Saviour once and afterward attaineth remission shall escape through that denial one penny the cheaper, but that he shall, ere he come to heaven, full surely pay for it.

VINCENT: He shall peradventure, uncle, afterward work it out in the fruitful works of penance, prayer, and almsdeed, done in true faith and due charity, and in such wise attain forgiveness well enough.

ANTHONY: All his forgiveness goeth, cousin, as you see well, but by "perhaps." But as it may be "perhaps yea," so may it be "perhaps nay," and where is he then? And yet, you know, he shall never, by any manner of hap, hap finally to escape from death, for fear of which he forsook his faith.

VINCENT: No, but he may die his natural death, and escape that violent death. And then he saveth himself from much pain and so winneth much ease. For a violent death is ever painful.

ANTHONY: Peradventure he shall not avoid a violent death thereby, for God is without doubt displeased, and can bring him shortly to as violent a death by some other way.

Howbeit, I see well that you reckon that whosoever dieth a natural death, dieth like a wanton even at his ease. You make me remember a man who was once in a light galley with us on the sea. While the sea was sore wrought and the waves rose very high, he lay tossed hither and thither, for he had never been to sea before. The poor soul groaned sore and for pain thought he would very fain be dead, and ever he wished, "Would God I were on land, that I might die in rest!" The waves so troubled him there, with tossing him up and down, to and fro, that he thought that trouble prevented him from dying, because the waves would not let him rest! But if he might get once to land, he thought he should then die there even at his ease.

VINCENT: Nay, uncle, this is no doubt, but that death is to every man painful. But yet is not the natural death so painful as the violent.

ANTHONY: By my troth, cousin, methinketh that the death which men commonly call "natural" is a violent death to every may whom it fetcheth hence by force against his will. And that is every man who, when he dieth, is loth to die and fain would yet live longer if he could.

Howbeit, cousin, fain would I know who hath told you how small is the pain in the natural death! As far as I can perceive, those folk that commonly depart of their natural death have ever one disease and sickness or another. And if the pain of the whole week or twain in which they lie pining in their bed, were gathered together in so short a time as a man hath his pain who dieth a violent death, it would, I daresay, make double the pain that is his. So he who dieth naturally often suffereth more pain rather than less, though he suffer it in a longer time. And then would many a man be more loth to suffer so long, lingering in pain, than with a sharper pang to be sooner rid. And yet lieth many a man more days than one, in well-near as great pain continually, as is the pain that with the violent death riddeth the man in less than half an hour—unless you think that, whereas the pain is great to have a knife cut the flesh on the outside from the skin inward, the pain would be much less if the knife might begin on the inside and cut from the midst outward! Some we hear, on their deathbed, complain that they think they feel sharp knives cut in two their heartstrings. Some cry out and think they feel, within the brainpan, their head pricked even full of pins. And those who lie in a pleurisy think that, every time they cough, they feel a sharp sword snap them to the heart.

## XXV

Howbeit, what need we to make any such comparison between the natural death and the violent, for the matter that we are in hand with here? Without doubt, he who forsaketh the faith of Christ for fear of the violent death, putteth himself in peril to find his natural death a thousand times more painful. For his natural death hath his everlasting pain so instantly knit to it, that there is not one moment of time between, but the end of the one is the beginning of the other, which never after shall have an end.

And therefore was it not without great cause that Christ gave us so good warning before, when he said, as St. Luke in the twenty-second chapter rehearseth, "I say to you that are my friends, be not afraid of them that kill the body, and when that is done are able to do no more. But I shall show you whom you should fear. Fear him who, when he hath killed, hath in his power further to cast him whom he killeth into everlasting fire. So I say to you, be afraid of him." God meaneth not here that we should not dread at all any man who can but kill the body, but he meaneth that we should not in such wise dread any such man that we should, for dread of them, displease him who can everlastingly kill both body and soul with a death ever-dying and that shall yet never die. And therefore he addeth and repeateth in the end again, the fear that we should have of him, and saith, "So I say to you, fear him."

O good God, cousin, if a man would well weigh those words and let them sink down deep into his heart as they should do, and often bethink himself on them, it would (I doubt not) be able enough to make us set at naught all the great Turk's threats, and esteem him not a straw. But we should be well content to endure all the pain that all the world could put upon us, for so short a while as all they were able to make us dwell in it, rather than, by shrinking from those pains (though never so sharp, yet but short), to cast ourselves into the pain of hell—a hundred thousand times more intolerable, and of which there shall never come an end. A woeful death is that death, in which folk shall evermore be dying and never can once be dead! For the scripture saith, "They shall call and cry for death, and death shall fly from them."

O, good Lord, if one of them were not put in choice of both, he would rather suffer the whole year together the most terrible death that all the Turks in Turkey could devise, than to endure for the space of half an hour the death that they lie in now. Into what wretched folly fall, then, those faithless or feeble-faithed folk, who, to avoid the pain that is so far the less and so short, fall instead into pain a thousand thousand times more horrible, and terrible torment of which they are sure they shall never have an end!

This matter, cousin, lacketh, I believe, only full faith or sufficient minding. For I think, on my faith, that if we have the grace verily to believe it and often to think well on it, the fear of all the Turk's persecution—with all this midday devil were able to do in the forcing of us to forsake our faith—should never be able to turn us.

VINCENT: By my troth, uncle, I think it is as you say. For surely, if we would often think on these pains of hell—as we are very loth to do, and purposely seek us childish pastimes to put such heavy things out of our thought—this one point alone would be able enough, I think, to make many a martyr.

## XXVI

ANTHONY: Forsooth, cousin, if we were such as we should be, I would scant, for very shame, speak of the pains of hell in exhortation to the keeping of Christ's faith. I would rather put us in mind of the joys of heaven, the pleasure of which we should be more glad to get than we should be to flee and escape all the pains of hell.

But surely God is marvellous merciful to us in the thing in which he may seem most rigorous. And that is (which many men would little think) in that he provided hell. For I suppose very surely, cousin, that many a man—and woman, too—of whom some now sit, and more shall hereafter sit, full gloriously crowned in heaven, had they not first been afraid of hell, would never have set foot toward heaven.

But yet undoubtedly, if we could conceive in our hearts the marvellous joys of heaven as well as we conceive the fearful pains of hell—howbeit, we can conceive neither one sufficiently. But if we could in our imagination approach as much toward the perceiving of the one as we may toward the consideration of the other, we would not fail to be far more moved and stirred to suffering for Christ's sake in this world, for the winning of those heavenly joys than for the eschewing of all those infernal pains. But forasmuch as the fleshly pleasures are far less pleasant than the fleshly pains are painful, therefore we fleshly folk, who are so drowned in these fleshly pleasures and in the desire of them that we have almost no manner of savour or taste for any pleasure that is spiritual, we have no cause to marvel that our fleshly affections are more abated and refrained by the dread and terror of hell than spiritual affections are imprinted in us and pricked forward with the desire and joyful hope of heaven.

Howbeit, if we would set somewhat less by the filthy voluptuous appetites of the flesh, and would, by withdrawing from them, with help of prayer through the grace of God, draw nearer to the secret inward pleasure of the spirit, we should, by the little sipping that our hearts should have here now, and that instantaneous taste of it, have an estimation of the incomparable and uncogitable joy that we shall have (if we will) in heaven, by the very full draught thereof. For thereof it is written, "I shall be satiate" or satisfied, or fulfilled, "when thy glory, good Lord, shall appear," that is, with the fruition of the sight of God's glorious majesty face to face. And the desire, expectation, and heavenly hope thereof, shall more encourage us and make us strong to suffer and sustain for the love of God and salvation of our soul, than ever we could be made to suffer worldly pain here by the terrible dread of all the horrible pains that damned wretches have in hell.

Therefore in the meantime, for lack of such experimental taste as God giveth here sometimes to some of his special servants, to the intent that we may draw toward the spiritual exercise too—for which spiritual exercise God with that gift, as with an earnest-penny of their whole reward afterward in heaven, comforteth them here in earth—let us labour by prayer to conceive in our hearts such a fervent longing for them that we may, for attaining to them, utterly set at naught all fleshly delight, all worldly pleasures, all earthly losses, all bodily torment and pain. And let us do this, not so much with looking to have described what manner of joys they shall be, as with hearing what our Lord telleth us in holy scripture how marvellous great they shall be. Howbeit, some things are there in scripture expressed of the manner of the pleasures and joys that we shall have in heaven, as, "Righteous men shall shine as the sun and shall run about like sparkles of fire among reeds."

Now, tell some carnal-minded man of this manner of pleasure, and he shall take little pleasure in it, and say he careth not to have his flesh shine, he, nor like a spark of fire to skip about in the sky. Tell him that his body shall be impassible and never feel harm, and he will think then that he shall never be ahungered or athirst, and shall thereby forbear all his pleasure of eating and drinking, and that he shall never wish for sleep, and shall thereby lose the pleasure that he was wont to take in lying slug-abed. Tell him that men and women shall there live together as angels without any manner of mind or motion unto the carnal act of generation, and he will think that he shall thereby not use there his old filthy voluptuous fashion. He will say then that he is better at ease already, and would not give this world for that. For, as St. Paul saith, "A carnal man feeleth not the things that be of the spirit of God, for it is foolishness to him."

But the time shall come when these foul filthy pleasures shall be so taken from him that it shall abhor his heart once to think on them. Every man hath a certain shadow of this experience in the fervent grief of a sore painful sickness, when his stomach can scant abide to look upon any meat, and as for the acts of the other foul filthy lust, he is ready to vomit if he hap to think thereon. When a man shall after this life feel in his heart that horrible abomination, of which sickness hath here a shadow, at the remembrance of these voluptuous pleasures, for which he would here be loth to change with the joys of heaven: when he shall, I say, after this life, have his fleshly pleasures in abomination, and shall have there a glimmering (though far from a perfect sight) of those heavenly joys which here he set so little by—O, good God, how fain will he then be, with how good will and how gladly would he then give this whole world, if it were his, to have the feeling of some little part of those joys!

And therefore let us all who cannot now conceive such delight in the consideration of them as we should, have often in our eyes by reading, often in our ears by hearing, often in our mouths by rehearsing, often in our hearts by meditation and thinking, those joyful words of the holy scripture by which we learn how wonderful huge and great are those spiritual heavenly joys. Our carnal hearts have so feeble and so faint a feeling of them, and our dull worldly wits are so little able to conceive so much as a shadow of the right imagination! A shadow, I say, for, as for the thing as it is, not only can no fleshly carnal fancy conceive that, but beside that no spiritual person peradventure neither, so long as he is still living here in this world. For since the very essential substance of all the celestial joy standeth in the blessed beholding of the glorious Godhead face to face, no man may presume or look to attain it in this life. For God hath said so himself: "There shall no man here living behold me." And therefore we may well know not only that we are, for the state of this life, kept from the fruition of the bliss of heaven, but also I think that the very best man living here upon earth—the best man, I mean, who is no more than man—cannot attain the right imagination of it; but those who are very virtuous are yet (in a manner) as far from it as a man born blind is from the right imagination of colours.

The words that St. Paul rehearseth of the prophet Isaiah, prophesying of Christ's incarnation, may properly be verified of the joys of heaven: "Oculus non vidit, nec auris audivit, nec in cor hominis adscendit, quae preparavit Deus diligentibus se." For surely, for this state of this world, the joys of heaven are by man's mouth unspeakable, to man's ears not audible, to men's hearts uncogitable, so far excel they all that ever men have heard of, all that ever men can speak of, and all that men can by natural possibility think on.

And yet, whereas such be the joys of heaven that are prepared for every saved soul, our Lord saith yet, by the mouth of St. John, that he will give his holy martyrs who suffer for his sake many a special kind of joy. For he saith, "To him that overcometh, I shall give him to eat of the tree of life. And I shall confess his name before my Father and before his angels." And also he saith, "Fear none of those things that thou shalt suffer . . . , but be faithful unto the death, and I shall give thee the crown of life. He that overcometh shall not be hurt of the second death." And he saith also, "To him that overcometh will I give manna secret and hid. And I will give him a white suffrage, and in his suffrage a new name written, which no man knoweth but he that receiveth it." They used of old in Greece, where St. John did write, to elect and choose men unto honourable offices, and every man's assent was called his "suffrage," which in some places was by voices and in some places by hands. And one kind of those suffrages was by certain things that in Latin are called calculi because, in some places, they used round stones for them. Now our Lord saith that unto him who overcometh he will give a white suffrage, for those that were white signified approving, as the black signified reproving. And in those suffrages did they use to write the name of him to whom they gave their vote. Now our Lord saith that to him who overcometh he will in the suffrage give him a new name, which no man knoweth but him who receiveth it. He saith also, "He that overcometh, I will make him a pillar in the temple of my God, and he shall go no more out thereof, and I shall write upon him the name of my God and the name of the city of my God, the new Jerusalem which descendeth from heaven from my God, and I shall write on him also my new name." If we wished to enlarge upon this, and were able to declare these special gifts, with yet others that are specified in the second and third chapters of the Apocalypse, then would it appear how far those heavenly joys shall surmount above all the comfort that ever came in the mind of any man living here upon earth.

The blessed apostle St. Paul, who suffered so many perils and so many passions, saith of himself that he hath been "in many labours, in prisons oftener than others, in stripes above measure, at point of death often times; of the Jews had I five times forty stripes save one, thrice have I been beaten with rods, once was I stoned, thrice have I been in shipwreck, a day and a night was I in the depth of the sea; in my journeys oft have I been in peril of floods, in peril of thieves, in peril by the Jews, in perils by the pagans, in perils in the city, in perils in the desert, in perils in the sea, perils by false brethren, in labour and misery, in many nights' watch, in hunger and thirst, in many fastings, in cold and nakedness; beside those things that are outward, my daily instant labour, I mean my care and solicitude about all the churches," and yet saith he more of his tribulations, which for the length I let pass. This blessed apostle, I say, for all these tribulations that he himself suffered in the continuance of so many years, calleth all the tribulations of this world but light and as short as a moment, in respect of the weighty glory that it winneth us after this world: "This same short and momentary tribulation of ours that is in this present time, worketh within us the weight of glory above measure on high, we beholding not these things that we see, but those things that we see not.

For those things that we see are but temporal things, but those things that are not seen are eternal."

Now to this great glory no man can come headless. Our head is Christ, and therefore to him must we be joined, and as members of his must we follow him, if we wish to come thither. He is our guide to guide us thither, and he is entered in before us. And he therefore who will enter in after, "the same way that Christ walked, the same way must he walk." And what was the way by which he walked into heaven? He himself showed what way it was that his Father had provided for him, when he said to the two disciples going toward the village of Emaus, "Knew you not that Christ must suffer passion, and by that way enter into his kingdom?" Who can for very shame desire to enter into the kingdom of Christ with ease, when he himself entered not into his own without pain?

## XXVII

Surely, cousin, as I said before, in bearing the loss of worldly goods, in suffering captivity, thraldom, and imprisonment, and in the glad sustaining of worldly shame, if we would in all those points deeply ponder the example of our Saviour himself, it would be sufficient of itself alone to encourage every true Christian man and woman to refuse none of all those calamities for his sake.

So say I now for painful death also: If we could and would with due compassion conceive in our minds a right imagination and remembrance of Christ's bitter painful passion—of the many sore bloody strokes that the cruel tormentors gave him with rods and whips upon every part of his holy tender body; of the scornful crown of sharp thorns beaten down upon his holy head, so strait and so deep that on every part his blessed blood issued out and streamed down; of his lovely limbs drawn and stretched out upon the cross, to the intolerable pain of his sore-beaten veins and sinews, feeling anew, with the cruel stretching and straining, pain far surpassing any cramp in every part of his blessed body at once; of the great long nails then cruelly driven with the hammer through his holy hands and feet; of his body, in this horrible pain, lifted up and let hang, with all its weight bearing down upon the painful wounded places so grievously pierced with nails; and in such torment, without pity, but not without many despites, suffered to be pined and pained the space of more than three long hours, till he himself willingly gave up unto his Father his holy soul; after which yet, to show the mightiness of their malice, after his holy soul departed, they pierced his holy heart with a sharp spear, at which issued out the holy blood and water, whence his holy sacraments have inestimable secret strength—if we could, I say, remember these things, in such a way as would God that we would, I verily suppose that the consideration of his incomparable kindness could not fail so to inflame our key-cold hearts, and set them on fire with his love, that we should find ourselves not only content but also glad and desirous to suffer death for his sake who so marvellously lovingly forbore not to sustain so far passing painful death for ours.

Would God that we would here—to the shame of our cold affection toward God, in return for such fervent love and inestimable kindness of God toward us—would God we would, I say, but consider what hot affection many of these fleshly lovers have borne and daily bear to those upon whom they dote. How many of them have not stinted to jeopard their lives, and how many have willingly lost their lives indeed, without any great kindness showed them before—and afterward, you know, they could nothing win! But it contented and satisfied their minds that by their death their lover should clearly see how faithfully they loved. The delight thereof, imprinted in their fancy, not only assuaged their pain but also, they thought, outweighed it all. Of these affections, with the wonderful dolorous effects following upon them, not only old written stories, but beside that experience, I think, in every country, Christian and heathen both, giveth us proof enough. And is it not then a wonderful shame for us, for the dread of temporal death, to forsake our Saviour who willingly suffered so painful death rather than forsake us? Considering that, beside that, he shall for our suffering so highly reward us with everlasting wealth. Oh, if he who is content to die for his love, of whom he looketh afterward for no reward, and yet by his death goeth from her, might by his death be sure to come to her and ever after in delight and pleasure to dwell with her—such a love would not stint here to die for her twice! And what cold lovers are we then unto God, if, rather than die for him once, we will refuse him and forsake him forever—him who both died for us before, and hath also provided that, if we die here for him, we shall in heaven everlastingly both live and also reign with him! For as St. Paul saith, "If we suffer with him, we shall reign with him."

How many Romans, how many noble hearts of other sundry countries, have willingly given their own lives and suffered great deadly pains and very painful deaths for their countries, to win by their death only the reward of worldly renown and fame! And should we, then, shrink to suffer as much for eternal honour in heaven and everlasting glory? The devil hath also some heretics so obstinate that they wittingly endure painful death for vain glory. And is it not then more than shame that Christ shall see his Catholics forsake his faith rather than suffer the same for heaven and true glory?

Would God, as I many times have said, that the remembrance of Christ's kindness in suffering his passion for us, the consideration of hell that we shall fall in by forsaking him, and the joyful meditation of eternal life in heaven that we shall win with this short temporal death patiently taken for him, had so deep a place in our breast as reason would that they should—and as, if we would strive toward it and labour for it and pray for it, I verily think they would. For then should they so take up our mind and ravish it all another way, that, as a man hurt in a fray feeleth not sometimes his wound nor yet is aware of it, until his mind fall more thereon (so much so that sometimes another man telleth him that he hath lost a hand before he perceive it himself), so the mind ravished in the thinking deeply of those other things—Christ's death, hell, and heaven—would be likely to diminish and put away four parts of the feeling of our painful death—either of the death or the pain. For of this am I very sure: If we had the fifteenth part of the love for Christ that he both had and hath for us, all the pain of this Turk's persecution could not keep us from him, but there would be at this day as many martyrs here in Hungary as there have been before in other countries of old.

And I doubt not but that, if the Turk stood even here with all his whole army about him; and if every one of them all were ready at hand with all the terrible torments that they could imagine, and were setting their torments to us unless we would forsake the faith; and if to the increase of our terror they fell all at once in a shout, with trumpets, tabrets, and timbrels all blown up at once, and all their guns let go therewith to make us a fearful noise; if then, on the other hand, the ground should suddenly quake and rive atwain, and the devils should rise out of hell and show themselves in such ugly shape as damned wretches shall see them; and if, with that hideous howling that those hell-hounds should screech, they should lay hell open on every side round about our feet, so that as we stood we should look down into that pestilent pit and see the swarm of poor souls in the terrible torments there—we would wax so afraid of the sight that we should scantly remember that we saw the Turk's host.

And in good faith, for all that, yet think I further this: If there might then appear the great glory of God, the Trinity in his high marvellous majesty, our Saviour in his glorious manhood sitting on the throne, with his immaculate mother and all that glorious company, calling us there unto them; and if our way should yet lie through marvellous painful death before we could come at them—upon the sight, I say, of that glory, I daresay there would be no man who once would shrink at death, but every man would run on toward them in all that ever he could, though there lay by the way, to kill us for malice, both all the Turk's tormentors and all the devils.

And therefore, cousin, let us well consider these things, and let us have sure hope in the help of God. And then I doubt not but what we shall be sure that, as the prophet saith, the truth of his promise shall so compass us with a shield that we shall never need to fear. For either, if we trust in God well, and prepare us for it, the Turk shall never meddle with us; or else, if he do, he shall do us no harm but, instead of harm, inestimable good. Wherefore should we so sore now despair of God's gracious help, unless we were such madmen as to think that either his power or his mercy were worn out already? For we see that so many a thousand holy martyrs, by his holy help, suffered as much before as any man shall be put to now. Or what excuse can we have by the tenderness of our flesh? For we can be no more tender than were many of them, among whom were not only men of strength, but also weak women and children. And since the strength of them all stood in the help of God; and since the very strongest of them all was never able to himself to stand against all the world, and with God's help the feeblest of them all was strong enough so to stand; let us prepare ourselves with prayer, with our whole trust in his help, without any trust in our own strength. Let us think on it and prepare ourselves for it in our minds long before. Let us therein conform our will unto his, not desiring to be brought unto the peril of persecution (for it beseemeth a proud high mind to desire martyrdom) but desiring help and strength of God, if he suffer us to come to the stress—either being sought, found, and brought out against our wills, or else being by his commandment, for the comfort of our cure, bound to abide.

Let us fall to fasting, to prayer, and to almsdeed in time, and give unto God that which may be taken from us. If the devil put in our mind the saving of our land and our goods, let us remember that we cannot save them long. If he frighten us with exile and flying from our country, let us remember that we be born into the broad world, not to stick still in one place like a tree, and that whithersoever we go, God shall go with us. If he threaten us with captivity, let us answer him that it is better to be thrall unto a man for a while, for the pleasure of God, than, by displeasing God, to be perpetual thrall unto the devil. If he threaten us with imprisonment, let us tell him that we would rather be man's prisoner a while here in earth than, by forsaking the faith, be his prisoners for ever in hell. If he put in our minds the terror of the Turks, let us consider his false sleight, for this tale he telleth us to make us forget him. But let us remember well that, in respect of himself, the Turks are but a shadow. And all that they can do can be but a flea-bite in comparison with the mischief that he goeth about. The Turks are but his tormentors, for he himself doth the deed. Our Lord saith in the Apocalypse, "The devil shall send some of you to prison, to tempt you." He saith not that men shall, but that the devil shall, himself. For without question the devil's own deed it is, to bring us by his temptation, with fear and force, into eternal damnation. And therefore saith St. Paul, "Our wrestling is not against flesh and blood," etc.

Thus may we see that in such persecutions it is the midday devil himself that maketh such incursion upon us, by the men who are his ministers, to make us fall for fear. For until we fall he can never hurt us. And therefore saith St. James, "Stand against the devil and he shall flee from you." For he never runneth upon a man to seize him with his claws until he see him down on the ground, willingly fallen himself. For his fashion is to set his servants against us, and by them to make us fall for fear or for impatience. And he himself in the meanwhile compasseth us, running and roaring like a ramping lion about us, looking to see who will fall, that he may then devour him. "Your adversary the devil," saith St. Peter, "like a roaring lion, runneth about in circuit, seeking whom he may devour."

The devil it is, therefore, who, if we will fall for fear of men, is ready to run upon us and devour us. And is it wisdom, then, to think so much upon the Turks that we forget the devil? What a madman would he be who, when a lion were about to devour him, would vouchsafe to regard the biting of a little fisting cur? Therefore, when he roareth out upon us by the threats of mortal men, let us tell him that with our inward eye we see him well enough, and intend to stand and fight with him, even hand to hand. If he threaten us that we be too weak, let us tell him that our captain Christ is with us, and that we shall fight with the strength of him who hath vanquished him already. And let us fence with faith, and comfort us with hope, and smite the devil in the face with the firebrand of charity. For surely, if we be of the tender loving mind that our Master was, and do not hate them that kill us but pity them and pray for them, with sorrow for the peril that they work unto themselves, then that fire of charity thrown in his face will strike the devil suddenly so blind that he cannot see where to fasten a stroke on us.

When we feel ourselves too bold, let us remember our own feebleness, and when we feel ourselves too faint, let us remember Christ's strength. In our fear, let us remember Christ's painful agony, that he himself would for our comfort suffer before his passion, to the intent that no fear should make us despair. And let us ever call for his help, such as he himself may please to send us. And then need we never doubt but that he shall either keep us from the painful death, or else strengthen us in it so that he shall joyously bring us to heaven by it. And then doth he much more for us than if he kept us from it. For God did more for poor Lazarus, in helping him patiently to die for hunger at the rich man's door, than if he had brought to him at the door all the rich glutton's dinner. So, though he be gracious to a man whom he delivereth out of painful trouble, yet doth he much more for a man if, through right painful death, he deliver him from this wretched world into eternal bliss. Whosoever shrinketh away from it by forsaking his faith, and falleth in the peril of everlasting fire, he shall be very sure to repent ere it be long after.

For I am sure that whensoever he falleth sick next, he will wish that he had been killed for Christ's sake before. What folly is it, then, to flee for fear from that death which thou seest thou shalt shortly afterward wish thou hadst died! Yea, I daresay almost every good Christian man would very fain this day that yesterday he had been cruelly killed for Christ's sake—even for the desire of heaven, though there were no hell. But to fear while the pain is coming, there is all our hindrance! But if, on the other hand, we would remember hell's pain into which we fall while we flee from this, then this short pain should be no hindrance at all. And yet, if we were faithful, we should be more pricked forward by deep consideration of the joys of heaven, of which the apostle saith, "The passions of this time be not worthy to the glory that is to come, which shall be showed in us." We should not, I believe, need much more in all this matter than one text of St. Paul, if we would consider it well. For surely, mine own good cousin, remember that if it were possible for me and you alone to suffer as much trouble as the whole world doth together, all that would not be worthy of itself to bring us to the joy which we hope to have everlastingly. And therefore, I pray you, let the consideration of that you put out all worldly trouble out of your heart, and also pray that it may do the same in me.

And even thus will I, good cousin, with these words, make a sudden end of mine whole tale, and bid you farewell. For now begin I to feel myself somewhat weary.

VINCENT: Forsooth, good uncle, this is a good end. And it is no marvel if you are waxed weary. For I have this day put you to so much labour that, save for the comfort that you yourself may take from having bestowed your time so well, and for the comfort that I have taken—and more shall, I trust—of your good counsel given, else would I be very sorry to have put you to so much pain.

But now shall our Lord reward and recompense you therefore, and many, I trust, shall pray for you. For to the intent that the more men may take profit of you, I purpose, uncle, as my poor wit and learning will serve me, to record your good counsel not only in our own language, but in the German tongue too.

And thus, praying God to give me, and all others who shall read it, the grace to follow your good counsel, I shall commit you to God.

ANTHONY: Since you be minded, cousin, to bestow so much labour on it, I would it had happed you to fetch the counsel at some wiser man, who could have given you better. But better men may add more things, and better also, thereto. And in the meantime, I beseech our Lord to breathe of his Holy Spirit into the reader's breast, who inwardly may teach him in heart. For without him little availeth all that the mouths of the world would be able to teach in men's ears.

And thus, good cousin, farewell, till God bring us together again, either here or in heaven. Amen.

www.ingramcontent.com/pod-product-compliance
Lightning Source LLC
Chambersburg PA
CBHW031642040426
42453CB00006B/181